Illustrator:
Ken Tunell

Editor:
Dona Herweck Rice

Editorial Project Manager:
Karen Goldfluss, M.S. Ed.

Editor in Chief:
Sharon Coan, M.S. Ed.

Creative Director:
Elayne Roberts

Art Coordinator:
Cheri Macoubrie Wilson

Associate Designer:
Denise Bauer

Cover Artist:
Sue Fullam

Product Manager:
Phil Garcia

Imaging:
Ralph Olmedo, Jr.

Publishers:
Rachelle Cracchiolo, M.S. Ed.
Mary Dupuy Smith, M.S. Ed.

INTERMEDIATE

Authors:
Deborah Shepherd-Hayes and Karyn Mazo

Teacher Created Materials, Inc.
6421 Industry Way
Westminster, CA 92683
www.teachercreated.com
ISBN-1-55734-464-4

©1999 Teacher Created Materials, Inc.   Made in U.S.A.

The classroom teacher may reproduce copies of materials in this book for classroom use only. The reproduction of any part for an entire school or school system is strictly prohibited. No part of this publication may be transmitted, stored, or recorded in any form without written permission from the publisher.

Table of Contents

The Wonderful World of Folk Tales and Fairy Tales 3
How to Use This Book 4
What Are Folk Tales and Fairy Tales? 10
Section 1—Around the World
   Momotaro: The Peach Warrior 21
   Sir Buzz 25
   Legend of the Poinsettia 28
   Seven Clever Brothers 34
   The Jolly Tailor Who Became King 38
   Kate Crackernuts 42
   The Tale of Sadko the Minstrel 46
   The Ox of the Wonderful Horns 50
   The Canary Prince 54
   The House in the Sky 58
   Fa Mulan 61
   The Little Seven-Colored Horse 65
Culminating Activities 68
Section Test 88
Section 2—Around the World with Cinderella
Introduction 90
   The Egyptian Cinderella 92
   Vasilisa the Beautiful: A Russian Tale . . . 95
   The Brocaded Slipper 99
   Yeh-Shen 102
   Poor Turkey Girl 105
   Hearth Cat 108
Culminating Activities 112
Section Test 122
Section 3—Animal Tales
   Ti-Jean and the White Cat 123
   Unanana and the Enormous One-Tusked Elephant 126
   The Enchanted Mule 132
   Buffalo Woman 137
   The Little White Dove 141

Culminating Activities 145
Section Test 155
Section 4—Comparative Tales
   Red Riding Hood 156
   Lon Po Po 158
   Beauty and the Beast 160
   The Lizard Husband 162
   The Frog King 164
   The Toad-Bridegroom 166
Culminating Activities 168
Section Test 172
Section 5—Tales with a Twist
   The Paper Bag Princess 173
   Sidney Rella and the Glass Sneaker . . . 175
   Sleeping Ugly 179
   The True Story of the Three Little Pigs . . 181
Culminating Activities 184
Section Test 196
Culminating Activities 197
Readers' Theater 219
   The Four Musicians 223
   Lazy Jack 235
   A Cat Is a Cat Is a Cat 242
   The Woodcutter and the Pine 248
   The Cat and the Parrot 255
   The Honey Gatherer's Three Sons 265
   Coyote Rings the Bell 274
   Beetle and Paca 283
   The Weary Spirits of Lanai 291
   Baba Yaga Bony-Legs 302
Bibliography 313
Country and Continent Index 316
Answer Key 317

The Wonderful World of Folk Tales and Fairy Tales

Somewhere between "once upon a time" and "happily ever after," something wonderful happens to the readers of folk and fairy tales. We are immediately transported to an enchanted world where humans and animals freely communicate, magic is found in all shapes and sizes, and good wins over evil. No matter in what trials and challenges our heroes and heroines find themselves, we find comfort and security in knowing that justice is served in the end. These tales take us to places beyond the imagination and introduce us to characters who often become lifelong friends.

One of the real life magical aspects of folk and fairy tales is that they connect us to people of different cultures and countries. Every place around the globe has its own tales, passed down from generation to generation and preserved throughout the years.

Every country and society tells tales for different reasons. Anthropologist William Bascom says there are four functions of such tales: amusement, the validation of cultures, the education of children, and the application of social control. Whatever the motive behind the tale, it is sure to be entertaining.

The term tale comes from the Anglo-Saxon word *talup,* meaning speech. Storytelling, that oldest of arts, has always been both an entertainment and a cultural necessity. Laws, news, customs, and celebrations have been passed down through the years, and storytellers have always been held in high regard by cultures and societies around the globe.

The stories in *Tales Around the World* have been selected from many different countries in the hope that we all can learn from and appreciate other cultures. Stories are powerful. They are both a journey and a joining. Folk and fairy tales provide us with the magical chain to connect us with one another. All we need is a listening ear and an open heart.

How to Use This Book

Tales Around the World is an extensive resource book with several strategies for classroom implementation. If you plan to launch a thematic-teaching semester with tales as the central theme, there are plenty of stories and activities available in this book to support you. If the number of activities is too many for your time and purposes, then consider conducting a mini-unit, using one section at a time. Even if you do not plan to teach specifically around this theme, there are a multitude of international and multicultural activities provided here which can be used for virtually any discipline area.

Whichever route you choose to follow, be sure to begin with the introductory pages 10–20. The information and activities provided will give your students a working understanding of the literary genres, which will be important for many other activities in the book. These pages can also serve alone as language-arts lessons.

Folk Tale and Fairy Tale Frames

Encourage students to take notes after reading each tale. There are many different stories to study; therefore, by keeping notes students will have ready access to the information for follow-up activities.

Note-taking is a good academic habit to acquire, and this unit can be the perfect place to begin note-taking skills. A Folk and Fairy Tale Frame for note-taking is provided on page 8. Duplicate plenty of copies for your students. (If your access to a photocopier is limited, students can easily create their own page by copying the frame information.) Create one for yourself on an overhead transparency (or scan the image for your computer) to use for class discussions upon completion of each tale.

Allow students to use their notes when they complete the culminating activities. This will give them a compelling reason to keep complete notes.

Folk and Fairy Tale Frame

Title: "Beauty and the Beast"
Country of Origin: France

Characters	Setting
father (merchant)	French countryside
Beauty	Beast's castle
Beast	merchant's home
2 sisters	Beast's Garden

Plot

Problems:	Solutions:
Beauty's family is poor.	Beauty becomes a wealthy princess and provides for her family.
One daughter must remain imprisoned by the beast in place of her father.	Beauty falls in love with the beast, and he and his court are changed back into original forms.
The beast and the objects in his castle have been placed under a magic spell. He is really a prince and the castle is his royal court.	

Points of Interest

How to Use This Book *(cont.)*

Gathering Resources

Plan a trip to the library, equipped with the Library List of titles (page 9) used in this book. All the books referenced here can probably be found at your public library. You may have some of the more traditional stories in your own classroom collection, and these are certainly acceptable to use in lieu of the books on page 9. However, if you do use books other than the ones suggested here, be sure to read through the activities beforehand to make any changes necessary, allowing for variations that frequently occur in the retelling of any traditional tale.

Sectional Groups

Each sectional group within this book is divided according to a particular commonality in the stories. If you have another use for them, you can certainly group them in ways that better meet your needs.

Within each group, publishing information is provided for each book, and the stories are summarized and followed with a variety of supporting activities. These include discussion questions, journal questions or prompts (for standard or reader-response journals), and one or more activities suited to the particular story and its country of origin.

Thematic Teaching

Research indicates that most students learn best in an integrated manner rather than by isolated, unrelated blocks of study. Thematic teaching provides students with an integrated approach to learning and is interesting for students and teachers. Use Folk and Fairy Tales as the theme for your class this term. There are countless stories available with natural ties to social studies, geography, language arts, and other content areas. By adopting this theme, you can integrate the different sections of the book into your course of study.

One Story at a Time

The stories and activities in *Tales Around the World* can be used for independent lessons as well as for an integrated unit of study. If your class or school participates in an International Faire, students can be assigned in groups to study countries or parts of the world. A group studying Africa could design a sponge stamp pattern on paper or cloth to represent the Adinkra fabric of Ghana. Anytime your class studies information from a particular country, the same idea can be applied. You can also take a folk and fairy tale break in between core literature units and spend a few days completing one of the sections.

How to Use This Book (cont.)

Pocket Charts

Whether you decide to cover all the tales for one extensive unit or for one section at a time, the use of pocket charts for story analysis is very helpful. As you and your students read each tale, use the pocket chart to hold information about the characters, settings, and plot. After reading several tales, the pocket chart will become a valuable resource for reference as well as a variety of extended language-arts activities.

If you plan to cover several stories, it is ideal to have three pocket charts for each area of story analysis.

Character Pocket Chart	Setting Pocket Chart	Plot Pocket Chart
Characters	**Settings**	**Plot**
Good	**Indoor**	**Problems**
Cinderella	stepmother's house	Cinderella's stepmother and stepsisters are mean to her.
prince	Cinderella's room	Cinderella must do all the work.
fairy godmother	palace ballroom	Cinderella has no dress for the ball and no way to get there.
		Cinderella's stepmother tries to keep her from trying on the glass slipper.
	Outdoor	**Solutions**
Evil	palace courtyard	The stepmother and stepsisters are punished.
stepmother	palace steps	Cinderella becomes a princess and doesn't have to do any more work.
stepsisters	stepmother's yard	The fairy godmother gives Cinderella a dress and a coach.
		Cinderella is freed just in time and tries on the slipper.

(**Note:** While commercial pocket charts are easy to use, in place of them you can simply use large sheets of butcher paper and write the information on the paper rather than the cards used in a pocket chart.)

How to Use This Book (cont.)

Around-the-World Map

If you plan to complete the entire book or at least one section, create a large bulletin board display with a world map. Make an overhead of a world map from an atlas and project it onto a large piece of white butcher paper. Have the students color the map and add various geographical and political features.

After reading a tale, let the students take turns completing the cards below and posting them on the map. As stories are read, the map becomes a visual reference for the students.

Folk Tale or Fairy Tale	Folk Tale or Fairy Tale
Country of Origin:	Country of Origin:
Folk Tale or Fairy Tale	Folk Tale or Fairy Tale
Country of Origin:	Country of Origin:

Culminating Activities

Most of the culminating activities require some preparation and will take a significant amount of time to do. In the interest of time management, you may want to consider coordinating two of the activities so that the students have the benefit of participating in a variety of unit closures. The following is an example of how this can be done.

1. Run the mock trial in the morning and celebrate with the Food Faire for lunch.
2. After students have written their modern-day tales and read them to their cross-age class, invite the other class to join yours for the Food Faire.
3. Host a Game Day and play Name That Character and Q & A on the same day.

How to Use This Book (cont.)

See page 4 for directions.

Folk and Fairy Tale Frame

Title: _____

Country of Origin: _____

Characters	Setting

Plot

Problems:	Solutions:

Points of Interest

How to Use This Book (cont.)

Tales Around the World Library List

Alderson, Brian. *The Brothers Grimm: Popular Folk Tales.* Doubleday & Company, 1978

Byron, Ashley. *The Ox of the Wonderful Horns and Other African Folktales.* Simon & Schuster Children's Books, 1993

Climo, Shirley. *The Egyptian Cinderella.* HarperCollins Children's Books, 1992

dePaola, Tomie. *Legend of the Poinsettia.* Putnam, 1994

Goble, Paul. *Buffalo Woman.* Simon & Schuster Children's, 1984

Haviland, Virginia. *Favorite Fairy Tales Told in India.* William Morrow & Company, 1994
  Favorite Fairy Tales Told in Poland. William Morrow & Company, 1995
  Favorite Fairy Tales Told in Spain. William Morrow & Company, 1995

Hearne, Betsy. *Beauties and Beasts: The Oryx Multicultural Folktale Series.* Oryx Press, 1993

Henius, Frank. *Stories from the Americas.* Charles Scribner's Sons, 1944

Louie, A-Ling. *Yeh-Shen: A Cinderella Story from China.* Putnam Publishing Group, 1996

Marshall, James. *Red Riding Hood.* Dial Books for Young Readers, 1987

Martin, Evan and Laszlo Gal. *Canadian Fairy Tales.* Douglas & McIntyre Ltd., 1984

Mayhew, James. *Koskka's Tales: Stories from Russia.* Larousse Kingfisher Chambers, 1993

Mayo, Margaret. *Magical Tales from Many Lands.* Dutton Children's Books, 1993

Munsch, Robert N. *The Paper Bag Princess.* Firefly Books Limited, 1986

Myers, Bernice. *Sidney Rella and the Glass Sneaker.* Simon & Schuster Children's, 1985

Nones, Eric Jon. *The Canary Prince.* Farrar Straus & Giroux, 1991

Sakurai, Gail. *Peach Boy: A Japanese Legend (Legends of the World).* Troll Associates, 1994

San Souci, Robert D. *Fa Mulan.* Hyperion Books for Children, 1998
  The House in the Sky: A Bahamian Folktale. Dial Books for Young Readers, 1996
  The Little Seven-Colored Horse: A Spanish American Folktale. Chronicle Books, 1995

Scieszka, John. *The True Story of the Three Little Pigs.* Scholastic, Inc., 1991

Sierra, Judy. *Cinderella: The Oryx Multicultural Folktale Series.* Oryx Press, 1992

Vuong, Lynette. *The Brocaded Slipper and Other Vietnamese Tales.* HarperCollins Children's Books, 1992

Winthrop, Elizabeth. *Vasilisa the Beautiful: A Russian Tale.* HarperCollins Children's Books, 1991

Yolen, Jane. *Favorite Folktales from Around the World.* Pantheon Books, 1988
  Sleeping Ugly. Houghton Mifflin Co., 1995

Young, Ed. *Lon Po Po: A Red Riding Hood Story from China.* Putnam Publsihing Group, 1989

What Are Folk Tales and Fairy Tales?

While most of your students are probably familiar with many European fairy tales, they will be delighted to discover a much broader and diverse world of folklore than even the well-loved tales of the Brothers Grimm and Hans Christian Andersen. Before beginning this multicultural folk-and-fairy-tale unit with your students, allow time to discuss and learn some background folklore and the different genres within folk and fairy tales. The following information is written for you as the teacher. You may want your students to read this section themselves or, depending on their grade level, you may pull out the appropriate information and share it with your students in a suitable format.

Fairy tale is the term most generally applied to the traditional tales popular with children. The German word for fairy tales is *marchen,* which implies that the tales were originally written for adult entertainment. Many of today's tales for children are merely fantasies based on the traditional models. Since most of what we call fairy tales do not contain actual fairies, *marchen* is a bit too technical; therefore, many researches began using the term folk tale. However, folk tale is too broad in its meaning since there are a variety of genres and tale types which can be classified as folk. Folk tale then is the governing term for any story that has been passed down from one generation to another, either orally or in writing. Fairy tales are a separate type of folk tale in that there are distinct components which must be included in the tale in order for it to be called a fairy tale.

Think of the term folk tale as being an umbrella with many panels. Each panel is a certain tradition or genre of story encompassed within the folk tale umbrella, including fairy tales, legends, myths, ballads, fables, epics, and nursery rhymes. (Activities for students who use the umbrella model to learn this concept can be found on pages 13–18.)

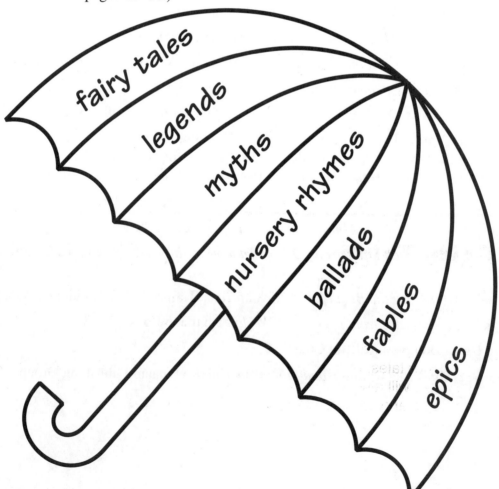

What Are Folk Tales and Fairy Tales? *(cont.)*

Folk tales are most commonly thought of as legends, myths, fairy tales, ballads, epics, fables, and nursery rhymes. The majority of folklore researchers divide folk tales into the following three primary areas:

Legends

A legend is an instructive tale with the intent of informing children about their ancestry. Legends also answer questions in nature and are generally specific to a certain locality. Folklorists call legends "adorned history."

Myths

A myth is a story which is based in ritual and is intended for religious reinforcement. Myths are concerned with gods and goddesses, heroes and heroines, and the acts of creation. Myths are less concerned with entertainment than they are with telling a sacred truth.

Fairy Tales

Fairy tales are purely fiction and designed for entertainment purposes only. They are complex tales with common themes and formulas. These wonder tales, or magical tales as they are also known, will always contain magic, good versus evil, and an unappreciated hero or heroine who finds happiness at the end of the story.

What Are Folk Tales and Fairy Tales? *(cont.)*

Folklorists think of the three folk tale divisions (legends, myths, and fairy tales) in the following ways:

"Legends are set in time, myths are before historical time, and fairy tales are 'once upon a time' or timeless."

Researchers realize that these categories are not absolute as there are, for example, mythical elements in fairy tales as well as fairy tale elements in legends. But for research and categorical purposes, these three divisions have been universally accepted.

While there is a definite framework and formula for all fairy tales, the individual incidents will vary, depending upon culture and storyteller. Fairy tales have magical elements, and the setting is a world in which, at first glance, anything can happen. Researchers have found that these tales of magic have strict rules as to what events may occur and by what means and how and what types of characters may take part in the stories. The logic of fairy tales is always inevitable. If a character is persecuted, he or she will be helped in the end. If he or she attempts to escape love, love will successfully seek him or her. If the character persecutes others, those persecuted will prevail.

There will be several references in this book to the fairy tale recipe. This is an easy way to remember these guidelines and components which must be included in a story in order for the story to be considered a fairy tale. These seven recipe ingredients are the following:

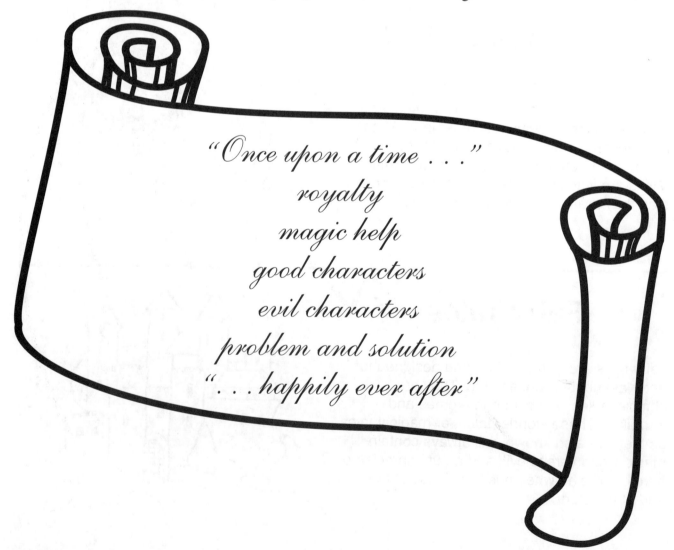

"Once upon a time . . ."
royalty
magic help
good characters
evil characters
problem and solution
". . . happily ever after"

What Are Folk and Fairy Tales?

Folk Tale Umbrella: Option I

Directions: Write each of the seven types of folk tales in the umbrella panels. Color the umbrella. Cut out and glue it to a piece of construction paper.

myth	legend	fairy tale	epic
ballad	fable	nursery rhyme	

© Teacher Created Materials, Inc.   #464 *Tales Around the World*

What Are Folk Tales and Fairy Tales?

Folk Tale Umbrella: Option II

Create a folk-tale mobile. The raindrops beneath the umbrella will represent each of the seven folk-tale types.

Materials:

- coat hanger (plastic or wire)
- string or yarn
- marking pens or crayons
- scissors
- glue
- patterns for raindrops, umbrella, and handle (pages 15–18)
- colored construction paper (umbrella)
- light-blue construction paper (raindrops)
- brown construction paper (handle)
- tape or stapler

Teacher Preparation:

Prepare the patterns ahead of time by copying them onto cardstock or manila folders which will be easier than paper for the students to trace. You will need to attach each half of the umbrella and handle patterns to make complete patterns. To minimize the number of patterns, make one set for each small group of students and allow them to share.

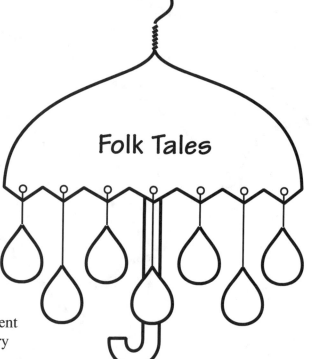

Directions:

1. Trace the umbrella pattern twice onto two pieces of colored construction paper.
2. Trace the handle pattern onto a piece of brown construction paper.
3. Trace the raindrop pattern seven times onto light-blue construction paper.
4. With a marking pen or dark crayon, write a different type of tale on each raindrop (myths, legends, fairy tales, epics, fables, nursery rhymes, ballads).
5. Cut seven pieces of string, varying the lengths, as shown.
6. Glue each raindrop to a piece of string. Let them dry for a few minutes.
7. On one of the umbrella patterns, write Folk Tales in large letters.
8. Lay the other umbrella pattern flat on the table. Next, lay the coat hanger on top of it. Be sure that the hook of the coat hanger is pointing out of the top of the umbrella. Tape the coat hanger onto the umbrella construction paper.
9. Place the labeled (Folk Tales) umbrella pattern on top of the coat hanger. Tape, staple, or glue the two patterns to the hanger. You now have a front and back to your mobile.
10. Glue each raindrop string to the bottom of the umbrella.
11. Glue or staple the handle to the mobile, as shown.
12. Hang your umbrella on a door, window, display wire, or bulletin board for everyone to see!

What Are Folk Tales and Fairy Tales?

Folk Tale Umbrella: Option II *(cont.)*

Note: Attach this half of the pattern to the half on page 16 to make one complete umbrella. The pieces can be glued together at the center strip. Make enough copies so that each mobile has two completed umbrella patterns, one for the front and one for the back of the mobile.

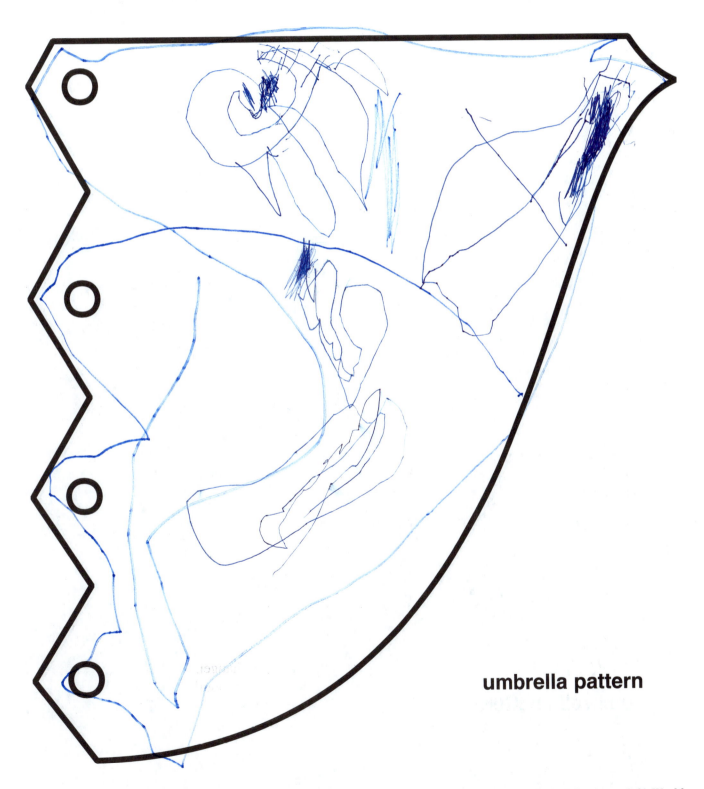

umbrella pattern

What Are Folk Tales and Fairy Tales?

Folk Tale Umbrella: Option II *(cont.)*

Note: Attach this half of the pattern to the half on page 15 to make one complete umbrella. The pieces can be glued together at the center strip. Make enough copies so that each mobile has two completed umbrella patterns, one for the front and one for the back or the mobile.

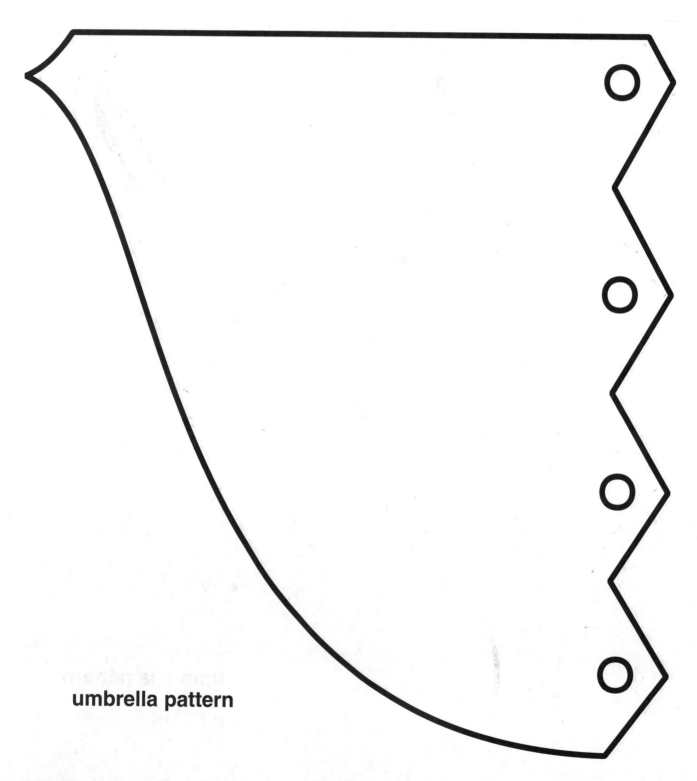

umbrella pattern

#464 Tales Around the World © Teacher Created Materials, Inc.

Folk Tale Umbrella: Option II *(cont.)*

Note: Make enough copies so that each mobile has seven raindrops.

raindrop patterns

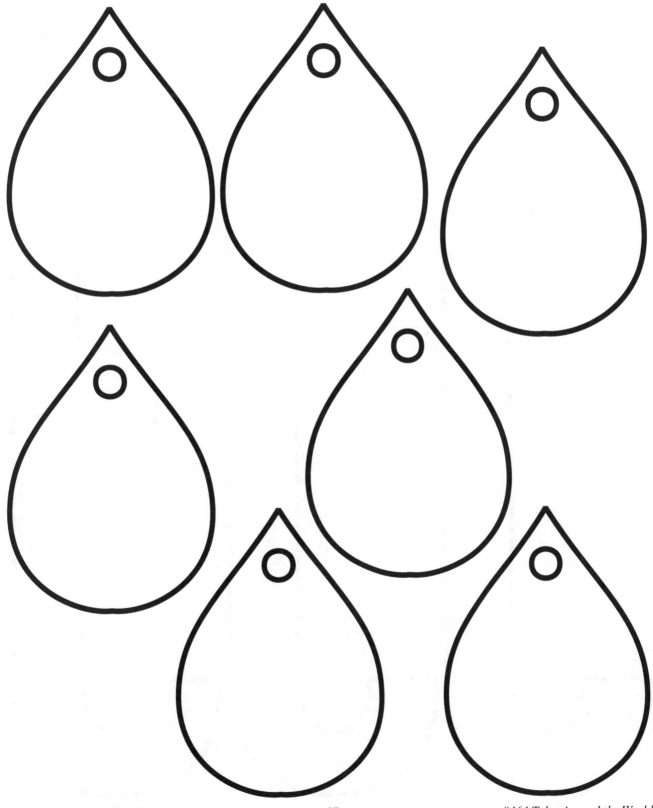

What Are Folk Tales and Fairy Tales?

Folk Tale Umbrella: Option II *(cont.)*

Note: Make enough copies so that each mobile has one handle.

handle patterns

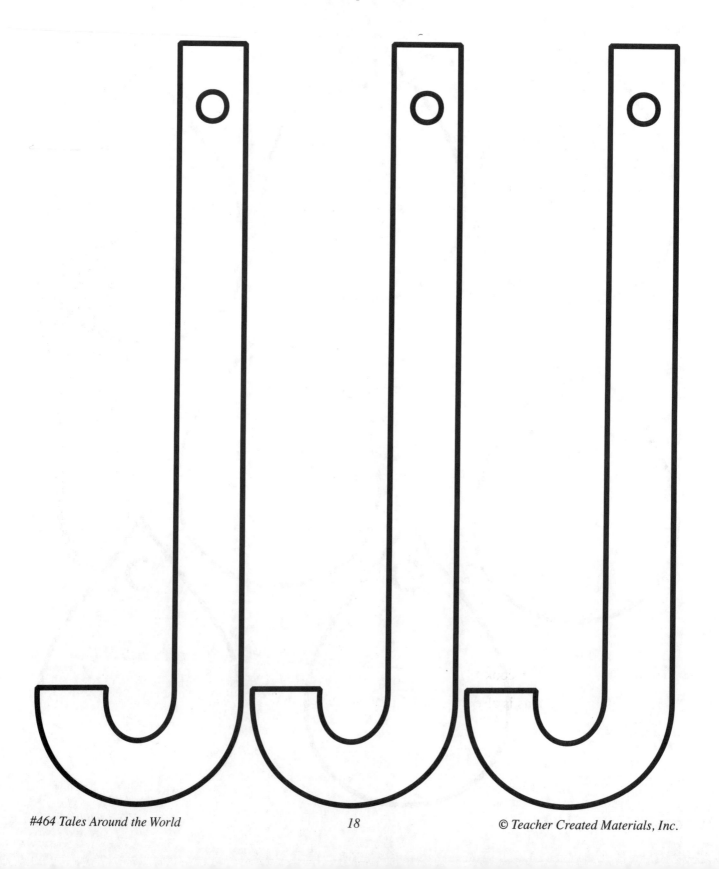

What Are Folk Tales and Fairy Tales?

Recipe for a Fairy Tale

As you read and listen to a variety of fairy tales, you are likely to notice the similar themes and ideas present in all the stories. A fairy tale written over a millennium ago and a fairy tale written just last week will have similar components. Even fairy tales based in different countries and cultures have these commonalities. The similarities have significance because they tell the readers what folk-tale genre they are reading.

What's Cookin' in the Kingdom?

An easy way to remember these important fairy-tale components is to think of them as ingredients in a recipe.

Fairy Tale Ingredients
- "Once upon a time..."
- royalty
- magic help
- good characters
- evil characters
- problem and solution
- "...happily ever after"

Instruct the students to work in cooperative learning groups to write their own recipe card for the creation of a fairy tale. Use words that are associated with recipes, such as the following:

- sprinkle
- mix
- fold in
- add
- beat
- stir
- cook
- pour
- bake
- chop

The amount of ingredients is also important. Use measuring terms such as the following:

- cup
- milliliter
- teaspoon
- dash
- liter
- tablespoon
- heaping

The recipe card can be found on page 20.

What Are Folk Tales and Fairy Tales?

Recipe for a Fairy Tale *(cont.)*

Directions: Using the seven ingredients you have learned, write a recipe for the creation of a fairy tale. Include words from recipes you have read, such as mix, blend, and bake.

Dish: _____

_____

From the kitchen of _____ Serves _____

Ingredients: _____

_____

_____

_____

_____

_____

_____

_____

_____

Preparation: _____

_____

_____

_____

_____

_____

_____

What Are Folk Tales and Fairy Tales?

Section 1: Around the World

Momotaro: The Peach Warrior

Japan

Book: *Peach Boy: A Japanese Legend (Legends of the World)* retold by Gail Sakurai (Troll Associates, 1994)

Summary: At the foot of Mount Fuji, there lives an old, poor, and childless couple. They work hard, but they are sad because they do not have a child. One day the wife finds a large peach floating in the river. When she and her husband open it, out pops a small boy who is sent to be their son. They love their son, Momotaro, and he grows to be a fine young man.

One day the son leaves his parents to seek his fortune. He heads to Demon's Island, much to his parents' dismay. However, the young man possesses magical powers to help him in his journey.

Along the way, Momotaro meets three animals who come along with him as his samurai warriors. They set out to Demon's Island to free the captives and to rid the land of the evil demons. With the help of his three friends and magical strength, Momotaro defeats the demons. The prisoners are freed, and he gathers all the treasure to disperse to the poor and to his parents. The whole country makes a hero of Momotaro. He finally returns to his parents, and his treasures allow them to live in peace and happiness to the end of their days.

Discussion Questions:

- What are the parents' names?
- How does the wife get the peach?
- What does Momotaro mean in English?
- What personality qualities does Momotaro possess?
- How does Momotaro recruit his three helpers?
- What do the two beautiful girls do to help?
- What happens to the chief of the Devils?

Journal Questions and Prompts:

- What would you do if you opened a peach and found a little baby inside?
- What do you think happens to Momotaro after he returns to his parents, and how do you think he lives out his life?
- Complete the sentence and write a short story: One day, I was surprised to see a large peach floating down the river near my house . . .

© Teacher Created Materials, Inc.   #464 *Tales Around the World*

Section 1: Around the World   Momotaro: The Peach Warrior

Samurai Warriors

Along the way to Demon's Island, Momotaro met up with three animals who became his samurai helpers in battle. In the boxes below, write the names of these helpers and draw a picture of each. You may want to read the story again for particular details about each one.

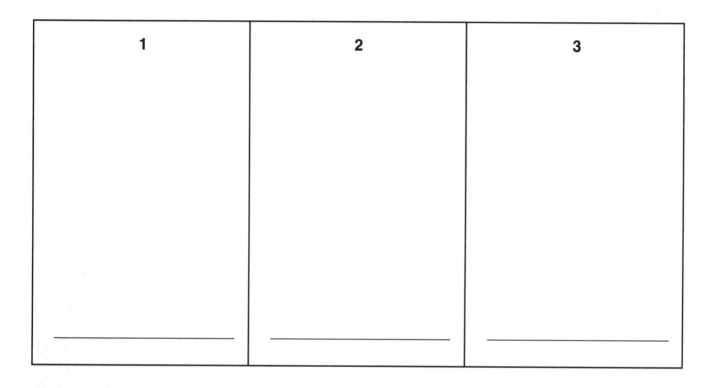

A samurai warrior is a traditional warrior of Japan. For seven centuries these warriors were the military force of Japan. The word *samurai* comes from the Japanese word *saburau*, which means service. Samurai involvement in Japanese government and culture began in 1156 A.D. The samurai costume is known for its brilliant colors and long, decorative swords. The first samurai warriors were generally illiterate, rural landowners who farmed between battles. The samurai evolved into military bureaucrats and became strong leaders trained in military arts. These warriors lived by a strict code of ethics called the *bushido,* which means the way of the warrior. Samurais became elite members of Japanese society.

After reading the paragraph above, answer these questions on the back of this paper.

1. How many centuries did the samurai reign in the military?
2. Where does the word *samurai* come from, and what does it mean?
3. When did samurai involvement begin?
4. What were the first samurai warriors like?
5. What did the samurai system evolve into?
6. What does *bushido* mean?

Kokeshi Doll

Japan holds many festivals throughout the year. Some of these festivals include Children's Day, New Year's, Doll's Festival, Flower Viewing, and All Soul's Day. An important part of many of these festivals is the dolls that are associated with the celebrations. The Kokeshi doll is usually made from the dogwood tree. The kimono is the traditional, wide-sleeved, ankle-length Japanese clothing that wraps around the body. Both men and women wear kimonos.

In honor of *The Peach Warrior*, the class can make Kokeshi dolls by following the directions below.

Materials:

- cardboard toilet-paper tube (one per child)
- 3" (7.5 cm) ball of aluminum foil, Styrofoam, or masking tape
- homemade papier-mâché mixture (See recipe below.)
- small newspaper strips
- tempera paint (white and black)
- printed origami paper, wrapping paper, or fabric
- ½" x 7" (1.25 cm x 17.5 cm) construction-paper strip
- kimono pattern (page 24)
- small piece of string or yarn
- paintbrushes
- glue
- scissors

Directions:

1. Glue the foil (or other) ball to one end of the cardboard tube.
2. Completely cover the tube and ball with papier-mâché strips. Let the doll dry overnight.
3. Paint the entire doll with white tempera paint. Allow ample time to dry.
4. Using the black tempera paint, paint on the hair, eyes, nose, and mouth of the doll. Give time for the figure to dry.
5. Using the kimono pattern, trace and cut out the kimono on either the origami paper or wrapping paper.
6. Wrap the kimono around the doll so that it overlaps in the front. Glue it in place.
7. Wrap the construction-paper strip (sash) around the waist of the doll. Tie with a small piece of yarn.

Homemade Papier-mâché

Pour ½ cup (125 mL) flour or white glue into a bowl. Add ½ cup (125 mL) water and stir. The paste should be the consistency of cream (not too thick). Add more water if necessary. Place newspaper strips into the mixture one at a time. With one hand hold the strip, and with the other hand use two fingers to squeeze out the excess mixture. Place the strips over the form. Press down completely so there will be no wrinkles when it dries. Let dry completely before painting.

Section 1: Around the World   Momotaro: The Peach Warrior

Kokeshi Doll (cont.)

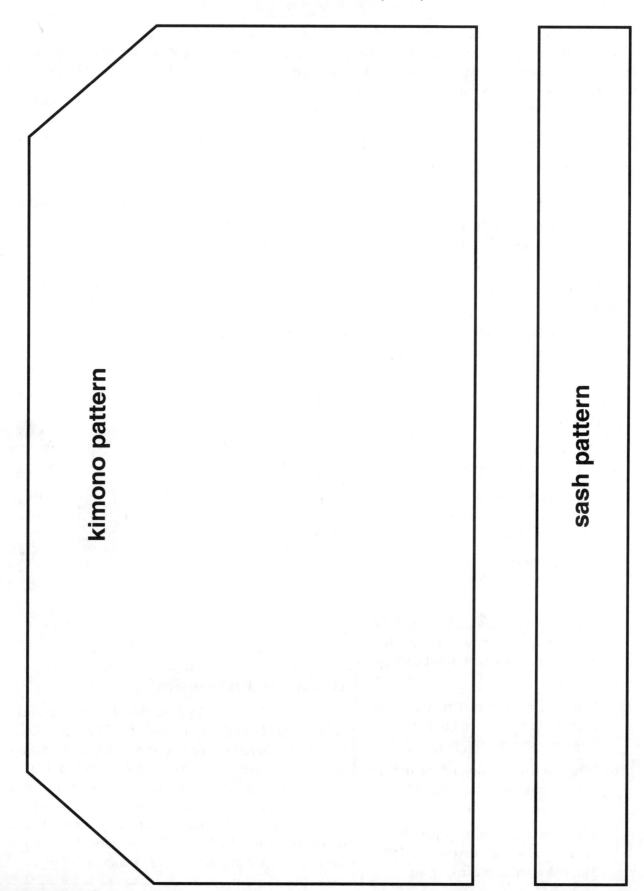

kimono pattern

sash pattern

Section 1: Around the World

Sir Buzz

India

Book: "Sir Buzz" from *Favorite Fairy Tales Told in India* retold by Virginia Haviland (William Morrow & Company, 1994)

Summary: Once upon a time a soldier dies, leaving behind his wife and only son. They become very poor, so the young lad decides to seek his fortune in the world. He comes across a tigress with a thorn in her paw. In exchange for befriending her, she gives him a box, instructing him to carry the box for nine miles (14.4 kilometers). Before the distance is covered, the boy opens the box. A little, troll-like man pops out. His name is Sir Buzz.

Sir Buzz, a grouchy manikin, is there to serve the boy. He helps him to get food and the attentions of Princess Blossom. Eventually the boy, princess, and Sir Buzz find themselves in trouble with the king, police chief, and a vampire. Sir Buzz saves the two from the evil vampire, gives the princess and soldier's son the gold and jewels that belonged to the vampire, and takes them home to the boy's mother. They lived happily ever after.

Discussion Questions:

- Where does the boy get the shillings to set about on his journey?
- What does the tigress do to withstand the pain of having the thorn removed?
- Where is the first place Sir Buzz goes for the boy?
- Describe the first meeting between the princess and the boy?
- What does the vampire pretend to be at first?
- How does Sir Buzz save them from the vampire?

Journal Questions and Prompts:

- Would you have helped the tigress? Why or why not?
- If you were the boy's mother, would you have let him leave to find his fortune in the world? Explain your answer.
- Complete the sentence and continue to write a short story: When I was a child, my father was killed in battle. My mother and I were left penniless, so I . . .

Section 1: Around the World   Sir Buzz

Go the Distance

Read the story of Sir Buzz and then respond to the following questions and prompts.

1. In the tale of Sir Buzz, the tigress gives the soldier's son a box and tells him not to open it until he travels nine miles (14.4 kilometers). What does the boy notice about the box with each passing step?

   _____

2. How far does he travel before he puts the box down?

   _____

3. Who does the boy think the tigress really is?

   _____

4. What happens when the boy flings the box on the ground?

   _____

5. The little manikin tells the boy that if he had carried the box the full nine miles (14.4 kilometers), he might have found something better inside. What (or who) do you think would have been in the box at the end of the distance? Draw a picture of what would have been in the box and write a few sentences describing this find.

   [   ]

   _____
   _____
   _____

6. How might this new character or thing have changed the story? On the back of this paper, write a short paragraph telling how the story would have changed.

Divali Festival Lamp

India is a country with many festivals and celebrations. Most of the celebrations are related to Hinduism, the predominant religion of India. The most important holiday is Divali, the festival of light, celebrated in honor of Lakshmi, the goddess of wealth and bliss. For the holiday, the entire family dresses in their best clothes and prepares an elaborate breakfast meal. Time is also put aside to set off firecrackers and watch festive parades in the streets. Painted clay items and paper toys are sold. In the evening thousands of the Divali lamps are lit on the edges of roofs. Glass flasks of colored water are placed in front of the lamps to give the city a colorful, twinkling look.

You can make your own Divali festival lamps by following these directions.

Materials:

- 3" (7.5 cm) ball of self-hardening clay (1 per student)
- 3" (7.5 cm) wick (found in candle shops, or use a piece of cotton string)
- salad oil
- pencil (1 per student)

Directions:

1. Roll the ball of clay and shape it into a flat bowl by pressing your thumb into the middle.

2. Make the wick holder by pulling one side of the clay bowl into a lip.

3. Rub the pencil with salad oil so it will not stick in the clay and then press the pencil into the lip of the clay bowl.

4. Let the bowl dry.

5. When it is dry, remove the pencil, fill the bowl with salad oil and lay the wick into the lamp.

6. Light the lamp. (**Caution:** Only an adult should light the lamp and handle it when there is a flame.)

7. While all the Divali lamps are glowing, enjoy the light while eating some traditional Indian bread called *chapati*, which can be found in many bakeries and specialty stores.

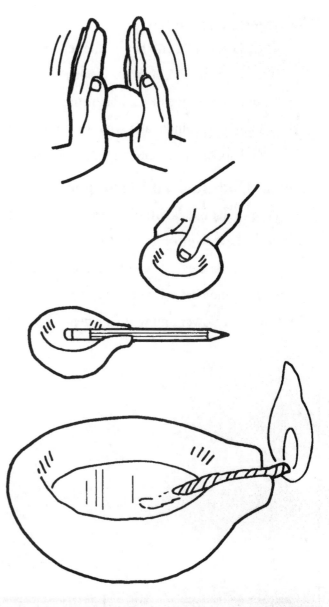

Section 1: Around the World

Legend of the Poinsettia

Mexico

Book: *Legend of the Poinsettia* retold by Tomie dePaola (Putnam, 1994)

Summary: Lucinda and her mother are weaving a new blanket for the Baby Jesus for their church's Christmas procession, but the mother becomes ill and is unable to finish it. Lucinda tries to do the work on her own, but she tangles the yarn and ruins the blanket. She is heartsick, and she feels she has ruined the procession. A mysterious old woman appears and tells her that any gift is beautiful because it is given. Lucinda takes her words to heart. After finding a patch of weeds, she gathers them to bring to the church. In the church she lays down the weeds and begins to pray. Miraculously, the weeds bud beautiful red flowers which cover the altar. The flowers are the poinsettias we know today, the traditional Christmas flower.

Discussion Questions:
- Why do Lucinda and her mother choose to weave a blanket?
- What happens to Lucinda's mother?
- What troubles does Lucinda encounter when she tries to work on her own?
- Who helps Lucinda, and why do you think this person offers her help?
- What happens to Lucinda's gift of weeds? Why?

Journal Questions and Prompts:
- Why is Lucinda's gift of weeds a special gift?
- Why is every gift precious?
- What is the best gift you have ever given? Why?
- What is the best gift you have ever received? Why?
- Choose a flower and write a legend about how it came to be.

Legend of the Poinsettia Section 1: Around the World

Lucinda's Gift

Make a weed turn into a poinsettia!

Materials:

- patterns (page 30)
- red, green, and yellow paper
- pencil
- scissors
- hole punch
- brass paper fastener
- glue

Directions:

1. Cut out and trace the leaf and stem patterns onto green paper. Make five leaves and one stem.

2. Cut out and trace the petal pattern onto red paper. Make five petals.

3. Cut out and trace the pistil-and-stamen pattern onto yellow paper. Make one copy.

4. Gather the leaves together and stack them. Also stack and gather the petals.

5. Punch a hole through the circle at the one end of the petal stack. Do the same to the leaf stack and the stem.

6. Push the fastener through the leaf stack, then the stem, and finally the petals.

7. Open the brass fastener. Glue the pistil-and-stamen piece to the legs of the fastener, being careful not to glue it to the petals.

8. Turn the flower over so only the leaves and stem are showing. This is the weed. Open the leaves to reveal the petals. Turn the flower over and spread the petals to make a poinsettia.

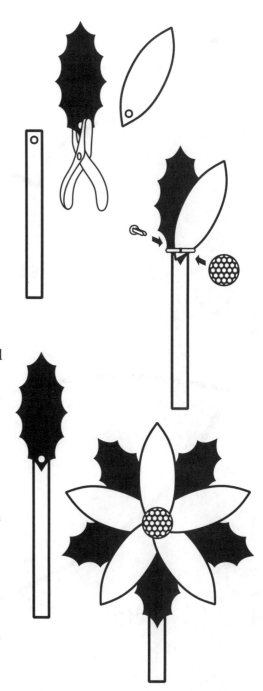

© Teacher Created Materials, Inc. 29 #464 Tales Around the World

Section 1: Around the World Legend of the Poinsettia

Lucinda's Gift *(cont.)*

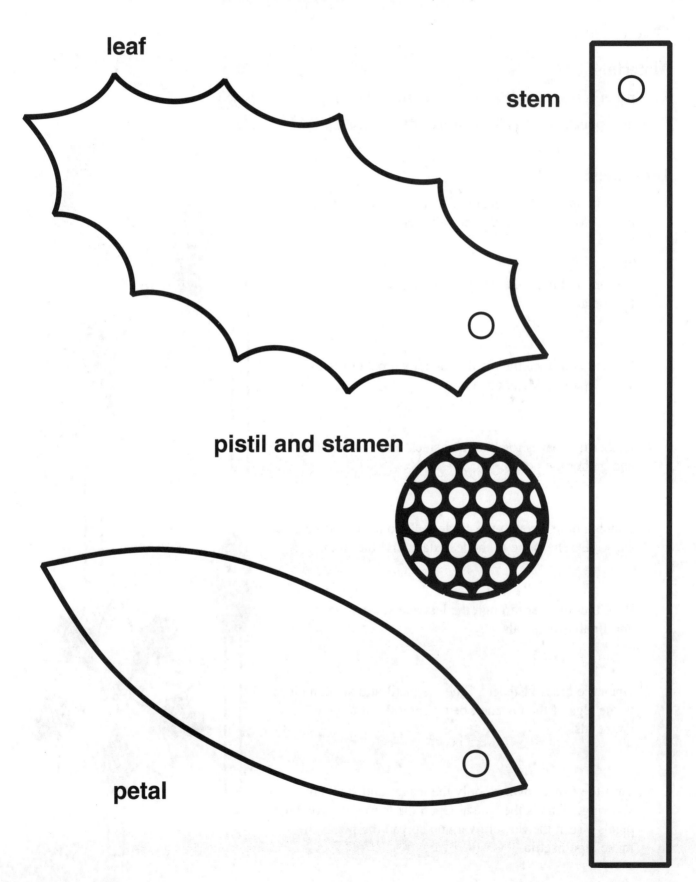

Legend of the Poinsettia Section 1: Around the World

Paper Flowers

A traditional craft and decoration found in Mexico is the popular paper flower. Paper flowers have been popular for hundreds of years. The flowers vary in size and color, the more variety the better. They are found everywhere, from ceremonies to street corners.

Materials:

- 7" (18 cm) square pieces of tissue paper (assorted colors)
- chenille sticks (assorted colors)
- pencils
- scissors
- flower patterns (page 32 and 33)
- manila folders or cardstock

Directions:

1. Use all three pattern sizes for each flower. Trace each pattern onto a manila folder or cardstock and cut it out.

2. Use the sturdy patterns to trace onto tissue paper. Use a different color for each size. Cut out the flowers.

3. Layer the flower pieces from largest to smallest.

4. Use scissors to poke two holes in the center of the flower.

5. Bend a chenille stick through the two holes so that the pipe cleaner is even at both ends. Begin twisting the stick to make the stem. This will bring the flower "petals" together.

6. Decorate a bulletin board with your flowers and save them for your Cinco de Mayo celebration. Plan a fiesta, serve traditional Mexican food, break a piñata, and place the flowers on tables as decorations!

© Teacher Created Materials, Inc. #464 Tales Around the World

Section 1: Around the World   Legend of the Poinsettia

Paper Flowers (cont.)

See page 31 for directions.

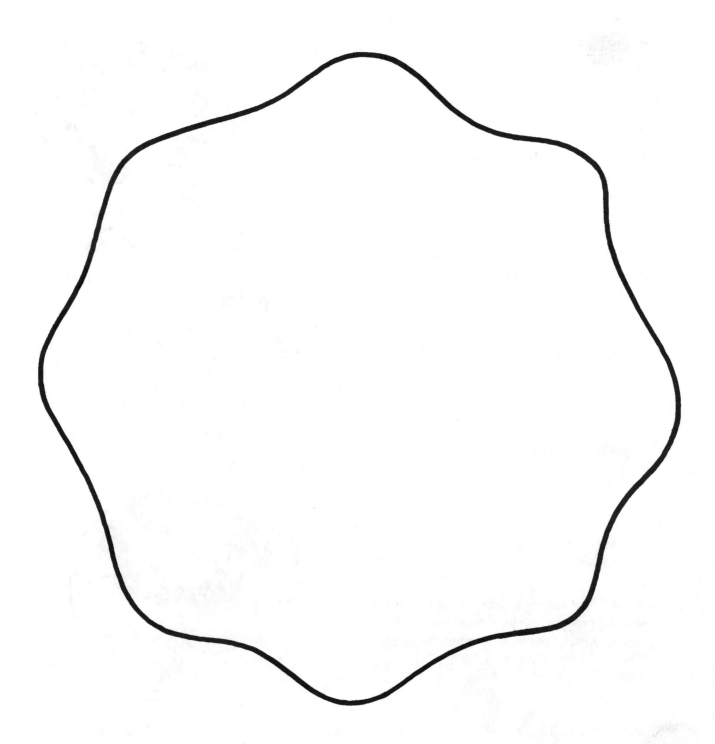

Legend of the Poinsettia   Section 1: Around the World

Paper Flowers (cont.)

See page 31 for directions.

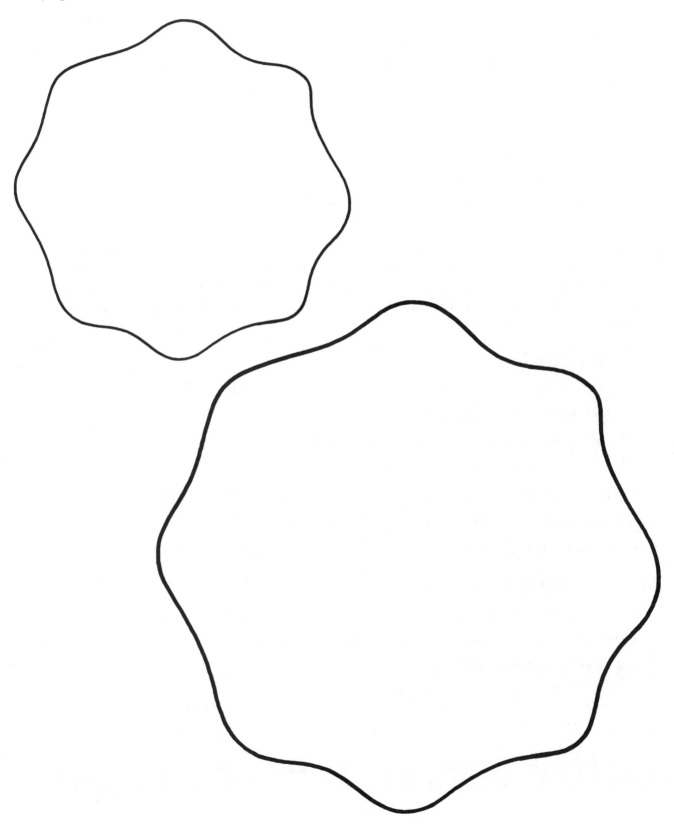

Section 1: Around the World

Seven Clever Brothers

Israel

Book: "Seven Clever Brothers" from *Magical Tales from Many Lands* retold by Margaret Mayo (Dutton Children's Books, 1993)

Summary: Once upon a time a king and queen had seven sons, all born on the different days of the week and so named. One day all the brothers decide to explore the world. Their father makes them promise that they will never quarrel and always remain friends.

As they travel, they come to a fork with seven roads. Each brother takes a different road and agrees to meet back at that spot one year later. When they meet again, the brothers each have found a special gift and power.

They continue to travel together and come upon a strange, silent city. The princess of that city has been kidnapped and is to wed an evil sorcerer. The king offers half his riches and (if his daughter is willing) her hand in marriage. The brothers set out to find her. Through the use of their gifts, they rescue the princess. She chooses to marry Saturday, the youngest, and the other brothers split the treasures. Celebrations ensue in both kingdoms.

Discussion Questions:

- Why do the king and queen name their sons after the days of the week?
- Who is the oldest, and who is the youngest?
- Why does the king want Saturday not to go with the brothers?
- What does the king make the brothers promise?
- What are the special gifts and powers that each brother finds on his journey?
- How does the evil sorcerer try to get the princess back?
- At what point do the brothers break their promise not to quarrel, and how is it resolved?

Journal Questions and Prompts:

- If you were the princess, which brother would you choose to marry and why?
- How do you resolve conflicts with your brother(s) or sister(s)?
- Who chose your name and why?

A Land Full of History

Israel is a very old land, filled with histories of people and times long ago. One city, Jericho, is believed to be the oldest city in the world. It is estimated to be 10,000 years old. Another important city, Jerusalem, also called the Holy City, is sacred to Jews, Christians, and Muslims. These are all different religious groups. Jewish citizens make up about 90% of Israel. From the beginning of their civilization to modern times, the Jewish people have struggled over their right to settle permanently on this land. Many battles, kings, and conquerors have taken a place in the history of this small but highly volatile country.

Work with a partner or small group to learn more about the land of Israel and its people. Choose a topic from the list below. You can get information from the library in books, encyclopedias, and the Internet. Describe your findings in at least three paragraphs. Be ready to present what you learn to the class.

Israel Research Topics

- Father Abraham
- Moses
- The Promised Land
- King David
- King Solomon
- Cyrus of Persia
- The Hasmonean Period
- Constantine the Great
- Constantinople and the Christian Crusades
- The Ottoman Empire

- The Diaspora (scattering of Jews outside Israel)
- Mount of Olives
- Jerusalem
- Jericho
- Babylonia
- Bar Kokhba
- Mount Zion
- King Herod
- Muhammad

Section 1: Around the World   Seven Clever Brothers

Menorah

In the Jewish religion, one of the most special holidays is Hanukkah. Hanukkah is the Jewish Festival of Lights, celebrating a famous and significant battle about religious freedom fought over two thousand years ago in Israel. The eight candles on the menorah are lit on eight consecutive nights to remind Jews to give thanks. Hanukkah is also a time of gift giving as gifts are exchanged on each of the eight nights.

Students can make their own menorahs by following these directions.

Materials:

- self-hardening clay
- triangle pattern (page 37)
- white paper
- newspaper
- water
- tempera paint (assorted colors)
- paintbrushes
- birthday candles
- pencils
- scissors

Directions:

1. Cut out the triangle pattern. Trace it onto another piece of paper so that you have two triangles.

2. Glue the two triangles together to form a star as shown. (This represents the Star of David.)

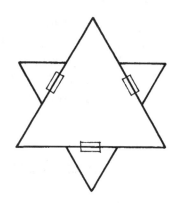

3. Place newspaper on the work area to protect the surface.

4. Roll a ball of clay into a snake shape about ½" (1.25 cm) thick and 5" (12.5 cm) long. Place it on one of the edges of your star.

5. Make five more snakes like the first one and place them on the star pattern.

6. Using a little bit of water, round and rub the corners of the clay pattern together to make the entire piece secure.

7. For the candleholders, roll eight small balls of clay approximately .75" (1.9 cm) round. Also roll one more ball but make it slightly larger.

8. Use the eraser end of a pencil to push into the center of each ball. This will allow the candles to stay in place.

Menorah (cont.)

9. Using water, mold the candleholders in place on the star. Look at the diagram to see where to place the candleholders.

10. Let your menorah dry undisturbed for two days. When your menorah is completely dry, you may paint it with the tempera paints.

11. When the paint is dry, place birthday candles into the holders, and the menorah is ready for the celebration of Hanukkah!

triangle pattern

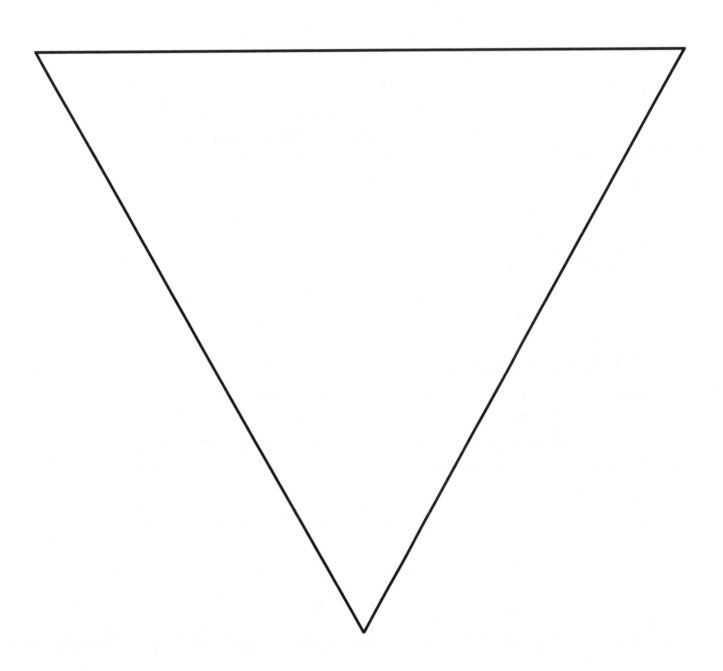

Section 1: Around the World

The Jolly Tailor Who Became King

Poland

Book: "The Jolly Tailor Who Became King" from *Favorite Fairy Tales Told in Poland* retold by Virginia Haviland (William Morrow & Company, 1995)

Summary: Once upon a time in the town of Taidaraida, there lives a merry little tailor named Mr. Joseph Nitechka. He is notable as both a very thin man and as an excellent tailor. He lives quite happily in his town. One day a gypsy comes to him with a cut in her foot. The tailor sews up her cut without a trace of a scar. She is so grateful that she reads his palm to tell him his fortune. She tells him that if he were to leave his town and head west, he would reach a place where he would be king.

He decides to go west, and along the way he meets a scarecrow who becomes his friend and joins him on his journey. They come upon an old town and find it in the midst of a rainstorm; yet, the weather is perfect everywhere else. The king of the town had just died, and his daughter, the princess, promises to marry the man who stops the rain. This man would become the king. The tailor figures out that when the king died, he left a great big hole in the sky on his way to heaven. Using many ladders, the tailor climbs to the hole and sews it shut. This stops the rain. The princess marries the tailor, and he becomes king.

Discussion Questions:

- What is the only kind of food the tailor can eat and why?
- What supplies does the tailor take with him?
- How do the scarecrow and tailor meet and become friends?
- How long does it take the tailor to figure out the problem of the town? (Tell in detail how he solves the problem.)

Journal Questions and Prompts:

- If you were the tailor, would you have trusted the gypsy and left your happy home in hopes of becoming king? Explain.
- If you could eat only one food for the rest of your life, what would it be and why?
- Complete the sentence and write a short story: No one in my town could figure out why it had been raining for a month . . .

The Jolly Tailor Who Became King   Section 1: Around the World

A Jolly Thank You

Mr. Nitechka, the jolly tailor who becomes king, is very happy for his good fortune. If it was not for the gypsy who read his future in the palm of his hand, he would never have found the lovely princess and become king of Pacanow.

Whenever someone gives us a gift or does something nice, it is customary to send him or her a thank-you note to express our gratitude. Pretend that you are Mr. Nitechka and you are writing a thank-you note to the gypsy. Decorate the space around the card. On the lines, express your thanks and share with her how you became king! You will need to figure out the gypsy's address. Since you are a clever king, you should have no trouble!

Section 1: Around the World
The Jolly Tailor Who Became King

Embroidery

Folk art, traditional art from a country, is alive and well in Poland. Polish people, especially in the countryside and small villages, are experts at tapestry weaving, woodcarving, pottery making, embroidery, and painting on glass. A feature of Polish art is that not only is the craft decorative and beautiful, but it is also functional. Folks may eat from pottery dishes turned out by a father, store their clothes in a chest painted by a mother, and stir their soup with a wooden spoon carved by an uncle.

Here is an opportunity for students to embroider, adding a touch of color and artistry to even the most utilitarian of objects.

Materials:

- 8" (20 cm) squares of muslin
- white tissue paper
- pencils
- patterns (page 41)
- straight pins
- embroidery needles
- embroidery floss

Directions:

1. Choose a pattern to embroider and select a muslin square.
2. Trace the pattern onto white tissue.
3. Pin the tissue pattern to the cloth.
4. Thread the needle with a desired color of floss. (Use an even number of strands. Floss comes in strands of six.) Tie a knot in the end.
5. Stitch over the pattern in the following sequence:
   a. Bring the needle through the fabric's underside.
   b. Keeping the thread loose enough to form a small loop, insert the needle down, beside the first insertion point.
   c. Push the needle back up again to start the next stitch at insertion point c.
6. Continue in this way until you have reached the end of your desired color. Tie off the floss below.
7. Switch colors and continue with another part of the pattern.
8. When your embroidery is complete, carefully tear away the tissue paper. The project is finished.

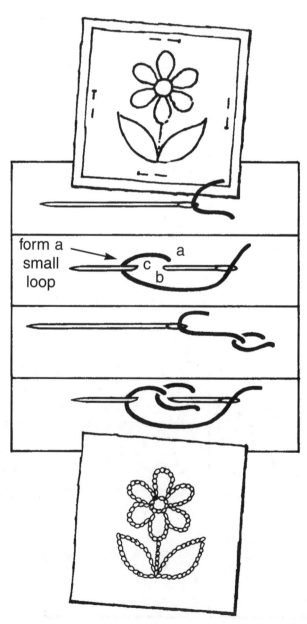

The Jolly Tailor Who Became King Section 1: Around the World

Embroidery (cont.)

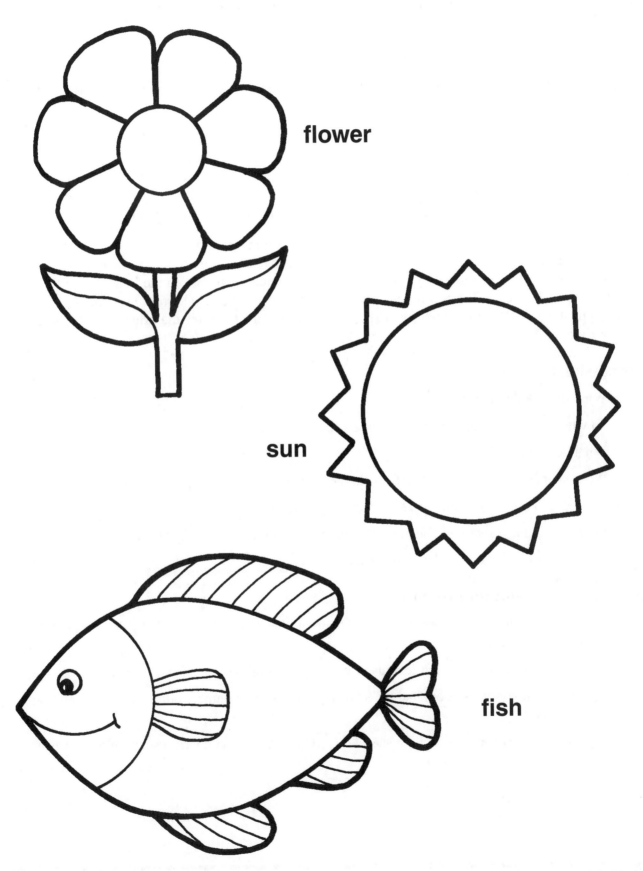

flower

sun

fish

Section 1: Around the World

Kate Crackernuts

Scotland

Book: "Kate Crackernuts" from *Magical Tales from Many Lands* retold by Margaret Mayo (Dutton Children's Books, 1993)

Summary: Long, long ago there lived a bonny (pretty) princess named Kate. After her mother dies, her father remarries another queen who has her own daughter, also named Kate. The two girls get along very well. Two Kates in the family is confusing, so the king's Kate, who is bonnier, is called Bonny Kate. This makes the queen jealous, so she has a spell cast upon the Bonny Kate and turns her head into a sheep's head. After this, both Kates run away, fearing what might happen next.

In the next kingdom, plain Kate takes a job in the castle as a maid, saying that her sister is sick so no one will see her sheep's head. The king of this castle has two sons, one of whom is very sick. Plain Kate watches over him one night and discovers that he is under a spell from the fairies. She finds out how to return her sister to her bonny self as well as how to save the prince from his sickness. The king is so happy, he gives Plain Kate whatever she wants. She wants to marry the prince, and her sister, Bonny Kate, marries the other prince. They all live happily ever after.

Discussion Questions:

- What does bonny mean?
- To whom does the queen go to find a spell for Bonny Kate?
- What does the spell do?
- What happens to all the people left in charge of watching the sick prince?
- What does Plain Kate do to solve everyone's problems?
- What two items does Plain Kate find that help her sister and the sick prince?
- How does Plain Kate earn the name "Kate Crackernuts?"

Journal Questions and Prompts:

- In most fairy tales, a sister is usually jealous of another sister's beauty. Why do you think Kate Crackernuts is not jealous?
- Tell about a time you have felt jealous of one of your siblings or friends.
- If everyone in your classroom had the same name, what nickname would suit you to tell you apart? Why?
- Complete the sentence and write a short story: The jealous queen cast a spell on me because . . .

Kate Crackernuts   Section 1: Around the World

Kate the Helper

In *Kate Crackernuts* Plain Kate is a great helper. She helps her sister escape her jealous mother and finds a way to cure her from the evil spell of the sheep's head. She also helps the sick prince while risking her own life in the land of the fairies. Kate is a good friend, sister, and helper.

Can you think of a time you helped a friend solve a problem? What did you do to help? Did your friend feel better after your help? Was the problem solved?

Work in small cooperative learning groups and role-play the following problems. Allow each group member to offer his or her suggestions for help. Decide as a group which would be the best solution to each problem and write it down in the spaces provided below.

Problems	Our Solution
Your friend cheated on a math test, got a good grade, and now feels guilty about the situation.	
You notice an older student picking on a younger one at recess. The younger child is upset.	
Your class has a substitute teacher for the day. The rest of the class is creating problems for her, and she cannot find the lesson plans.	
Your friend was unkind to a new student and now feels badly about it.	
(Write a problem of your own.)	

Scottish Plaid

A traditional folk costume in Scotland is the kilt. The kilt is a wool skirt which comes to the knee. A decorative belt is worn around the waist. Both men and women wear kilts for festive occasions. During times of ancient wars between clans, the male soldiers wore kilts to battle. The pattern of the kilt is known as plaid. Plaid is a rectangular piece of wool designed in a pattern called a tartan pattern. The design is created in a criss-cross pattern made from lines of different widths. Scotland is known for its red, green, and yellow, blue, and black plaid designs.

You will make your own Scottish plaid piece by weaving yarn in a cardboard loom. To make a piece of Scottish plaid, use mostly red yarn, and then green, black, and yellow. You may use other colors if you wish.

Materials:

- 5" x 6" (12.5 cm x 15 cm) cardboard rectangles (one per student)
- assorted yarn colors such as blue, brown, green, red, black, or yellow
- scissors
- ruler
- pencil

Directions:

1. Cut nine ½" (1.25 cm) slits on both ends of the cardboard. The slits should be ½" apart and ½" long.

2. Take a long length of two yarn colors (approximately 7' or 2 m). Slip one end into the first slit on the bottom left side of the cardboard. Bring the yarn up to the top and slip the yarn into the first slit on the top left side. Continue wrapping the yarn top to bottom until you reach the end on the right side.

3. Finish by slipping the last of the yarn into the bottom right slit. Trim the remainder with scissors.

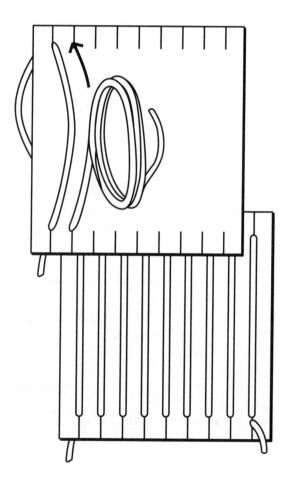

Kate Crackernuts   Section 1: Around the World

Scottish Plaid (cont.)

4. Begin weaving with long lengths of yarn, approximately 2' (60 cm) long. Start at the bottom of the loom by weaving in an under-over-under-over pattern until you reach the bottom of the row.

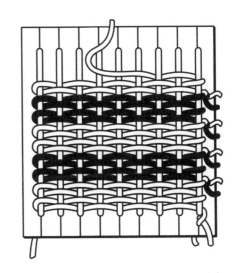

5. When you get to the end of the row, return in the other direction, following the same pattern. Keep the yarn loose as you weave, but push each row close to the one before it when you finish a row.

6. When you run out of the colored piece of yarn you are currently using, cut a new piece of yarn and tie the old end to the new end to continue weaving.

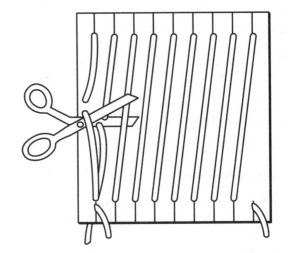

7. When you have almost reached the top, finish the last row and stop. Turn the weaving loom over and cut the back yarn strands through the middle.

8. Carefully pull the end strands away from the cardboard and lay the plaid piece flat.

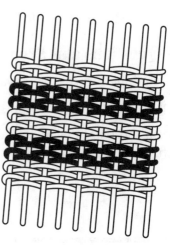

9. Trim the fringe at the top and bottom to whatever length you desire. Now you have your own piece of Scottish plaid! You can use this piece as a small table mat or as a wall hanging.

© Teacher Created Materials, Inc.

Section 1: Around the World

The Tale of Sadko the Minstrel

Russia

Book: "The Tale of Sadko the Minstrel" in *Koskka's Tales: Stories from Russia* retold by James Mayhew (Larousse Kingfisher Chambers, 1993)

Summary: There is a poor minstrel whose only source of income is playing his *goosli* (harp-like instrument played on the lap) for the enjoyment of others. One late night while he is playing his music by the lake, he hears a fair voice singing back. It is Princess Volkova, daughter of the Tsar of the Sea, and she has fallen in love with him and his voice. She gives him gold and brings him so much luck that he soon becomes a wealthy sea merchant, owning three magnificent ships.

Sadko becomes richer and richer, promises to marry a beautiful girl, Lubasha, and continues to sail the seas. On one trip, the Tsar of the Sea is angry with Sadko and creates a huge storm, tossing Sadko to the bottom of the ocean. The Princess Volkova rescues Sadko, and the Tsar is so happy he offers his daughter to be Sadko's bride. However, Sadko longs to be on the land with his beautiful Lubasha. Saint Nikolai of Mozhaysk, the patron saint of all sailors, saves him from the ocean kingdom, but the princess follows. The saint tells her she must stay in the sea, but he takes pity upon her broken heart. He transforms her into a shining river that flows near Sadko's town. Sadko names the river Volkova. Sadko returns home, marries Lubasha, and sings along the Volkova River, much to the enjoyment of the princess.

Discussion Questions:

- How does Sadko get his *goosli*?
- What does Sadko first believe the voice from the lake to be?
- What does the princess promise Sadko?
- Who are the three men who come with Sadko to the lake, and what do they give him?
- Why is the Tsar of the Sea angry with Sadko?
- How is it determined which sailor should jump overboard?
- What does Sadko do which pleases the Tsar of the Sea?
- When Sadko returns to the land, what does he do, and how is his life different?

Journal Questions and Prompts:

- Do you think Princess Volkova was happy with how the tale ended? Explain.
- What do you think of the sailor's idea to determine who was a jinx among them?
- Write a short story beginning with this sentence: I was walking through the woods when I heard a soft, beautiful voice calling to me . . .

The Tale of Sadko the Minstrel Section 1: Around the World

Water, Water Everywhere!

Water is a focal point in *The Tale of Sadko the Minstrel.* There are lakes, rivers, seas, ships, and an underwater kingdom. The land of Russia is a place full of lakes, seas, and rivers. Study this map and answer the questions about this water-filled land.

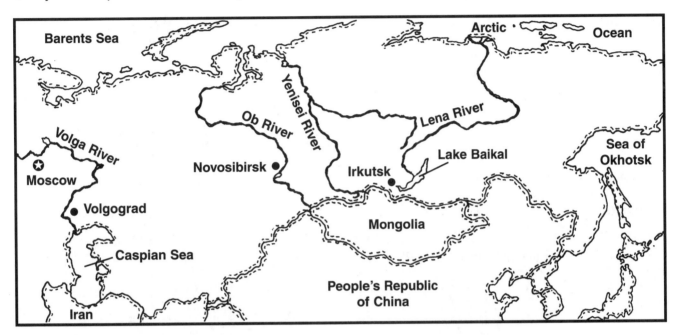

1. What is the capital city of Russia? _____

2. What river flows into the Caspian Sea? _____

3. What river flows into Lake Baikal? _____

4. What flows through the city of Moscow? _____

5. What river is west of the Yenisei River? _____

6. What is the easternmost sea? _____

7. What other country shares a border with the Caspian Sea? _____
   _____

8. What is the name of the town through which the Ob River flows? _____
   _____

9. Lake Baikal is closest to what city? _____

10. What ocean touches the northern borders of Russia? _____

© Teacher Created Materials, Inc.   #464 *Tales Around the World*

Section 1: Around the World   The Tale of Sadko the Minstrel

Straw Doll

Dolls are popular in virtually every culture around the world. Some dolls are elaborately decorated and expensive while others are more simple, less costly, and easy to make. This Russian farm doll is made from straw and leftover material scraps.

Materials:

- handful of 8" (20 cm) straw for each student (width should be approximately 1–2" or 2.5–5 cm)
- 2 chenille sticks per student
- fabric scraps and yarn
- scissors
- needle and thread, or glue

Directions:

1. Gather about three-quarters of the bunch of straw. Use a chenille stick to tie off the "head." Cut away the chenille stick since you will need the scraps later.

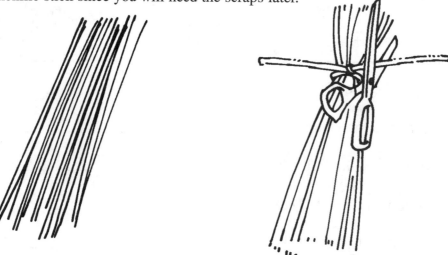

2. Separate the straw at the bottom into two equal bunches. Use the small pieces of chenille stick to tie off the bunches into two legs.

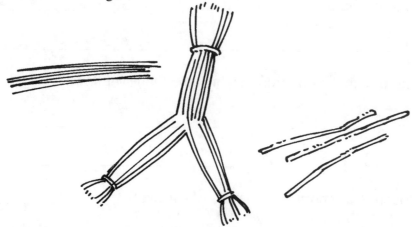

The Tale of Sadko the Minstrel Section 1: Around the World

Straw Doll *(cont.)*

3. Gather the rest of the straw for the the "arms." This bundle will be smaller than the bundle for the body. Attach it across the body of the doll using extra pieces of the chenille stick. Use short pieces of the chenille stick to tie off the arms.

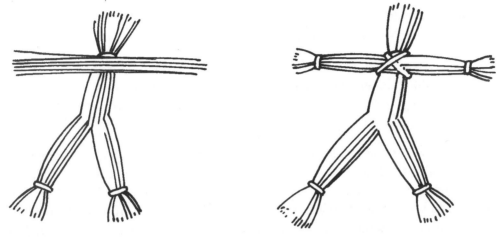

4. Determine if you will be making a boy or a girl doll. Choose from various material scraps to make clothes for the doll. Use needle and thread or glue to attach the clothes.

5. Generally, traditional straw dolls are faceless and hairless, but you can create a face and hair with fabric and yarn scraps if you like.

Section 1: Around the World

The Ox of the Wonderful Horns

Africa

Book: "The Ox of the Wonderful Horns" in *The Ox of the Wonderful Horns and Other African Folktales* retold by Ashley Byron (Simon & Schuster Children's Books, 1993)

Summary: In a village in Africa, a chief and his favorite wife have a boy named Mungalo. All of the other wives are jealous of Mungalo and are cruel to him, especially after his mother dies. As promised, the day comes for the chief to give Mungalo the most beautiful ox of the herd. This ox has wonderful horns and is the finest of Mungalo's cattle.

However, Mungalo becomes so unhappy at his general mistreatment, he mounts the ox one day and leaves the village. Eventually, they run out of food and water, and Mungalo thinks they will die. The ox tells Mungalo that if he rubs his horns three times to the right, he will have anything he wants, but rubbing two times to the left will make the item vanish. The two continue on their journey. Eventually, the ox gets into a fight with a fierce bull and dies. Mungalo takes the horns from his cherished beast and wears them on his belt, finding that the magic still works. He meets many people along his journey, some who try to steal the magical horns; however, the magic only works for Mungalo.

At one village, Mungalo finds favor with the chief and his daughter. He marries the daughter and returns to his village, finding that the evil mothers have mended their ways and welcome Mungalo and his new bride back into their village.

Discussion Questions:

- Why are the other wives jealous of Mungalo's mother?
- What does his mother promise him before she dies?
- Does the ox know of his death before it happens? How do you know?
- Why won't the first man let Mungalo into his hut?
- How does Mungalo get his wonderful horns back from the thief?
- How does Mungalo win the heart of the chief's daughter?
- Where does the couple live at the end of the story?

Journal Questions and Prompts:

- Why do you think the ox's magic works only with Mungalo?
- List animal helpers in other stories you have read. How have they helped?
- Write a short story that begins with this sentence: My pet ox told me his horns had magical powers . . .

The Ox of the Wonderful Horns　　　　　　　　　　　　　Section 1: Around the World

Chain of Events

The journeys of Mungalo lead him to many places, people, and adventures. Reread the story and place each event in its proper order on the chain of Mungalo's life.

Events

　　The ox tells Mungalo the magic of his horns.

　　Mungalo finds a village with no real food.

　　The chief's daughter becomes fond of Mungalo and agrees to marry him.

　　The singer turns out to be a thief and takes the horns.

　　Mungalo's mother gives him little clay oxen toys to play with.

　　Mungalo and the great ox leave the village.

　　Mungalo and his wife return to his father's village and settle there.

　　The ox beats the fierce bull in a fight.

　　Mungalo is treated like royalty in this village.

　　Mungalo's father gives him the great white ox.

Chain of Events

Section 1: Around the World The Ox of the Wonderful Horns

Adinkra Sponge Stamps

In *The Ox of the Wonderful Horns*, Mungalo magically changes his dirty clothes into those of royal appearance. He wears beautiful garments and shiny, decorative ornaments and jewels.

In the African country of Ghana, beautiful fabric patterns are made from symbols that are stamped onto cloth in repeated patterns. The fabric is called *adinkra*.

Materials:

- dry, clean household sponges
- cardstock or manila folder scraps
- black, fine-point, felt-tip pen
- manila or light tan construction paper (one per student)
- assortment of tempera paints
- black (or dark-colored) felt marker
- sharp scissors and/or stencil knife (for adult use only)
- paper plates or small, shallow bowls
- symbols (page 53)

Directions:

1. Trace the four symbols onto the heavy paper and cut them out.
2. Place one of the patterns on a dry sponge. Using the fine-tip pen, trace the pattern onto the sponge, using dots.
3. Cut around the dots with the sharp scissors. The stencil knife may make the cutting easier. (An adult should do this.) Trim any extra pieces away from the desired symbol.

The Ox of the Wonderful Horns Section 1: Around the World

Adinkra Sponge Stamps *(cont.)*

4. Prepare the construction paper "cloth" by dividing it into four squares. Mark these squares with the dark marking pen.

5. Squeeze some tempera paint on a paper plate or bowl. Have a variety of colors available.

6. Carefully dip the sponge symbol into the paint. Be sure only to dip enough so that no more than half of the sponge is submerged in paint.

7. Gently press the painted sponge symbol into the square. Repeat until you have a pattern for that symbol. Continue doing this, using all the symbols.

Patterns:

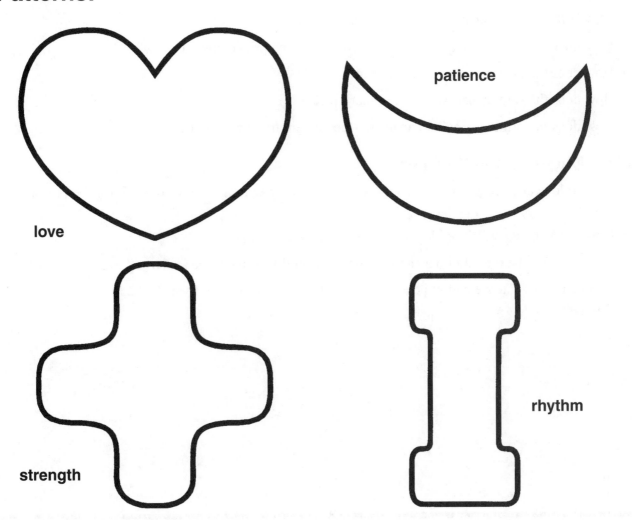

love

patience

strength

rhythm

Section 1: Around the World

The Canary Prince

Italy

Book: *The Canary Prince* retold by Eric Jon Nones (Farrar Straus & Giroux, 1991)

Summary: There lives a beautiful, Italian princess who, like so many lovely princesses, is envied by her wicked stepmother. The stepmother manages to imprison the girl in a tower. It is there that a handsome young prince discovers her. Through the use of a magic charm, the princess is able to turn the prince into a canary so that he can fly to the heights of her tower and visit her there. Once in the tower, he again becomes a man.

It does not take long for the stepmother to learn about the canary prince, and she contrives to have him wounded. The princess learns of his jeopardy, and she finds a way to climb from the tower to find her wounded love. Disguising herself, she gets near to the prince and heals him. As is the case with any good fairy tale, the couple live happily ever after.

Discussion Questions:

- Why is the princess locked in the tower?
- Why is the princess unable to get out of the tower?
- How does the princess acquire the magic to change the prince into a canary?
- How does the prince again become a man?
- How does the stepmother wound the canary prince?
- How does the princess finally manage to free herself and save the prince?

Journal Questions and Prompts:

- Do you love anything or anyone so much you would be willing to risk your life for the person? Explain.
- How is *The Canary Prince* like the fairy tale *Rapunzel*?
- If you were to be turned into an animal, which would you like to be and why?
- Complete the sentence and write a short story: Once upon a time, I was locked in a tower by an evil queen . . .

The Canary Prince   Section 1: Around the World

Canary and Prince

Color and cut out the patterns. Glue them back to back, placing a craft stick at the bottom between the two patterns. Turn the puppet from canary to prince to retell the story of *The Canary Prince*.

Section 1: Around the World   The Canary Prince

Pasta Making

Pasta is a traditional dish served in Italy. While pasta originated in China, Italian explorers brought back the recipe to their country and created their own special types of pastas. Pasta is the Italian word meaning dough. The best pasta is made from durum (hard) wheat and is full of low-fat carbohydrates. There are several types of pasta available in a variety of shapes and sizes that are served in many different ways. This recipe will tell you how to make homemade pasta without a pasta machine.

Ingredients:

- 2½ cups (625 mL) flour
- ⅓ cup (85 mL) water
- 1 tablespoon (15 mL) olive oil
- butter and salt (or another topping or sauce)
- 2 eggs
- 1 egg yolk
- 1 teaspoon (5 mL) salt

Materials:

- large bowl and spoon (or electric mixer)
- pasta cutter or serrated knife
- large saucepan filled with water
- rolling pin
- clean dishcloths
- colander

Preparation:

1. In a large bowl, mix 1 cup (250 mL) flour with all the remaining ingredients.

2. When the mixture is thoroughly mixed, stir in enough of the remaining flour to make a soft dough.

3. Turn the dough onto a lightly floured surface and knead it until it is smooth and elastic (about 10 minutes).

4. Cover the dough with a towel and let it sit undisturbed for thirty minutes.

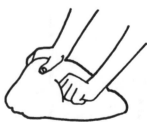

The Canary Prince   Section 1: Around the World

Pasta Making *(cont.)*

5. Cut the dough in half. Take one half and use a rolling pin to roll out the dough onto a floured surface. Form the dough into a rectangular shape about ¼" (.6 cm) thick.

6. Use the pasta cutter or serrated knife to cut the dough into thin strips.

7. Place the dough strips in a single layer onto the clean dishcloths.

8. Repeat with the remaining dough. Let the strips dry for at least two hours before cooking them.

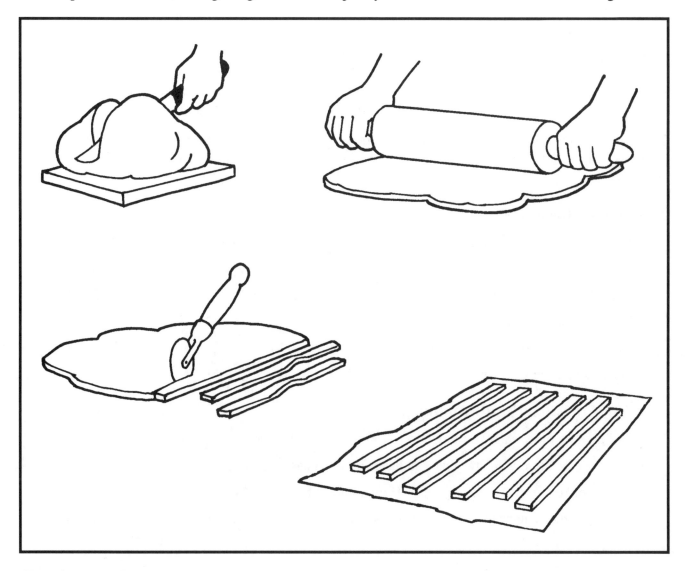

Cooking the Pasta

Fill the saucepan with water and add a dash of oil. Bring the water to a boil. Add the noodles into the boiling water and cook about 5–8 minutes or until tender but firm. Drain the noodles in the colander. Serve your pasta with some butter and salt or add your own special sauce, and enjoy this Italian tradition.

Section 1: Around the World

The House in the Sky

Bahamas

Book: *The House in the Sky: A Bahamian Folktale* by Robert D. San Souci (Dial Books for Young Readers, 1996)

Summary: Two lazy brothers want to find a way to feed their families without having to work. Rabby, the clever brother, discovers that one can steal food from the sky spirits. He goes to their dwelling, quickly fills his bag, and leaves with plenty of supplies. His brother, Boukee, equally lazy, is not equally clever. Boukee also goes to the house of the sky spirits, but he remains inside and gorges himself on all he can eat. He stays so long that the spirits return to find him eating their food. Boukee is caught because of his greed, and he barely manages to escape with his life.

The author of this book notes that he has combined elements from a few traditional tales to create this composite tale. Nonetheless, he tells it with a Caribbean flavor that adds to the authenticity of the story.

Discussion Questions:

- How are Rabby and Boukee supposed to provide for their families?
- What makes the brothers so lazy?
- Why does Boukee not follow the express advice of his brother?
- Why is Boukee captured?
- How does Boukee manage to escape?
- What does Rabby do when Boukee is caught?

Journals Questions and Prompts:

- Tell about a time when you failed to follow some good advice.
- Is there any chore you have that you have found an easy way to avoid?
- Does Boukee deserve what he gets? How about Rabby?
- Complete the sentence and write a short story: Quietly I crept into the home of the sky spirits . . .

The Home of the Sky Spirits

Imagine the home of the sky spirits has something you could use to make your life easier. Draw how you imagine the home to appear with whatever bounty you would like to find there.

Section 1: Around the World   The House in the Sky

My Island

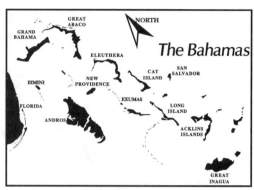

The Bahamas consist of an archipelago of approximately 700 islands and islets. While the islands are known for their subtropical climates and beautiful beaches, only about 40 of them are inhabited.

Imagine that one of the islands was given to Rabby and Boukee. What do you think they would do with it? Think about how they act in the story and then write your ideas here.

_____
_____
_____
_____
_____
_____

Now imagine that you became the owner of one island in the Bahamas, and you could do with it whatever you chose. Would you build on the island? Would you live there? Would you use it for any special purpose? Think about these questions and then write about your Bahamian paradise in the space below.

_____
_____
_____
_____
_____
_____

Section 1: Around the World

Fa Mulan

China

Book: *Fa Mulan* retold by Robert D. San Souci (Hyperion Books for Children, 1998)

Summary: This book is based on an ancient Chinese ballad thought to stem from the Northern and Southern Dynasties of 420 A.D.—589 A.D. The story has been told in many forms over the years with some variation, although the basic story remains the same. The protagonist is called Mulan, Mu-lan, or Mu Lan, depending on the version. Fa is the family name, which in the Chinese culture is written first.

San Souci's retelling of the classic ballad is modeled after the earliest recorded versions of the story. It begins with Mulan and Elder Sister arguing about the role of women in war. While the two are shopping in their village, they hear a call to arms for Chinese men to fight with the Khan against the invading Tartars. Mulan's father is drafted, but he is old and weak. Mulan convinces her parents to let her go in his place, disguised as a man.

Cutting her hair and wearing her father's armor, Mulan joins Khan's army. A determined and able soldier, she rises in rank and skill, earning the respect of her colleagues and superiors. Although she is proud of her service and the honor she brings to her family, she misses her home and wishes one day to return and become a wife and mother.

For twelve years Mulan fights and lives as a man, and when the war is over, the Khan offers her money and anything else she wishes in gratitude for her brave and victorious service. She asks to be discharged and allowed to return home. The Khan thanks her and releases her with an honor guard of her five closest comrades. Once home, Mulan dresses in her former clothes, and her peers see that she is a woman. They honor her, stating in effect that on a field of battle, men and women are indistinguishable. The story ends with the suggestion that Mulan and one of her fellow soldiers with whom she has had a close bond will marry and begin a life together.

Discussion Questions:

- Why does Elder Sister say that Mulan should not play with swords?
- Who are the Tartars, and what do they do?
- Why does Mulan take her father's place in the Khan's army?
- How does Mulan distinguish herself in the war?
- What does Mulan mean when she talks about the male and female rabbits in the field?
- What do you think will happen next for Mulan?

Journal Questions and Prompts:

- Imagine that you were to spend twelve years pretending to be someone else. Write about your experiences.
- Do you think the story of Mulan could have really happened? Could it happen today?
- Tell about a situation when you did something different from your friends. Were you honored or criticized for it?
- What would you most like to do when you are grown?
- Write a short story, starting with this sentence: I looked up and saw the powerful army riding toward us on hundreds of stallions . . .

Section 1: Around the World   Fa Mulan

The Same or Different?

Many stories you have heard have been passed down from one generation or group of people to another. Such stories are told for many reasons but particularly to help explain events, to teach lessons, or simply to entertain. *Fa Mulan* is a story with an important message about the equality—and yet differences—between men and women.

When Mulan goes to war, no one believes that a woman can be a soldier. Mulan proves them wrong because not only is she an excellent soldier, but she also becomes the general, and ultimately wins the war for China.

You have probably heard many things in your life about what boys and girls can and cannot do because of who they are. Together with a partner, make a list of these things. Write down everything you have heard, whether or not you think it is true. (For example, some people believe that only boys should play football and only girls should wear long hair.) Write these and other things on your lists. When you have finished, follow the directions below.

Just for Boys	Just for Girls

Choose one item from your list. On the back of this paper, write why you agree or disagree with the statement. Give lots of information to support your ideas. Later, you will share your arguments with the class.

Fa Mulan   *Section 1: Around the World*

Chinese Moon Festival Lantern

While she is away at war, Mulan misses everything about her home and family life. One of the things families do together is to celebrate special occasions. In the Chinese culture, one prominent celebration is the Moon Festival. Held on the fifteenth day of the eighth month of the lunar calendar (usually October) the Moon Festival takes place in honor of a good harvest. Families gather to create beautiful lanterns, eat traditional foods, and participate in a community-wide lantern parade. The lantern symbolizes the glow of the harvest moon.

Materials:

- 4 sheets of red construction paper (4.5" x 6" or 11.5 cm x 15 cm)
- 4 sheets of white paper (3" x 4½" or 7.5 cm x 11.5 cm)
- scissors
- hole punch
- gold glitter
- white glue
- stapler or clear tape
- red or black crayon or marking pen
- thick, black or red yarn
- Chinese writing (page 64)

Directions:

1. On each sheet of white paper (in a vertical direction), choose and draw a Chinese word (page 64) with crayon or pen.
2. If desired, cut a fancy edge or curved shape to the bottom of each white paper.
3. Glue each white rectangle to the center of each red sheet of paper.
4. Draw a border pattern around the edges of the red paper. Apply glitter as desired.
5. To form the sides of the lantern, staple or tape the rectangles together as shown.
6. Punch a hole in the top center of each rectangle. Attach yarn to hang the lantern.
7. *Option:* Make tassels from the yarn and suspend them from the bottom corners of the lantern.

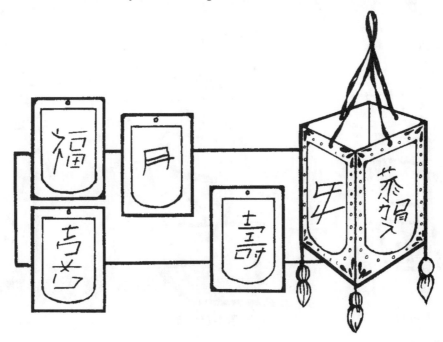

Section 1: Around the World Fa Mulan

Chinese Moon Festival Lantern (cont.)

Section 1: Around the World

The Little Seven-Colored Horse

Spain

Book: *The Little Seven-Colored Horse: A Spanish American Folktale* retold by Robert D. San Souci (Chronicle Books, 1995)

Summary: Juanito is the youngest of three brothers. The older boys are mean-spirited and selfish, but Juanito has a good and loving heart. When the family farm is in jeopardy, Juanito comes to the rescue by capturing the magical, seven-colored horse. However, after the horse promises to always help Juanito whenever he needs it, Juanito frees the horse and is ridiculed and threatened by his brothers. True to his word, the horse helps the boy flee from his siblings. The two begin to travel around the world, having wonderful adventures. Eventually, Juanito is challenged to accomplish three difficult tasks which the horse helps him to manage. The result is that Juanito wins the hand of the mayor's daughter.

Discussion Questions:

- What are the differences between Juanito and his brothers?
- What amazing feat does Juanito accomplish to help his family?
- What is special about the horse?
- How does Juanito flee his brothers?
- What are some adventures had by Juanito and the horse?
- What three challenges does Juanito face?

Journal Questions and Prompts:

- Tell about a time you helped your family.
- Tell about a time when you were brave.
- Have you ever received a reward for something you did? Tell about it.
- Write a short story that begins with the sentence: I couldn't believe my eyes when I saw a beautiful, seven-colored horse standing in the field . . .

Section 1: Around the World   The Little Seven-Colored Horse

Horse of Seven Colors

Color the seven-colored horse as you think it might appear. Remember to use seven colors!

Gazpacho

A traditional Spanish food is *el gazpacho,* a popular summer dish which is like a cold vegetable soup. It is prepared in several different ways and usually contains bread, oil, garlic, water, and tomato. Other ingredients such as cucumber and fresh pepper are often added.

As a class project try preparing some gazpacho. Follow the recipe below, asking each student to contribute a portion of the ingredients or any equipment or serving items needed for preparation. Fresh ingredients work best, but canned ones may be used. Serve croutons along with the soup.

Ingredients:

- 9 oz. (265 mL) tomatoes
- 1 clove garlic
- 2 tablespoons (30 mL) vinegar
- pinch of salt
- 2 green peppers
- 5 tablespoons (75 mL) oil
- 1 cup (236 mL) bread crumbs
- cold water

Materials:

- large sauce pan
- knife (for adult use only)
- mixing bowls
- stirring spoons
- cutting board

Directions:

1. Peel and crush the garlic.
2. Take the seeds out of the peppers and chop them.
3. Cut the tomatoes into small pieces and add the bread crumbs.
4. Mix everything together and add olive oil a little at a time, stirring continuously.
5. When the oil is absorbed, add cold water and then strain it off.
6. Add vinegar and a pinch of salt. Serve cold.

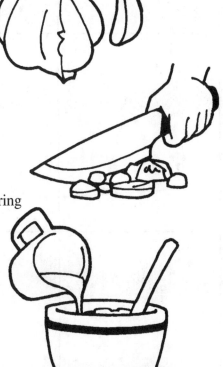

Section 1: Culminating Activities

Folk Tale Map

Having read this section's twelve tales from different countries all over the world, use your geography skills and creative art ideas to complete a Folk Tale Map.

First, draw a symbol for each tale. A symbol is a picture or design that represents something else. For example, a glass slipper could be a symbol representing the story or character of Cinderella.

After you have drawn and colored your symbols for each fairy tale, locate on the map (pages 69–70) the country from which the tale originated. (Use your social studies book or atlas to help you find the countries on the blank map on the next pages. You will need to paste together the two halves of the map.)

Cut out the symbol, glue it on the correct country location, and label the country as well as the tale. When you have finished, glue your Fairy Tale Map onto a piece of construction paper to create a frame.

Section 1: Culminating Activities

Folk Tale Map *(cont.)*

Directions: Cut out and assemble the map sections below and on page 70. Use the map to complete the activity on page 68.

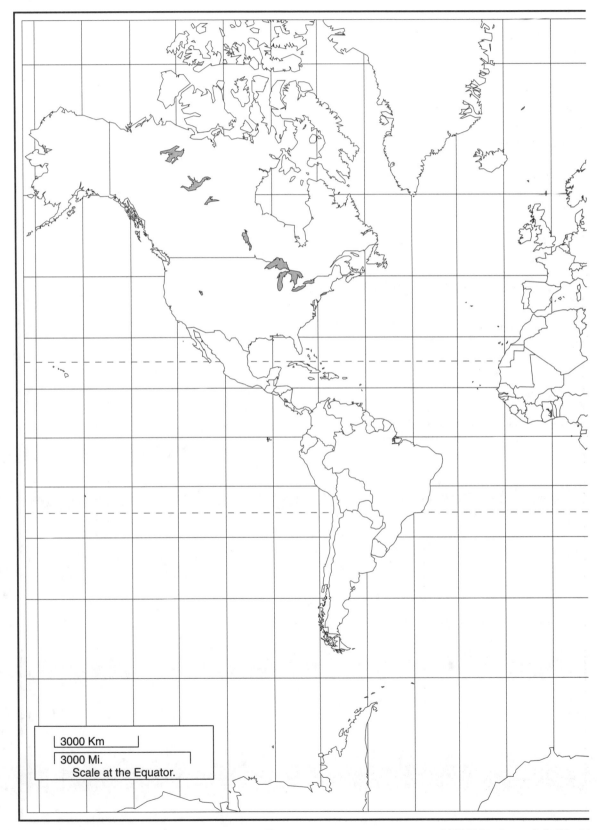

© Teacher Created Materials, Inc.　　　　　#464 *Tales Around the World*

Section 1: Culminating Activities

Folk Tale Map (cont.)

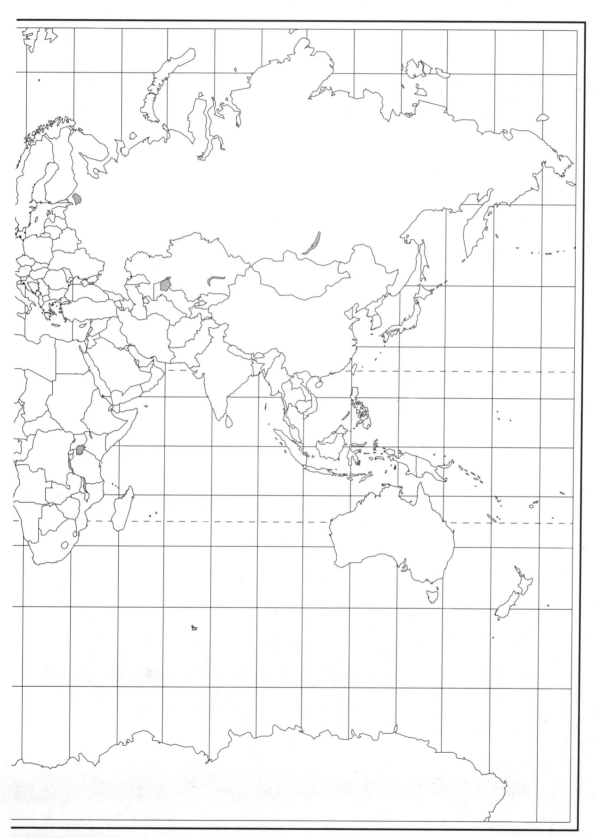

Section 1: Culminating Activities

Help Is on the Way

In all fairy tales and many folk tales, there is a magical helper who assists the hero or heroine. In the tales you have read, these magical helpers came in many shapes and sizes! Write the helpers for each tale listed here. (**Hint:** In some tales the main characters already have magical and not-so-magical powers of their own which help them.)

Tale	Helper
1. Momotaro: The Peach Warrior	_____
2. Sir Buzz	_____
3. Legend of the Poinsettia	_____
4. Seven Clever Brothers	_____
5. The Jolly Tailor Who Became King	_____
6. Kate Crackernuts	_____
7. The Tale of Sadko the Minstrel	_____
8. The Ox of the Wonderful Horns	_____
9. The Canary Prince	_____
10. Fa Mulan	_____

Who was your favorite helper? _____

   Why? _____

Who was your least favorite helper? _____

   Why? _____

In your opinion, which character needed the most help? _____

   Why? _____

_____

_____

Section 1: Culminating Activities

Heroes and Heroines, Villains and Villainesses

Most stories, and folk tales specifically, have two kinds of characters in them. One kind of character is good, kind, smart, helpful, and trustworthy. These characters are known as the heroes (males) and heroines (females). The other kind of character is just the opposite—evil, mischievous, destructive, and harmful to others. These are known as the villains (males) and villainesses (females). One way to think of these two types of characters is in simple terms of good people versus bad people.

Choose five folk tales you know. (You may choose five of the twelve you studied in this section or any others.) Write the names of the heroes/heroines and villains/villainesses from each tale in the chart provided below.

Tale	Hero/Heroine	Villain/Villainess

Section 1: Culminating Activities

Character Qualities

(**Note:** Complete the activity on page 72 first.)

When an author describes a character, he or she will use special words so that the reader has a good understanding of what the character's personality is like. These types of descriptive words are called adjectives. For example, in the traditional Cinderella story, adjectives used to describe her might be kind, helpful, gentle, obedient, beautiful, and wishful.

From your list on the previous page, choose one hero or heroine and one villain or villainess. Think about these characters and what words you would use to describe each one. Use adjectives that describe their physical appearances and personality traits. Come up with as many adjectives as possible.

Hero/Heroine	Adjectives

Villain/Villainess	Adjectives

Section 1: Culminating Activities

Word Webs

(**Note:** Complete the activity on page 73 first.)

Use the adjectives from the previous activity to create word webs about each character. Write the character's name in the middle and then fill in the web with descriptive adjectives.

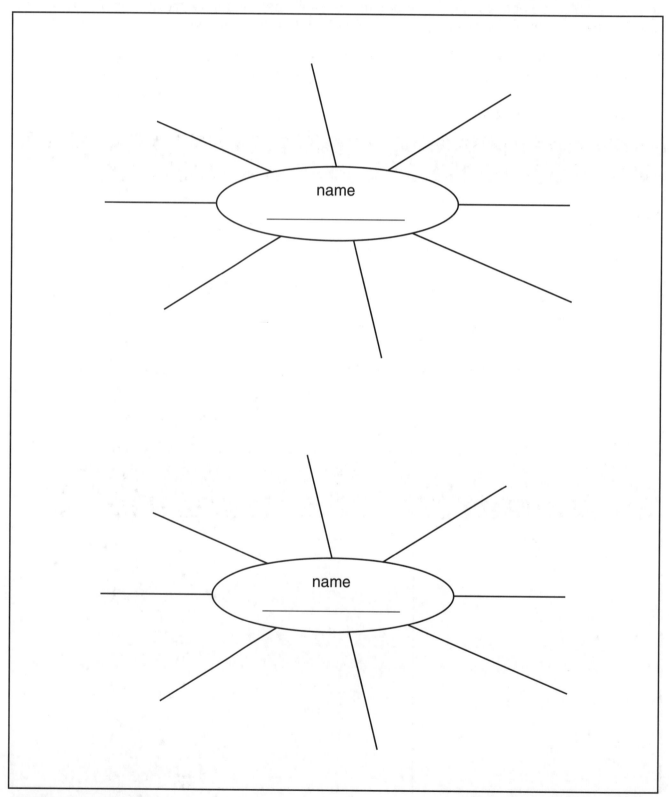

Section 1: Culminating Activities

Character Cinquains

A cinquain poem is a special type of poem. The word *cinq* in French means five. A cinquain is a poem with five lines, but it does not have to rhyme. Each line should have a certain number of words and describe something in particular.

Character Cinquain Formula:

Line 1:   one word (names the character the poem is about)

Line 2:   four words (describes the character of the poem)

Line 3:   six words (an action taken by the character)

Line 4:   eight words (your observation of the character)

Line 5:   one or two words (another describing word for the character)

Example:

Cinderella

Patient, kind, hopeful, loving

Lost glass slipper at the ball

Patience and kindness pay off in the end

Happy princess!

From the folk tales you read in this section, choose a character to write about in a character cinquain. When you have finished, write one about yourself on the back of this paper!

_____

_____ _____ _____ _____

_____ _____ _____ _____ _____ _____

_____ _____ _____ _____ _____ _____ _____ _____

_____ _____

Section 1: Culminating Activities

Happy Endings

As you know, in order for a fairy tale truly to be a fairy tale, there must be a happy ending with the good characters all living "happily ever after." Read the titles of the tales you have read in this section and match the happy endings to each.

Tale

1. _____ Momotaro: The Peach Warrior

2. _____ Sir Buzz

3. _____ Legend of the Poinsettia

4. _____ Seven Clever Brothers

5. _____ The Jolly Tailor Who Became King

6. _____ Kate Crackernuts

7. _____ The Tale of Sadko the Minstrel

8. _____ The Ox of the Wonderful Horns

9. _____ The Canary Prince

10. _____ The House in the Sky

11. _____ Fa Mulan

12. _____ The Little Seven-Colored Horse

Happy Ending

A. They all save the princess, and she marries the youngest man, named Saturday.

B. The clever stepsister saves the enchanted prince and her sister.

C. This musician is saved from death, returns to his love, and keeps the water princess happy.

D. The young girl's gift of weeds becomes beautiful red flowers.

E. The lazy brothers escape the spirit dwelling with their lives.

F. He defeats the demons and brings back treasure for his parents.

G. The hero accomplishes three challenging tasks and marries the mayor's daughter.

H. The princess heals the wounded prince.

I. This young boy finds both a princess and wealth and is welcomed back to his village.

J. The big hole in the sky is closed, and the princess marries the smart man.

K. Princess Blossom marries the boy, and they are saved from the vampire.

L. She returns home and is honored as a hero.

Section 1: Culminating Activities

Your Happy Ending

Think about your day today. Is it going the way you want it to go? Could it stand improvement? Would a little magic perk it up?

If you could choose the perfect happy ending to your day today, what would it entail? Would you go to another place? meet someone new? pass a challenging test? Write your happy ending here, just as though you were a character in a story and this was your tale. Afterwards, the class can share its happy endings.

Section 1: Culminating Activities

Around-the-World Research Ideas

One of the best things about traditional tales is that they bring us closer to our neighbors around the world. What an excellent opportunity to learn more about them!

Choose one of the tales you read in this section of the book and then complete a research project on the country from which the tale originates. Work with a partner to conduct the research and to complete the report. Choose your research topic from the ideas below and on the next pages. If you have another idea or topic in mind, discuss it with your teacher and get his or her approval.

You can get the information you need for your research from the library (in encyclopedias, country books, and other reference books), computer online services, CD-ROM encyclopedias, and interviews with people from the country you are researching.

Note to the Teacher: Research forms for this report and for a traditional country report can be found on pages 82–87.

Japan *(Momotaro: The Peach Warrior)*

- geographical features of Japan
- bullet train
- major religions of Japan (Shintoism and Buddhism)
- samurai warrior and shogun systems
- Japan's involvement in World War II (such as Pearl Harbor and the effects of the atomic bombs on Hiroshima and Nagasaki)
- traditional Japanese foods including rice, seaweed, and sushi
- popular sporting events like sumo wrestling and the martial arts
- Executive Order 9066, the American law removing Japanese Americans from their homes and placing them in detention camps

India *(Sir Buzz)*

- Himalayas, the tallest mountain range in the world
- Bengal tiger
- Islamic religion
- mosques
- British control of the country
- Mohandas K. Gandhi
- traditional Indian foods, especially those involving the use of curry

Mexico *(Legend of the Poinsettia)*

- ancient Mexican civilizations of the Aztec and the Maya
- Mayan calendar
- pyramids of Mexico
- Cinco de Mayo and Mexican Independence Day
- Day of the Dead
- Catholicism and its history in Mexico
- General Antonio Santa Anna and the Battle of the Alamo
- soccer, the most popular sport in Mexico
- Mexican history in the United States
- traditional Mexican foods, such as those which use beans, rice, and corn

Section 1: Culminating Activities

Around-the-World Research Ideas (cont.)

Israel (Seven Clever Brothers)

- Judaism, Islam, and Christianity, as related to Israel
- struggle of the Jewish people over rights to land in Israel
- Palestine Liberation Organization
- Jerusalem
- Tel-Aviv
- Yom Kippur, Rosh Hashanah, Hanukkah, and Purim
- Star of David
- kibbutz living
- Wailing Wall
- Dead Sea Scrolls
- Jordan River
- Hebrew and Arabic
- Mediterranean Sea
- Red Sea
- Dead Sea

Poland (The Jolly Tailor Who Became King)

- Krakow
- why Poland is called the "Land of Lakes"
- early Slavic tribes
- Jewish death camps during WWII: Auschwitz, Treblinka, and Majdanek
- All Hallow's Eve
- Nicolaus Copernicus
- Marie Curie (Marja Sklodowska)
- Solidarity and Lech Walesa

Scotland (Kate Crackernuts)

- golf (originated in Scotland at St. Andrews)
- famous Scottish writers such as Sir Walter Scott, Robert Louis Stevenson, and J. M. Barrie
- bagpipes
- lochs and firths
- legendary Loch Ness monster
- Hebrides
- coal
- Glasgow
- kilts
- Duncan I and Macbeth
- Sir William Wallace
- Stuart dynasty
- Mary, Queen of Scots
- Harris tweed fabric

Section 1: Culminating Activities

Around-the-World Research Ideas *(cont.)*

Russia *(The Tale of Sadko the Minstrel)*

- geographical components to the land
- Commonwealth of Independent States
- Union of Soviet Socialist Republics
- Russian Revolution
- Moscow
- Siberia
- Mikhail Gorbachev
- Tzar Nicholas II
- Kirov Ballet
- caviar
- matrioshka nesting dolls
- extensive national sports programs, especially gymnastics, ice skating, and ice hockey
- Peter Tchaikovsky
- Yuri Gagarin
- Leo Tolstoy

Africa *(The Ox of the Wonderful Horns)*

- pharaohs
- Chaka Zulu
- Alexander the Great
- Cleopatra VII
- African slave trade
- African art such as sculpting, carving, cloth dyeing, mask and basket making, and bronze casting
- animals of Africa
- Sahara Desert
- Nile River
- Masai
- Bedouins

Italy *(The Canary Prince)*

- major monuments of Rome such as the Coliseum and Pantheon
- chariot races
- Leaning Tower of Pisa
- Benito Mussolini
- Galileo
- Leonardo da Vinci and Michaelangelo
- Dante
- Sicily
- Florence
- Venice and its waterways
- traditional foods of Italy
- olives
- the Mafia
- the Roman Empire

Section 1: Culminating Activities

Around-the-World Research Ideas (cont.)

Bahamas (The House in the Sky)

- Andros
- San Salvador
- subtropical climate
- economy (known as an international banking center)
- Arawaks and Christopher Columbus
- Blackbeard
- Lynden O. Pindling
- Hubert Ingraham
- Free National Movement
- Progressive Liberal Party
- folk guitar
- Biminis
- Nassau

China (Fa Mulan)

- Beijing
- Yellow Sea
- communism
- Taiwan
- Gobi Desert
- Confucius
- Tang Dynasty
- Great Wall of China
- Boxer Rebellion
- Mao Zedong
- Tian'an Men Square
- traditional foods

Spain (The Little Seven-Colored Horse)

- Madrid
- Gibraltar
- Canary Islands
- Miguel de Cervantes Saavedra
- Pyrenees Mountains
- bullfighting
- traditional foods
- Basques
- Roman Catholicism
- El Greco
- Pablo Picasso
- flamenco guitar and dancing
- grapes and olives
- Francisco Franco
- Roman Iberia

Section 1: Culminating Activities   Around-the-World Research Ideas

Country Research Report

Name(s): _____

Topic: _____

Country: _____

Country Map

(Draw the map yourself or trace it from a book.)

Around-the-World Research Ideas   Section 1: *Culminating Activities*

Country Research Report (cont.)

The topic of my (our) research is _____.

This is what I (we) have learned.

(Write the information you have learned in complete sentences and paragraphs. Use additional paper as needed.)

_____
_____
_____
_____
_____
_____
_____
_____
_____
_____
_____
_____
_____
_____
_____
_____
_____
_____
_____
_____
_____

Section 1: Culminating Activities   Around-the-World Research Ideas

Country Research Report (cont.)

Name: _____

Country: _____

Famous Landmark *(Draw it in the space below.)*

Name of Landmark

Around-the-World Research Ideas   Section 1: *Culminating Activities*

Country Research Report *(cont.)*

Capital City: _____

Primary Language(s): _____

Population: _____

Climate: _____

_____

Highest and Lowest Elevations: _____

_____

Major Religions: _____

Natural Landmarks: _____

_____

_____

_____

_____

_____

_____

_____

Manmade Landmarks: _____

_____

_____

_____

_____

_____

_____

_____

Section 1: Culminating Activities   Around-the-World Research Ideas

Country Research Report (cont.)

Country Flag

(Draw and color it here.)

Traditional Dress

(Draw and color an example here for both a man and a woman.)

Country Research Report *(cont.)*

Significant Historic Events

(List at least seven and write a short description of each one. Use additional paper as needed.)

_____
_____
_____
_____
_____
_____
_____
_____
_____
_____
_____
_____
_____
_____
_____
_____
_____
_____
_____
_____
_____

Section 1: Section Test

Around-the-World Test

I. Matching: Match each tale with the action that takes place in it.

_____ 1. Momotaro: The Peach Warrior

_____ 2. Sir Buzz

_____ 3. Legend of the Poinsettia

_____ 4. Seven Clever Brothers

_____ 5. The Canary Prince

_____ 6. The Jolly Tailor Who Became King

_____ 7. Kate Crackernuts

_____ 8. The Tale of Sadko the Minstrel

_____ 9. The House in the Sky

_____ 10. The Ox of the Wonderful Horns

_____ 11. The Little Seven-Colored Horse

_____ 12. Fa Mulan

A. A girl brings a gift of weeds to the Baby Jesus.

B. A princess becomes a river.

C. A lonely boy uses the magic powers of an animal who befriends him.

D. An evil stepmother locks a princess in a tower.

E. Two lazy brothers devise a plan to avoid work.

F. A boy escapes from his mean brothers.

G. Two sisters share the same name.

H. A boy defeats demons.

I. A hole in the sky is sewn to stop the endless rain.

J. A girl fights in the army as a boy.

K. A manikin appears from a box and helps a boy.

L. The brothers are named for the days of the week.

II. Name that Country: Write the country of origin for each tale.

1. Momotaro: The Peach Warrior _____

2. Sir Buzz _____

3. Legend of the Poinsettia _____

4. Seven Clever Brothers _____

5. The Jolly Tailor Who Became King _____

6. Kate Crackernuts _____

7. The Tale of Sadko the Minstrel _____

8. The Ox of the Wonderful Horns _____

9. The Canary Prince _____

10. The House in the Sky _____

11. Fa Mulan _____

12. The Little Seven-Colored Horse _____

Section 1: Section Test

Around-the-World Test *(cont.)*

III. Short Answer Essay: Write your responses to these questions and prompts on the back of this paper.

1. What makes Momotaro a hero?
2. Compare and contrast Juanito of *The Little Seven-Colored Horse* with Mungalo of *The Ox of the Wonderful Horns*.
3. Compare and contrast the princess of *The Canary Prince* with Plain Kate of *Kate Crackernuts*.

IV. Draw and Write: Draw a picture of a memorable scene from one of the twelve tales. Write the title of the story below the picture. Write a sentence that describes the scene you have drawn.

Title: _____

Sentence: _____

_____

_____

Section 2: Around the World with Cinderella

Introduction

The fairy tale *Cinderella* is a story with which many people are familiar. Children and adults from around the world know about the young girl who lives with her wicked stepmother and stepsisters, and nearly everyone knows that one day a fairy godmother pays Cinderella a visit and assists her in magical ways to find her prince and happiness.

When you think of Cinderella, you probably remember her glass slipper, pumpkin coach, and the clock striking midnight. However, there are some things about Cinderella that you probably do not know, such as the following:

- There are over 500 different *Cinderella* stories worldwide.
- The first *Cinderella* story ever told was more than 1,000 years ago.
- Some *Cinderella* stories have a magical fish or turkey instead of a fairy godmother.
- The Disney *Cinderella* is based on a French version of the tale from 1697.
- Some *Cinderella* stories are about young men instead of young women.

As you start reading some of the many different versions of *Cinderella,* you will see both similarities and differences in the stories. There will be unique traditions, clothing, customs, and scenery, depending on the country of the tale. Yet, even though the various stories have differences, all *Cinderella* stories have basic elements in common.

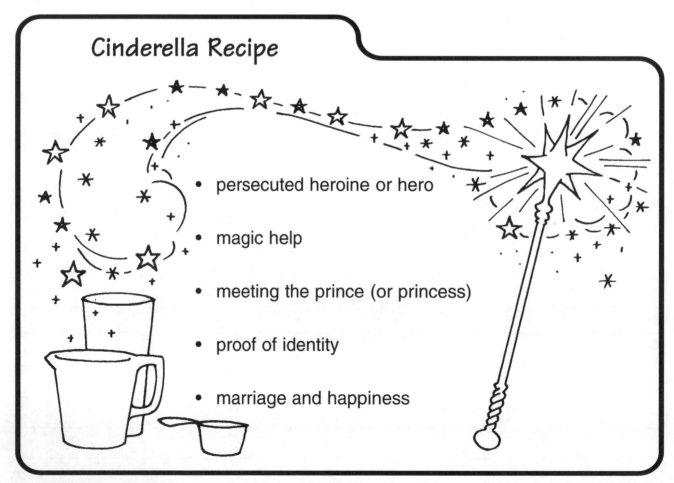

Cinderella Recipe

- persecuted heroine or hero
- magic help
- meeting the prince (or princess)
- proof of identity
- marriage and happiness

Section 2: Around the World with Cinderella

Cinderella Survey

I. In the space below, list as many facts, ideas, and thoughts you remember from the *Cinderella* story you know.

_____
_____
_____
_____
_____
_____
_____
_____
_____
_____

II. Using the information from your list, write ideas into fairy-tale ingredients groups.

Heroes/Heroines	Magical Symbols	Setting
Problem/Solution	**Villains/Villainesses**	**Miscellaneous**

Section 2: Around the World with Cinderella

The Egyptian Cinderella

Egypt

Book: *The Egyptian Cinderella* retold by Shirley Climo (HarperCollins Children's Books, 1992)

Summary: In the land of Egypt along the Nile River, there lives a fair maiden named Rhodopis. When she was a child, pirates stole her from her home in Greece and sold her in Egypt as a slave. Because she has fair hair, fair skin, and looks different from Egyptians, the other servant girls tease her and treat her poorly.

Her master gives her a pair of rose-red slippers, but one day a great falcon swoops down and takes one of them. The falcon flies to the festival and drops the slipper right into the Pharaoh's lap. At once the Pharaoh sets about to find the owner of this shoe. When he finally reaches the shores of the Nile and instructs Rhodopis to try on the shoe, the Pharaoh proclaims her a true Egyptian and takes her with him on the royal barge.

This story is based on both fact and fiction. There was a girl named Rhodopis born in Greece and kidnapped by pirates, and she later married Pharaoh Amasis, and became his queen.

Discussion Questions:

- From what country does Rhodopis originate?
- Describe how Rhodopis is different from the other women.
- What prompts the master to give Rhodopis the slippers?
- How does Rhodopis feel when the falcon takes one of her slippers?
- What happens after the falcon flies away?
- How does the Pharaoh explain that Rhodopis is a true Egyptian?

Journal Questions and Prompts:

- If a large bird flew down and took something of value from you, what would you do?
- Why do you think the Pharaoh decided to marry the woman who could fit the shoe?
- Would you marry someone whom you had never met? Explain your answer.

The Egyptian Cinderella   Section 2: Around the World with Cinderella

Where in the World?

Use the map to help answer the questions. Write your answers on a separate piece of paper.

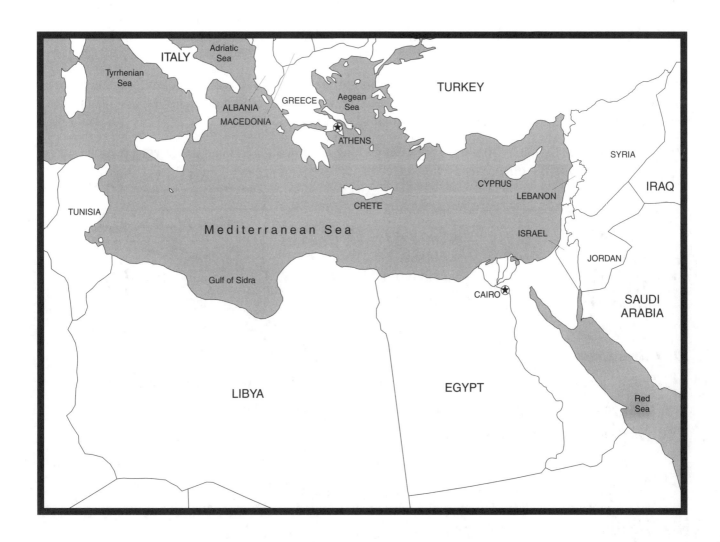

1. Rhodopis is from Greece. What direction is Greece from Egypt?
2. What island is just southeast of Greece?
3. What country shares a western border with Egypt?
4. What is the capital of Egypt?
5. What is the name of the largest river in Egypt?
6. Why do you think the large city of Cairo is located on the Nile River?
7. What country is directly north of Egypt?
8. What is the capital of Greece?
9. In what direction is the island of Cyprus from Crete?
10. In what direction does the Nile River mainly flow?

Section 2: Around the World with Cinderella   The Egyptian Cinderella

Papyrus Papermaking

Ancient Egypt was a highly complex, cultured, and artistic civilization. This ancient society demonstrated an extraordinary blend of art, education, medicine, recreation, transportation, religion, government, and language. Egyptians developed the earliest known writing system, which is the basis for many modern languages, including today's Western alphabet. This picture writing was known as hieroglyphics.

Hieroglyphics were often carved on wood and stone surfaces. They were also frequently painted on wood, clay tablets, and a unique type of paper called papyrus. Not only did the Egyptians invent this advanced language, they also invented this special type of paper.

Papyrus was originally made from a reed growing along riverbanks. You can make your own version of papyrus by following the directions on this page.

Materials:

- large bowl
- water
- white glue
- newspapers
- tissue paper (various colors)
- spoon or mixing stick
- sand screen sifter (or a piece of wire mesh)

Directions:

1. Fill a large bowl with water and add about half a cup (125 mL) white glue. Stir the mixture.
2. Tear up many small pieces of tissue paper. You can use one color or a blend of colors.
3. Put the tissues in the water/glue mixture.
4. Grab a handful of the soaked tissues and gently squeeze out some water. Lay the tissues flat on the wire screen.
5. Use a piece of newspaper to press the tissue paper on the screen and squeeze out the excess water.
6. Carefully remove the "papyrus" paper and let it dry on newspaper.
7. When the paper dries (in a few hours), paint your own hieroglyphic message on it.

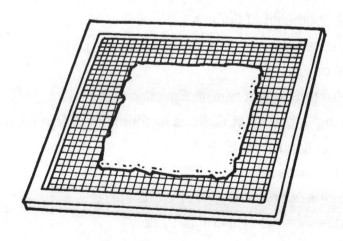

Section 2: Around the World with Cinderella

Vasilisa the Beautiful: A Russian Tale

Russia

Book: *Vasilisa the Beautiful: A Russian Tale* retold by Elizabeth Winthrop (HarperCollins Children's Books, 1991)

Summary: In a certain tzardom there is a widowed merchant with a daughter named Vasilisa the Beautiful. Right before her mother dies, she gives Vasilisa a small, magical doll who would later help her with many tasks and chores. When the merchant remarries, Vasilisa is treated unkindly by his wife and her two daughters.

One day the stepmother sends Vasilisa into the woods to Baba Yaga's house in search of fire. The witch makes Vasilisa do a variety of impossible chores in order to get the fire, but with the help of the doll, she is able to complete the tasks. When she returns home with a scull full of fire, her stepmother and sisters are immediately burned and turned to ashes.

Vasilisa then lives with an old woman and learns to weave beautiful materials. The old woman takes her cloth to the tzar who is so impressed that he asks Vasilisa to make him clothes from the material. When the tzar meets Vasilisa, he immediately falls in love with her, and they are married.

Note: Many Russian tales include the bony-legged grandmother witch, Baba Yaga.

Discussion Questions:

- What does Vasilisa's mother tell her about the doll?
- What does the stepmother hope to accomplish by giving Vasilisa all the hard chores?
- What happens instead?
- As the suitors begin asking for Vasilisa's hand, what does the stepmother tell them?
- What is Baba Yaga's hut like?
- What are some of the chores that Baba Yaga gives to Vasilisa?
- What do the white and red horseback riders represent?
- Why do you think the old seamstress will not take any money from the tzar?

Journal Questions and Prompts:

- The little doll that Vasilisa's mother gives to her provides her with safety and comfort. Tell about a special toy, doll, stuffed animal, or other object that has offered you comfort.
- Tell about an older person who has helped you in your life.
- What chores do you do at home?

Section 2: Around the World with Cinderella   Vasilisa the Beautiful: A Russian Tale

Three Horses and Baba Yaga's Hut

Read the directions and complete the following.

1. When Vasilisa journeys into the woods in search of fire, she comes across three horsemen. What color is each, and what does each represent? List them in the order in which they appear to her.

A	B	C
color:_____	color:_____	color:_____
represents:	represents:	represents:
_____	_____	_____
_____	_____	_____
_____	_____	_____
_____	_____	_____
_____	_____	_____
_____	_____	_____

2. Baba Yaga promises to give Vasilisa fire, but she will have to stay at the hut and do some chores for Baba Yaga first. Name three of the tasks that she asks Vasilisa to do.

   _____
   _____
   _____

3. Baba Yaga's hut is a mysterious and magical place.

   a. What kind of legs does it stand on? _____
   b. What is lit up along the walls? _____
   c. What kinds of things instantly appear to help Baba Yaga? _____
   _____

4. On a piece of construction paper, draw your interpretation of Baba Yaga's house. Be sure to include the details in the story, including the magical hands that instantly appear.

Vasilisa the Beautiful: A Russian Tale   Section 2: Around the World with Cinderella

Matrioshka Nesting Dolls

In *Vasilisa the Beautiful,* Vasilisa's mother gives her a good-luck doll before she dies. This doll befriends Vasilisa and saves her life many times.

A popular craft for many years in Russia is Russian nesting dolls, or *matrioshka*. These brightly and beautifully hand-painted dolls usually come in a set of five and are made from wood. All of the dolls look alike, but they come in different sizes. The smallest doll can be covered by the next largest doll and so on until the largest doll covers all four of the other dolls. The matrioshkas are still given today for good luck.

Materials:

- white or manila-colored cardstock paper
- circle patterns (page 98)
- fine-tipped colored pens, pencils, or paints and paintbrushes
- transparent tape
- scissors

Directions:

1. Duplicate the patterns onto the cardstock.

2. Cut out each circle.

3. Cut along a radius (the line from the outer circle to the midpoint).

4. Fold the circles until ¼ of the circle is completely tucked to make a cone. Tape the seam of the cone on the outside.

5. With fine-tipped colored pens, pencils, or paints, decorate each nesting doll. Be sure to use bright colors and to make every doll look alike.

6. Stack your nesting dolls in order!

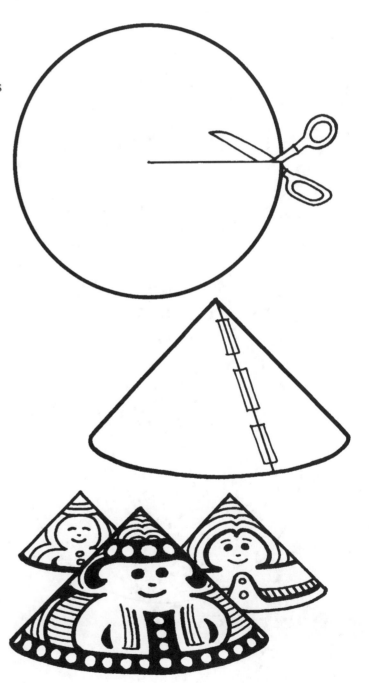

© Teacher Created Materials, Inc.

Section 2: Around the World with Cinderella   Vasilisa the Beautiful: A Russian Tale

Matrioshka Nesting Dolls (cont.)

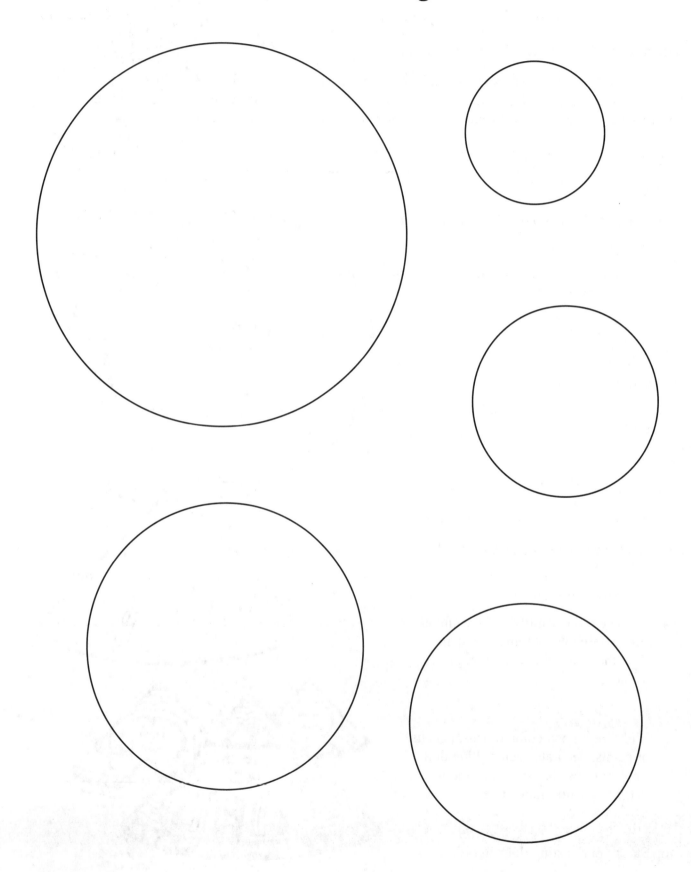

Section 2: Around the World with Cinderella

The Brocaded Slipper

Vietnam

Book: "The Brocaded Slipper" in *The Brocaded Slipper and Other Vietnamese Tales* retold by Lynette Vuong (HarperCollins Children's Books, 1992)

Summary: A widowed man with a beautiful daughter named Tam marries a woman with a daughter of her own. The other daughter is named Cam, and she is an ungainly and unkind girl. When Tam's father dies, she is left to live with her cruel stepmother and stepsister.

Feeling sad for Tam after she falls victim to one of her stepmother's many tricks, a fairy appears and places a magical fish into Tam's basket. The fish provides magic even after its death at the hands of Tam's stepmother and stepsister. The bones of the magical fish lead Tam to the prince and eventually to marriage. However, Tam's evil stepfamily kills Tam. Her spirit lives on in a variety of creatures, and finally she is reunited with the prince. The stepmother and stepsister are punished for their evil ways.

Discussion Questions:

- Why do you think the stepmother and Cam are mean to Tam?
- How does Cam trick Tam at the river?
- How does Tam go about finding the bones of her fish?
- What are the instructions the fairy gives Tam about the bones?
- How does the prince find Tam?
- Describe what actions the stepmother and Cam take after Tam and the prince are married.
- How are the prince and Tam finally reunited?

Journal Questions and Prompts:

- Cam will often compete with Tam in an unfair way. Write about a time that your sister, brother, or friend competed with you unjustly.
- If Cam had been caught at the end of the story and taken to court, what might the defense's and prosecution's arguments be?
- Write a short story about a magical animal who comes to your rescue.

Section 2: Around the World with Cinderella The Brocaded Slipper

Poetry Picks

In *The Brocaded Slipper* Tam calls to her pet fish by using poetry.

> *Come and eat, come and eat*
> *Little fish, pretty fish.*
> *Good rice, fine rice,*
> *From my gold and silver dish.*

Others, such as the prince, also use poetry. For centuries poetry has been a valued art and custom in the country of Vietnam. Even today, poetry is much more common in Vietnam than in most other countries. For example, a Vietnamese boy who is interested in a girl will speak to her poetically. If she is interested, she will speak back to him in the same fashion.

Poetry extends beyond courtship as well. A great deal of poetry for and against warfare has been produced during national conflicts. Among many dead and wounded soldiers' belongings have been found poems written to express their sentiments and determination about a war or revolution. Vietnam's most famous epic poem is "Kim Van Kieu," the story of a girl's struggle to maintain the honor of her family. Even though the plot is long and involved, many Vietnamese have memorized the poem in its entirely. "Kim Van Kieu" is such an accurate reflection of the Vietnamese soul and culture that government officials have told Americans to pay more attention to this poem than any statistics they may find.

The poetry patterns used in *The Brocaded Slipper* are quatrains and couplets. A quatrain consists of four lines with the second and fourth lines rhyming.

> *Mary had a little lamb,*
> *Its fleece was white as snow,* ⎤
> *And everywhere that Mary went,* ⎬ **rhyming words**
> *The lamb was sure to go.* ⎦

A couplet is any two lines that end in rhyme.

> *Percy is a very chubby pig.* ⎤
> *He likes to eat and likes to dig.* ⎦ **rhyming words**

Create your own quatrain and couplet to fit the story by choosing two of the scenes listed below. As you write your poetry for the given scenarios, do so from the character's perspective. Use a separate piece of paper and illustrate your poems.

- **Cam:** the day that Cam sees her stepsister and the prince walking back to the palace
- **the fish:** when he is first placed in Tam's bucket
- **the fairy:** giving instructions to Tam about the bones
- **the stepmother:** the day she persuades the prince to marry Cam
- **the prince:** at the old woman's house when he discovers that Tam is alive
- **Tam:** the day she discovers the finery in her four jars

Non la Hat

In *The Brocaded Slipper,* Tam sneaks out to her special fish in the well to share a few grains of rice with it. Most of the people of Vietnam today eat rice with every meal. Rice is an important product in Vietnam, and the rice harvest is a busy time for the Vietnamese people. The rice is pounded until the small grains fall from the stalks. The stalks are then used for fuel, but some are set aside to make a Non la, the traditional hat of the Vietnamese.

Materials:

- 18" (45 cm) square tagboard or stiff paper
- scissors
- glue
- stapler
- paint, markers, or crayons
- string, yarn, or ribbon
- hole punch

Directions:

1. From the stiff paper, cut a circle with an 18" (45 cm) diameter.

2. Paint the circle a neutral color.

3. When the paint is dry, color a simple flower design or write a poem on the underside of the circle.

4. Draw a radius line of 9" (22.5 cm) to the center of the circle.

5. Cut the radius.

6. Overlap the edges about 1" (2.5 cm) and staple them together to form a cone-shaped hat.

7. Punch two holes on both sides of the hat, midway from the rim to the top.

8. To make the chin strap pull a piece of yarn through one hole and knot it. Pull the free end through the other hole until the strap feels secure. Knot the other end.

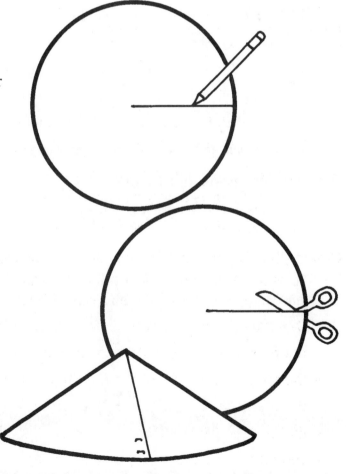

Section 2: Around the World with Cinderella

Yeh-Shen

China

Book: *Yeh-Shen: A Cinderella Story from China* retold by A-Ling Louie (Putnam Publishing Group, 1996)

Summary: Created some time between 618 and 907 A.D., this is the first complete *Cinderella* story ever recorded. In the dim past of southern China, there lives a cave chief who is married to two wives. Each wife has a baby daughter. One of the daughters is full of goodness and beauty. Her name is Yeh-Shen. The other daughter is ugly and unkind, as is her mother. When the father dies, Yeh-Shen is left in the care of her stepmother who treats her badly.

Yeh-Shen finds comfort and help in her pet fish, even after the fish is killed and eaten by her stepmother and stepsister. The fish, although dead, still has the power to help her attend the spring festival. On the way home from the festival, Yeh-Shen loses her shoe. By a strange twist of fate, the loss of the shoe enables her to meet the king, whom she marries. Her stepmother and stepsister continue to live in the caves until they meet their demise.

Discussion Questions:

- What is the name of Yeh-Shen's father?
- Where do Yeh-Shen and her family live?
- How does Yeh-Shen's sister trick the fish?
- Why does Yeh-Shen call the old man "kind uncle?"
- How does Yeh-Shen become transformed for the festival?
- Why does Yeh-Shen return to the pavilion for her other slipper?
- What happens to Yeh-Shen's stepmother and stepsister?

Journal Questions and Prompts:

- If you just found out that your favorite pet died and an old man told you to bury its bones in four jars, what would your reaction be?
- Write your thoughts and feelings about a man having two wives.
- Very often in fairy tales, beauty means goodness, and ugliness means a person is evil. Do you think appearance has to do with a person's character? Explain.

Yeh-Shen Section 2: Around the World with Cinderella

Sequence Storytelling

Read through the events listed below. Place them in the proper story order and write them in complete sentences on the lines provided.

Yeh-Shen talks to the bones of her dead fish.

The king and Yeh-Shen are married.

Chief Wu and Yeh-Shen's mother both die.

Yeh-Shen loses a shoe when running home.

The king follows her home and has her try on the shoe.

Her stepmother and stepsister are crushed to death in their cave.

Many women try on the shoe, but it will not fit any of them.

The fish creates a beautiful blue gown and golden, fish-like, magical shoes for Yeh-Shen to wear to the festival.

Yeh-Shen's stepmother uses her coat to trick the fish.

A merchant finds the shoe and gives it to the king of the island.

Yeh-Shen's tears in the pond make an old man appear.

In the middle of the night, Yeh-Shen goes to the pavilion and takes the shoe.

1. _____
2. _____
3. _____
4. _____
5. _____
6. _____
7. _____
8. _____
9. _____
10. _____
11. _____
12. _____

© Teacher Created Materials, Inc. #464 Tales Around the World

Section 2: Around the World with Cinderella   Yeh-Shen

Watercolor Scrolls

Observe the beautiful watercolored illustrations in the book *Yeh-Shen*. (Also note that they each depict a fish in some way.) In many parts of Asia, artists use bright watercolors to express themselves. Their paintings tell stories about the country. Artists also paint pictures closely tied to their religious beliefs. Around 1100 A.D. Asian artists began painting on scrolls instead of flat paper.

For this activity, you will choose a scene from *Yeh-Shen* and paint it on a scroll.

Materials:

- 6" x 9" (15 cm x 22.5 cm) white construction paper
- watercolor paints and brush
- dark, fine-tipped marking pen or dark chalk
- yarn
- pencil

Directions:

1. Using watercolors, paint some form of a fish on the paper scroll.

2. When it is dry, go back over the painting with a dark marking pen or piece of chalk, adding details about the scene you are retelling.

3. With a pencil, roll the top ends of the painting once around the body of the pencil. This should curl the painting, giving it the look of a scroll.

4. Cut a piece of yarn approximately 18" (45 cm) long. Loop the yarn through the top roll of the painting and then tie it in a bow at the top. This is how you will hang the scroll.

#464 Tales Around the World   © Teacher Created Materials, Inc.

Poor Turkey Girl

Native American Zuni

Book: "Poor Turkey Girl" from *Cinderella: The Oryx Multicultural Folktale Series* retold by Judy Sierra (Oryx Press, 1992)

Summary: This Native American Cinderella tale was recorded in Zuni, New Mexico, in the late 19th century. Here the teller connects the tale to the local landscape.

In the story, the ancient people of the plains around Thunder Mountain do not have sheep, cattle, or horses, but they do have many turkeys. In a little, tumble-down town nearby, there lives a very poor girl who herds the turkeys for a meager living. She wears only shabby clothes and subsists on little food, but she has a kind heart.

The Dance of the Sacred Bird is scheduled to take place soon, and the poor little turkey girl wishes to attend. The turkeys decide to help their "mother maiden" by transforming her shabby clothes into beautiful, white, embroidered, cotton garments.

The turkeys warn the girl about being late, but she ignores their warning. When she finally returns home, the turkeys have left the valley, and she becomes again a poor, dingy girl.

Discussion Questions:

- Describe the custom of the wealthy families in Matsaki regarding the turkeys.
- How do the turkeys feel about the poor girl?
- How does she react when the turkeys begin talking with her?
- Explain how the birds transform the girl.
- What do the turkeys fear will happen when she goes to the dance?
- Why does the girl stay late at the dance?
- What happens when she returns?
- Do you think the turkeys should have given her another chance? Explain your reasoning.

Journal Questions and Prompts:

- In this *Cinderella* story, the maiden stays out too late. Describe what you think would have happened in the traditional French version (by Perrault and adapted by Disney) if Cinderella had stayed at the ball past midnight.
- How does the choice of animal (turkey, fish, mice, etc.) affect the feeling of the *Cinderella* story?
- How do you feel about the ending of this story as compared to other *Cinderella* stories you know?

Turkey Tidbits

Read the information about turkeys and then answer the Turkey Tidbits at the bottom of the page.

The magical turkey friends of the turkey girl were very different from the turkeys you see at Thanksgiving dinner or other holiday feasts! The kind of turkey that most people eat is called a "domestic" turkey and is raised on farms. The turkeys in *Poor Turkey Girl* are wild turkeys and are very different.

The turkey is a large game bird originally from the central part of the United States and Mexico, but it is now raised commercially all over the world. There are two species of wild turkey: the Meleagris and the Agriocharis. The Meleagris turkey is about four feet (1.2 m) long with green-brown feathers and long, slim, spurred legs. The fleshy growth on top of its head is called a snood. The pouch-like area on its throat is called the wattle. The Agriocharis turkey is smaller but has beautifully colored feathers with bright eye spots on the tips of each feather, like the peacock.

Turkeys eat acorns, seeds, berries, and insects. A female turkey, called a hen, lays between 11 and 20 eggs and sits upon them for about 28 days until they hatch. Young turkeys are called poults.

Farming of turkeys began first in Mexico a few hundred years ago. Spanish explorers took turkeys to Europe for trade, and the pilgrims brought several turkey breeds back with them to North America in 1620.

Turkey Tidbits Questions

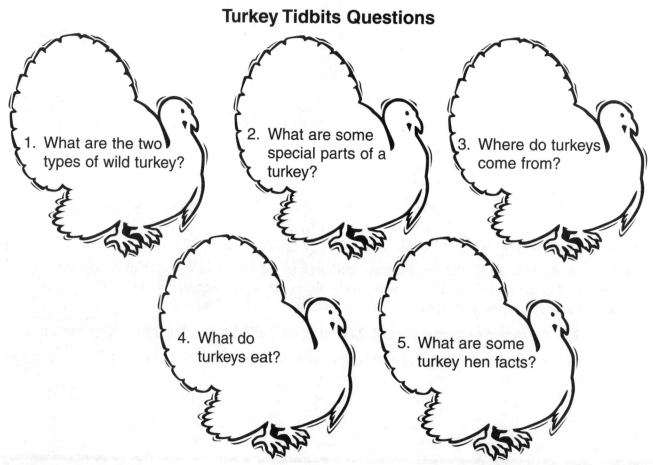

1. What are the two types of wild turkey?
2. What are some special parts of a turkey?
3. Where do turkeys come from?
4. What do turkeys eat?
5. What are some turkey hen facts?

Poor Turkey Girl

Section 2: Around the World with Cinderella

Zuni Hand Mask

Like many Native American tribes of the United States, the Zuni tribe of the southwest region made and wore special masks during different ceremonies and celebrations. One such mask is the hand mask which was worn during ceremonies centering around the changing seasons. Archaeologists have found many caves in the southwest desert with drawings of hands on the walls that date back thousands of years.

Materials:

- 24" x 9" (60 cm x 22.5 cm) construction paper (light colored)
- large piece of black construction paper
- pencil
- scissors
- tape

Directions:

1. On the black paper, use a pencil to trace your hand three times. Round out the bottom of your hand shape to complete the line.

2. On one of the hands, cut out two eye holes and one mouth hole as shown.

3. Wrap the light construction-paper strip around your head to find a good fit. Tape it together at that size.

4. Glue the hand with the eye and mouth holes on the front part of the mask. Glue the other two hands on the back.

5. Slip the mask over your head so that it rests on your shoulders.

© Teacher Created Materials, Inc.

Section 2: Around the World with Cinderella

Hearth Cat

Portugal

Book: "Hearth Cat" from *Cinderella: The Oryx Multicultural Folktale Series* retold by Judy Sierra (Oryx Press, 1992)

Summary: Like many other *Cinderella* stories, this Portuguese fairy tale involves a magical fish. However, unlike other stories the fish is actually the prince in this case.

The story begins with a widower and his three daughters. The youngest is always teased and treated badly by her sisters. They call her Hearth Cat. When her father comes home with a fish for dinner one day, Hearth Cat begs him to keep the fish for a pet. He agrees.

The fish lives in the well and calls to Hearth Cat to come down to him. When she eventually falls in, she discovers an underground palace of treasures and finery. Hearth Cat follows the fish's instructions and eventually attends the king's ball. Later, she discovers that the fish is a prince under an enchantment. The two become married and live a happy life at the palace on land.

Discussion Questions:

- Why does Hearth Cat take a liking to the fish?
- What prompts Hearth Cat to throw the fish in the well?
- Explain how she ends up at the bottom of the well.
- Why do you think Hearth Cat finally says yes to the fish's offer of marriage?
- How does the prince react when Hearth Cat declines his offer of marriage?

Journal Questions and Prompts:

- In this tale the fish is really a prince who is put under a spell. What other stories can you think of where the prince is turned into some kind of animal?
- Hearth Cat is the youngest daughter, yet she must do most of the chores. What do you think would be a fair system for three siblings to do chores? Give examples.
- Tell about a special pet you have had or have dreamed of having.
- Have you ever been the youngest (in the family, in a group of friends, in the class, etc.)? What was it like?

Hearth Cat   Section 2: Around the World with Cinderella

A Fishy Interview

The prince is lucky enough not to get eaten by Hearth Cat's family, and he is even luckier that Hearth Cat agrees to marry him. What would he have done if she had not helped him? Pretend you work for a magazine and are interviewing the prince/fish. Write his answers next to your questions.

1. What is your name? _____

2. How and when did you turn into a fish? _____
_____

3. Sometimes princes are not very nice, and they get a curse placed upon them. Did you do anything bad that might have led to you being turned into a fish?
_____
_____

4. How did Hearth Cat's father end up catching you?
_____
_____

5. Why have you picked Hearth Cat for your bride-to-be?
_____
_____

6. Why did you help Hearth Cat get all dressed up for the festival at the palace when you knew that you could not go with her?
_____
_____

7. What would you have done if your father had not believed Hearth Cat?
_____
_____

8. How did you get Hearth Cat to agree to marry you?
_____
_____

9. If Hearth Cat had not married you, how would you have spent your life?
_____
_____

10. What advice would you give other princes in your situation?
_____
_____

Glazed Pottery

Portugal is famous for its glazed tiles and pottery. These shiny handicrafts are brilliantly colored and painted and used widely in architecture as well as for interior decoration. Glazed earthenware from Coimbra is produced in the 13th century by a method that is still used today.

Each region of the country has its own colors and designs. Alcobaco pottery, for example, has a typical dark-blue color while products from Caldas da Rainha are distinguished by their vivid grass-green color.

Materials:

- salt dough (page 111)
- rolling pin
- bright colors of tempera paint
- plastic knife, toothpicks, craft sticks, and other items for etching designs
- acrylic gloss varnish (spray or paint on)
- access to an oven
- paintbrushes

Directions:

1. Knead the dough until it is smooth and firm.

2. Pull a handful of dough from the large piece and roll it into a ball (approximately 5" or 12.5 cm).

3. Pound your fist into the center of the ball.

4. Hold the ball of dough in one hand and with the other hand continue to work the dough into the shape of a bowl as shown.

5. Use two small pieces of the dough to create handles for your pot. To do so, roll small dough balls (approximately 2" or 5 cm) into snake-like coils.

6. Curve the coils and attach them to the sides of the bowl. Use a little bit of water to smooth out the ends and attach them.

7. Add designs with the etching tools along the sides.

8. Before baking your bowl, be sure that you have smoothed out all of the cracks with water and that the handles are secure.

9. Put your bowl into the oven, preheated to 250° F (130° C). Small projects take about 45 minutes to one hour to bake, and large projects take about two hours. When the project begins to turn golden, use a pot holder to remove it from the oven. (**Note:** Only adults should handle objects going in and out of the oven.)

10. When the bowl is cool, paint your project with a bright tempera color.

11. Let the bowl dry overnight and then spray it with the acrylic to give it a shine.

Hearth Cat

Section 2: Around the World with Cinderella

Homemade Salt-Dough Recipe

When you do not have enough money to use commercial potter's clay or you would just rather have the fun of making the dough yourself, this recipe is easy to make and inexpensive.

Ingredients:
- 3 cups (750 mL) white flour
- 1¼ cups (310 mL) warm tap water
- 1 cup (250 mL) salt

Materials:
- large bowl
- mixing spoon

Directions:
1. Pour the salt into a bowl.

2. Add the warm tap water to the salt. Stir until the salt is completely dissolved.

3. Add the flour to the mixture and stir.

4. Mix and knead the dough by working it with your hands. If you keep some flour on your hands, this will help keep the dough from sticking to your fingers. Keep working the dough until you are able to form it into a smooth, firm ball.

5. It is best to use the dough right away. If you decide not to, store it in a covered container in the refrigerator. It will keep for up to a week.

Section 2: Culminating Activities

Fairy Godmothers, Fish, and Other Helpers

Part 1

In all fairy tales there is always a magical helper who assists the hero or heroine. In the *Cinderella* stories you have read, these magical helpers come in many shapes and sizes. Write the helpers for each fairy tale in the chart below.

Fairy Tale	Helper
The Brocaded Slipper	_____
The Egyptian Cinderella	_____
Yeh-Shen: A Cinderella Story from China	_____
Poor Turkey Girl	_____
Hearth Cat	_____
Vasilisa the Beautiful: A Russian Tale	_____

Part 2

Answer these questions.

Who was your favorite helper? _____

   Why? _____

Who was your least favorite helper? _____

   Why? _____

If you wrote a *Cinderella* fairy tale, who (or what) would the helper be?

_____

Tell what magical powers this helper would possess and how he/she/it would help the heroine or hero.

_____

_____

_____

Section 2: Culminating Activities

Who Does What?

Read the clues below and write down which helper did what action. (Since two of the helpers are both fish bones, be sure to indicate from which story it comes.) You will use some helpers more than once.

| **fish bones** (*The Brocaded Slipper*) | **turkeys** | **doll** |
| **falcon** | **fish** | **fish bones** (*Yeh-Shen*) |

1. brings a shoe to a prince
   _____

2. makes golden shoes with fish-like scales
   _____

3. creates a jar full of gold, silver, and jewels
   _____

4. takes the girl to an underwater palace
   _____

5. weeds the garden, brings water from the well, and does other chores
   _____

6. turns old clothes into beautiful garments by stomping on them
   _____

7. warns the girl not to forget her friends and not to stay out too late
   _____

8. creates beautiful, red, silk slippers
   _____

9. cleans a large amount of poppy seeds one by one
   _____

Section 2: Culminating Activities

If the Shoe Fits

In most *Cinderella* fairy tales, there is a pair of shoes involved which become important in establishing Cinderella's true identity. In practically every *Cinderella* tale around the world, one of her (or his) shoes ends up missing for a short time. Many people try on this shoe, but since it is a magical shoe, it does not fit correctly until it is on Cinderella.

Shoes today are measured in sizes, not by magic. There is a size scale for children and one for adults. There are also different sizes for men's and women's shoes. When you go to the shoe store to get fitted for shoes, the salesperson brings out a device which has ruler markings on it to determine your shoe size. Without this device, what other ways can you think of to measure your foot?

For this class activity, you will conduct a survey of the other students in your "kingdom" to find out their shoe sizes and what kinds of shoes they are wearing today. Then you will make two shoe line graphs to display the results.

The royal helpers in *Cinderella* tales often have to look at many different feet before they find the person for whom they are looking. What a tough job! After sorting through all the feet and shoes in your classroom kingdom, you will have a good idea what these helpers had to go through!

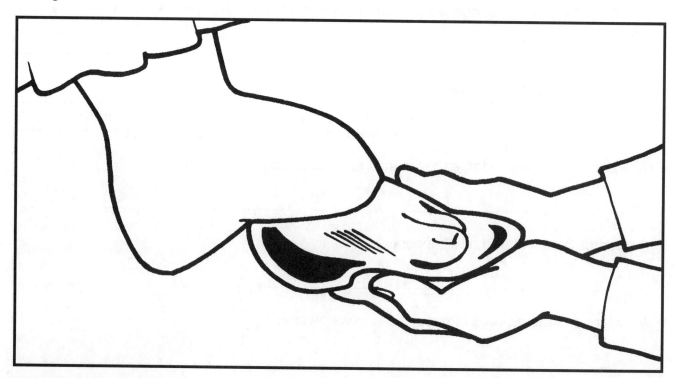

Section 2: Culminating Activities

If the Shoe Fits (cont.)

You will need to travel to each person in your classroom kingdom to get the information you need. Keep track of the information on this piece of paper and then transfer the data to the graph paper on the next page. Use tally marks to keep track. To help you stay organized, mark the size and shoe type at the same time for each person. If you need more room for information, use the back of this paper.

Shoe Size

1 _____

2 _____

3 _____

4 _____

5 _____

6 _____

7 _____

8 _____

9 _____

10 _____

11 _____

12 _____

13 _____

high-top sneaker	low-top sneaker
sandal	boot
high heel	loafer (slip-on)
other	

© Teacher Created Materials, Inc.   115   #464 Tales Around the World

Section 2: Culminating Activities

If the Shoe Fits (cont.)

Shoe Size Line Graph

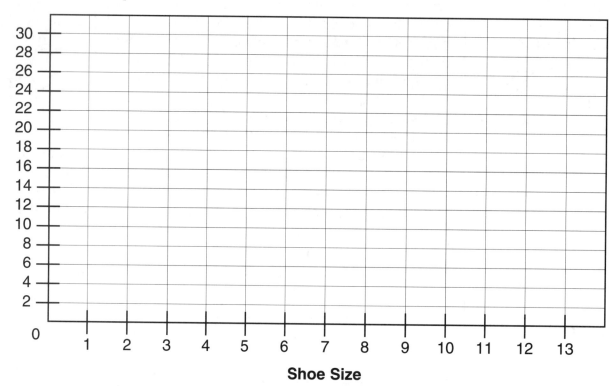

Shoe Type Line Graph

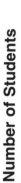
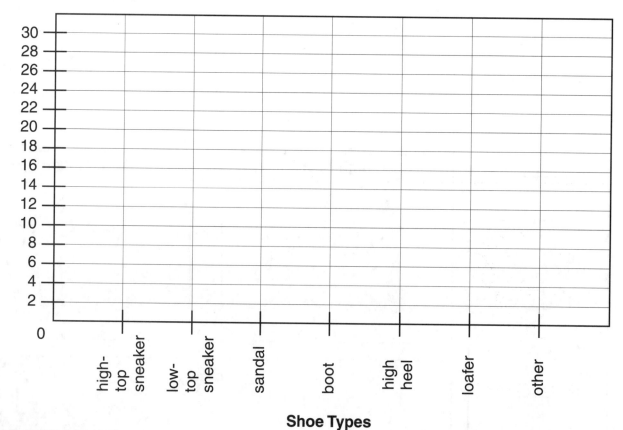

Section 2: Culminating Activities

Cinderella Venn Diagram

Complete the Venn diagram by comparing and contrasting the commonly told French *Cinderella* story written by Charles Perrault (adapted by Walt Disney) with one of the six versions you have just read. Be sure to include as many details as possible.

Walt Disney Version

both

Other Version

title: _____
_____

© Teacher Created Materials, Inc.   117   #464 Tales Around the World

Section 2: Culminating Activities

Venn Diagram Deluxe

For this deluxe Venn diagram, you will compare and contrast all six of the *Cinderella* stories you have just read. All of the tales have certain elements in common. Some have aspects in common with one or two versions but not all of them. You may want to use some scratch paper to make a list of story details before you complete this challenging *Cinderella* task! (Use the lines below to write notes on how all of the versions are similar.)

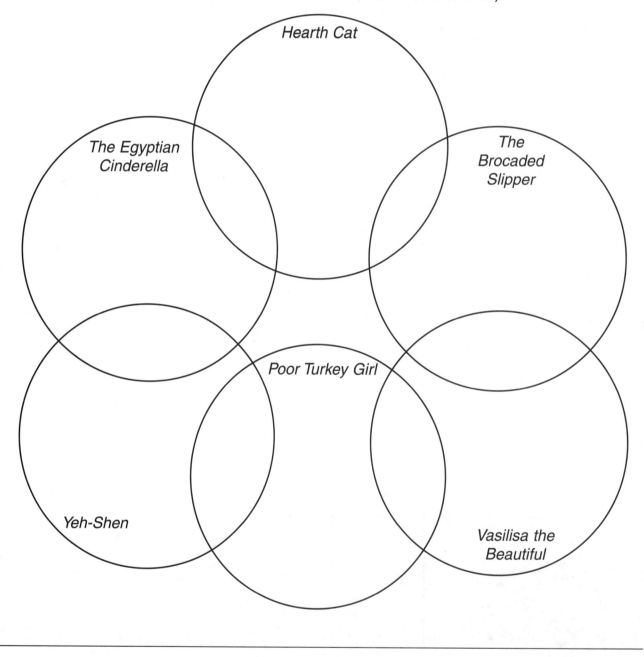

_____

_____

_____

#464 *Tales Around the World*   © *Teacher Created Materials, Inc.*

Section 2: Culminating Activities

Cinderella Word Search

Find the names of all the *Cinderella* characters and other related words in the puzzle below. When you are done, put the words in alphabetical order on the back of this paper.

Cinderella Word Bank

Hearth Cat	Nile	China	azure	Yeh-Shen
beautiful	Rhodopis	stepmother	tzar	Baba Yaga
Cam	well	fish bones	turkey	slipper
Pharaoh	Russia	Tam	Vasilisa	Egypt
chief				

```
D I O R E H T O M P E T S A M D H G J S F A D T A M
M S A F N K L F U A Z U R E D K E O Q N A H M V R E
M S J I O B A M N D W I C H I E F L E N D E N S M A
L E L E M E W P A K Z X A M F W J L D K N A V C R A
B A B A Y A G A R O L D M F L Y I V X I U R E R E S
K L H D S U W R T Y U N M I S D F A H J K T L I P W
S X O T N T P T Z A R Q U S R F G S C S J H H R P H
M L A S D I R S F B H U T H C A N I H C V C R T I S
B G R D R F S N I L E W R B A L O L N Z O A R I L C
E I A S A U G O W O D R H O D O P I S B O T Y A S N
D W H E R L E G E L O D T N O K N S O W M H I D S A
H E P R E I M A L C A L I E G E I A T U R K E Y O R
E G Y P T G I A L A R R U S S I A I M N E E X W I O
M A S D J H S G F N E H S H E Y M Z C A K L D Q W C
```

Section 2: Culminating Activities

Cinderella Research Ideas

Choose one of the tales you read in this section of the book and then complete a research project on the country from which the tale originates. Work with a partner to conduct the research and to write the report. Choose your topic from the ideas below and on the next page. If you have another idea, discuss it with your teacher and get his or her approval. You can get the information you need from the library (in encyclopedias, country books, and other reference books), computer online services, CD-ROM encyclopedias, and interviews with people from the country you are researching.

Note to the Teacher: Research forms for this report and for a traditional country report can be found on pages 82–87.

Egypt *(The Egyptian Cinderella)*

- gods, goddesses, and myths of ancient Egypt (especially Horsu)
- King Tut
- great pyramids of Egypt
- Nile River
- animals of Egypt
- Cairo
- Sahara desert

Russia *(Vasilisa the Beautiful)*

- the Kremlin and other significant structures
- how Russians obtain their names
- Russian Revolution
- Moscow
- Mikhail Gorbachev
- Tzar Nicholas II
- Kirov Ballet
- matrioshka nesting dolls

Vietnam *(The Brocaded Slipper)*

- Ho Chi Minh
- Le Loi
- Trung Sisters
- rice farming
- religions and philosophies of Vietnam (Confucianism, Taoism, Buddhism, Catholicism, Cao Dai, and Animism)
- Vietnam War
- Hanoi

Section 2: Culminating Activities

Cinderella Research Ideas (cont.)

China (Yeh-Shen)

- Ch'n and Han dynasties
- fishing industry of China
- cave dwelling people of China
- the abacus
- traditional food
- Great Wall of China
- Beijing
- Shanghai

Zuni Tribe, North America (Poor Turkey Girl)

- turkeys
- turkeys compared to other birds
- geological formation of mesas and canyons in the southwestern United States
- multifamily adobe houses of the Zuni
- Pueblo Revolt in 1680 against Spanish missionaries
- pottery
- weaving
- New Mexico

Portugal (Hearth Cat)

- the Azores
- explorers from Portugal
- colonization quest of Portugal
- Portugal's slave trade
- Triumphal Arch
- Lisbon
- Goths (Visigoths)

Section 2: Section Test

Cinderella Test

I. Matching: Match each Cinderella with the action taken.

_____ 1. Egyptian Cinderella   A. Her good luck doll saves her many times.

_____ 2. Hearth Cat   B. She keeps the bones of her fish in four jars.

_____ 3. Poor Turkey Girl   C. A falcon takes her shoe from her.

_____ 4. Yeh-Shen   D. This "Cinderella" finds her own shoe and takes it home.

_____ 5. Vasilisa the Beautiful   E. She does not follow the directions given to her and loses her special friends in the end.

_____ 6. Tam   F. Her special fish turns out to be the prince.

II. Name That Country: Write the country of origin for each Cinderella.

1. Yeh-Shen _____

2. Vasilisa _____

3. Tam _____

4. Hearth Cat _____

5. Rhodopis _____

6. Turkey Girl _____

III. Short Answer Essay: Respond to each of the following using complete sentences.

1. In the Egyptian Cinderella, how does Pharaoh explain that Rhodopis is a true Egyptian?

2. Describe Baba Yaga's hut in detail.

3. Write about the Cinderella character you admire most. What qualities does she possess which you think are important? Give examples.

Section 3: Animal Tales

Ti-Jean and the White Cat

Canada

Book: "Ti-Jean and the White Cat" from *Canadian Fairy Tales* retold by Eva Martin and Laszlo Gal (Douglas & McIntyre, 1984)

Summary: There lives a king who has neither sons nor daughters to inherit his crown. He chooses three men of the kingdom to compete in three tasks to help him decide who should be the next king.

The first task is to bring back the finest horse of the land. The three men travel down three different roads. Ti-Jean, one of the three men known to be a rascal, comes upon a cottage. There he sees a white cat jump into a tub of water. The cat turns into a beautiful princess. Ti-Jean asks her for a horse, and the princess gives him an ugly toad to take back to the king. The other two men laugh, but the toad turns out to be a beautiful horse.

Ti-Jean continues going to the white cat/princess for help on the other two tasks. The last task is to bring back a beautiful princess. Ti-Jean asks the white cat to come, but she says she can only be a princess permanently if she marries a king. He takes her back to the king, the king gives him the crown, and Ti-Jean and the princess are married.

Discussion Questions:

- Why does the king send these three men on the tasks?
- What are the three tasks?
- How does the white cat help Ti-Jean?
- How do the other two mean react when they see Ti-Jean's toad and walnut?
- What happens when the king opens the walnut?
- Why does the king select Ti-Jean to be the next king?

Journal Questions and Prompts:

- Why do you think Ti-Jean believes the white cat/princess in regards to the toad and walnut?
- How do you think the princess came to have the curse of being a white cat?
- Imagine you lived most of your life as an animal. Which would you want to be?
- Tell about another tale you know in which a princess is also an animal.

Section 3: Animal Tales *Ti-Jean and the White Cat*

Pet Profile

In many fairy tales there are animals who play important characters. Sometimes the animal is a helper, other times it is the recipient of a curse, and still other times it is a creature of great magical powers. In *Ti-Jean and the White Cat*, the cat has two identities: a cat and a beautiful princess who helps Ti-Jean become king.

What if your pet was a magical animal from a fairy tale? What would your life be like if your pet hamster could grant you wishes or if your loyal dog could take you flying instead of for a walk? Use your imagination to complete this Pet Profile for your magical pet.

What kind of animal is your pet? _____

What is your pet's name? _____

What magical powers or gifts does your pet possess? _____
_____

How did your pet receive these magical powers? _____
_____

Give examples of how your pet helps you. _____
_____

Is there any way that your pet could lose these powers? Explain. _____
_____

Who are some of your pet's magical friends from other fairy tales? _____
_____

Draw a picture of your pet.

Ice Sculptures

Canada is a large country divided into several provinces and territories. The early people of Canada came from many Indian tribes, and they were followed by many European immigrants.

The majority of the first Europeans to be settled in Canada were from France, and the French influence remains strong today. Ti-Jean, from the fairy tale, is a French name. Quebec, the oldest city in Canada, is a French-speaking city.

The most famous Canadian carnival is held in Quebec, and it is called the Winter Carnival. A popular activity at the carnival is ice sculpting.

Materials:

- freezer (with plenty of room for student pieces)
- several odd-shaped containers (paper cups, pie plates, rubber gloves, balloons, spice jars, butter containers, plastic bags, party ice trays, etc.)
- several rubber bands
- food coloring
- water
- cookie trays or large cake pans

Directions:

1. Decide what colors you want to use in your sculpture.

2. Mix water and the desired food coloring into containers.

3. Choose the shapes you want to use for the sculpture. Pour the water into the containers and rubber gloves, using rubber bands to tie off loose containers (such as plastic bags and rubber gloves).

4. Place the water-filled items in the freezer overnight. (If you live in a very cold environment, you can just place them outside!)

5. When the shapes are completely frozen, remove them from their containers by running a little warm water over them. You may need to cut some of the containers (plastic cups, bags, and gloves) to remove the ice.

6. Stack the pieces anyway you like on the cookie tray or cake pan. Invite another class in to view your Winter Wonderland! (Hurry, these sculptures are a little like the white cat and will change their forms quickly!)

Section 3: Animal Tales

Unanana and the Enormous One-Tusked Elephant

Zulu, South Africa

Book: "Unanana and the Enormous One-Tusked Elephant" from *Magical Tales from Many Lands* retold by Margaret Mayo (Dutton Children's Books, 1993)

Summary: In the southern part of the African bush, a mother named Unanana builds a house for herself and her two beautiful children in the middle of a wide road. This is the animals' road and a dangerous place, but Unanana is not afraid.

One day Unanana goes out to collect firewood, so the children's older cousin comes to watch them. While she is away, an enormous, one-tusked elephant comes along the road and eats both of Unanana's children whole. When Unanana returns, she cooks a big pot of corn porridge, takes her knife, and sets about to get her children back.

When she comes upon the elephant, he swallows her, too. She finds her children inside the elephant, along with some other people, and they all dance around so as to give the elephant a bellyache. Unanana cuts a doorway from the side of the elephant, and everyone escapes. The people are so happy, they bring many gifts to Unanana and she becomes rich. The elephant lives but never bothers her and her children again.

Discussion Questions:

- What do the people of the village say about Unanana's children?
- What two animals come down the road before the elephant?
- Why does the elephant eat her children?
- How does Unanana get the elephant's attention?
- Who and what does she find inside the elephant?

Journal Questions and Prompts:

- Why do you think Unanana builds a house in the middle of the road?
- Where would you like to build a house and live? Give details.
- Write a story (real or imaginary) about an animal with whom you have trouble.

Unanana and the Enormous One-Tusked Elephant Section 3: Animal Tales

Extra! Extra! Read All About It!

In *Unanana and the Enormous One-Tusked Elephant,* the two beautiful children of Unanana are eaten whole! They must have been very frightened inside of this large animal. They also meet other people and animals inside the belly of the enormous beast. Fortunately, Unanana is clever and brave enough to save everyone. What a story!

Pretend you are a reporter for a newspaper, and you are the first to arrive at the scene after the people are freed from the elephant's belly. It is your job to interview Unanana and her two children, possibly even the elephant, and to get as much information as possible for a story. What questions will you ask? What will the responses be? Before you write your newspaper article, conduct your interviews to obtain information.

Interview Information

Character	Questions	Responses
Unanana		
Boy		
Girl		
Elephant		
Other Person		

If you need more room, continue your interview on the back of this paper.

Section 3: Animal Tales   Unanana and the Enormous One-Tusked Elephant

Extra! Extra! Read All About It! *(cont.)*

Use the information you gained from the interviews to help you write a front-page story about this fascinating event. Include a picture with your story.

Zulu News

Date _____   Edition _____

Unanana and the Enormous One-Tusked Elephant   Section 3: Animal Tales

Akua-ba Doll

Unanana is a strong, brave woman who is very proud of her two beautiful children. In African cultures children are considered a blessing. The Akua-ba doll is a special doll made by the Astante people of Ghana. This doll is carried by girls who hope to have children in the future and by women who hope that their children will be healthy and beautiful.

Materials:

- 8" x 18" (20 cm x 45 cm) cardboard
- yarn (any colors)
- tempera paint (brown and black)
- bowl
- glue
- tape
- paintbrushes
- sharp scissors or mat knife (for adult use only)

Directions:

1. Cut out the patterns.
2. Tape the patterns onto the piece of cardboard. Be sure to tape the head and body together at the neck by overlapping them at the dotted lines. Do not forget to trace the slot.
3. Ask an adult to cut the pieces from the cardboard. It is helpful to place a cutting board beneath to protect the tabletop.
4. In a bowl, mix the black and brown tempera paint together to achieve the desired skin tone for your doll. Lay the head, body, and stand on newspaper. Paint one side, allow time to dry, and then paint the other side.
5. Cut small pieces of yarn to fit into the facial features of the doll. When you have decided what color will go where, apply glue to the facial lines. Press the yarn down on top of the glue. Allow time to dry thoroughly.
6. Using tape, connect the head to the body. Fit the entire body into the slot at the bottom of the doll.
7. Decorate your Akua-ba doll with beads around the neck and waist.
8. Set up a display with all the Akua-ba dolls. Bring in (or make) other dolls from different countries and cultures to compare.

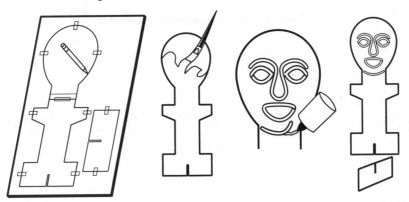

Section 3: Animal Tales　　　　　　　　　Unanana and the Enormous One-Tusked Elephant

Akua-ba Doll (cont.)

head

Unanana and the Enormous One-Tusked Elephant — Section 3: Animal Tales

Akua-ba Doll (cont.)

body

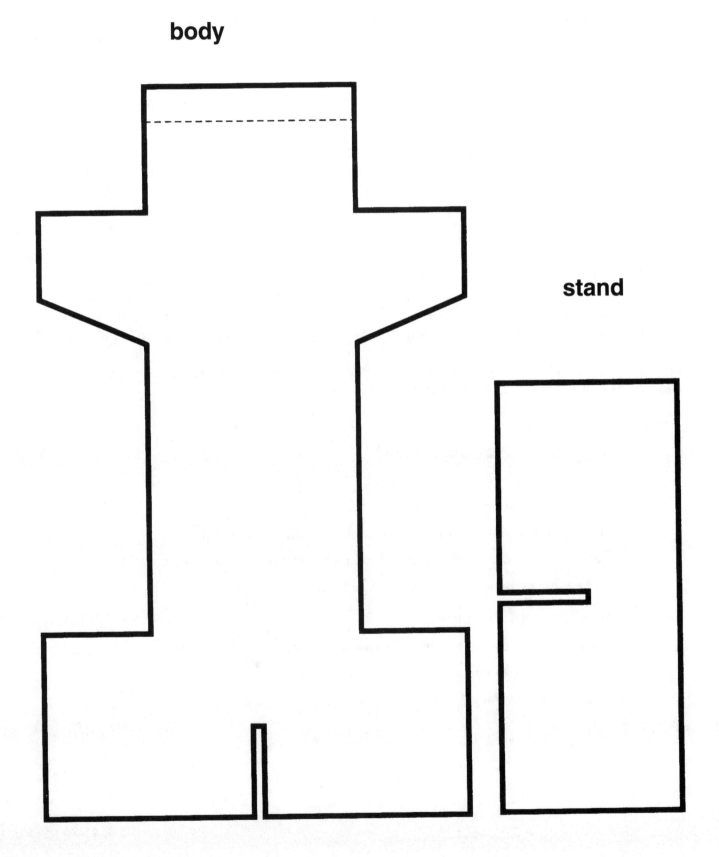

stand

Section 3: Animal Tales

The Enchanted Mule

Spain

Book: "The Enchanted Mule" from *Favorite Fairy Tales Told in Spain* retold by Virginia Haviland (William Morrow & Company, 1995)

Summary: There lives a poor man in Spain named Pedro. His job is to care for horses at an inn. Pedro is an unhappy man with a scolding wife. One day an archbishop riding a richly outfitted mule comes to the inn. The archbishop tells Pedro to take especially good care of the mule, feeding him the best oats. Pedro becomes angry that a mule should live a better life than him. The mule tells Pedro that he will gladly switch places with him. With the help of some magic, the two switch places.

Pedro tries to go back to his family to say goodbye, but they are frightened of the mule. Pedro is unaccustomed to being a mule and does not know how to carry the fat archbishop. He creates all kinds of trouble for the man on their journeys. He soon realizes that his life as a poor man was better than that of a mule, so one day he escapes and runs all the way back to the inn. The mule (in the form of Pedro) is at the inn and is very unhappy with his new life, too. The two agree to return to their original forms. Pedro learns that if he is kinder to his wife, she will not scold him so much. The archbishop, in the meantime, decides to sell his silly mule to the innkeeper. Pedro ends up taking care of the mule, and both are happy for the rest of their days.

Discussion Questions:

- How do the mule and Pedro change places?
- What is the first thing Pedro misses as a mule?
- Who does Pedro run to first, and what is that person's reaction?
- What are some of the antics that Pedro as the mule does to the archbishop?
- Eventually Pedro, the mule, grows to care for the archbishop. How do you know this?
- Why does Pedro never speak crossly to his wife again?

Journal Questions and Prompts:

- If you could trade places with an animal, which animal would it be and why?
- What would be the first thing you would do as an animal?
- What would be the advantages and disadvantages of being an animal?

The Enchanted Mule   Section 3: Animal Tales

Trading Places

Pedro and the mule in *The Enchanted Mule* have an opportunity to see what life is like in each other's shoes. They both learn valuable lessons and decide that their original lives are the best after all.

The story tells of the adventures of Pedro, but it does not tell what life is like for the mule. Describe what you think happens to the mule when he is in Pedro's form.

1. When the mule leaves the stall, where does he go first and why?

2. When the mule goes to Pedro's home, how do he and Pedro's mother get along?

3. When Pedro's wife begins scolding the mule, how does the mule as Pedro react and what does he do?

4. What kinds of events happen when the mule reports for work at the inn and takes care of the other mules?

5. How does the mule feel about wearing Pedro's clothes?

6. How did the mule feel about human food compared to hay and oats?

7. How does the mule find sleeping in a bed compared to a stall?

8. What is the worst thing about being a human, according to the mule?

9. What is the greatest thing about being a human, according to the mule?

10. What is the deciding factor in making up the mule's mind that he wants to be a mule again?

Section 3: Animal Tales   The Enchanted Mule

Spanish Tile

The art of brightly painted, glazed tiles has long been a popular as well as useful craft in Spain. Tiles are used decoratively to cover walls and floors. This art was brought to Spain by the Moors (Moslems) during their 750 years of reign in the country.

The tile design you will be using is a copy from the tiled walls of the Alhambra Palace in Granada, Spain, which was built by the Moors in the fourteenth century. It was at this famous place in 1492 that King Ferdinand and Queen Isabella met with Christopher Columbus and agreed to send him on his first journey to the "New World."

Materials:

- oven-bake clay (enough for one 6" or 15 cm square per student)
- tempera (or acrylic) paints (dark red, dark blue, and white)
- paintbrushes
- clay tools (rolling pin, ruler)
- sharp-pointed knife (for adult use only)
- access to an oven
- waxed paper
- tile pattern (page 135)
- light graphite paper
- pottery glaze (spray or paint)

Directions:

1. Trace the tile pattern onto the graphite paper. Keep the graphite paper in a safe, flat place until it will be needed again.

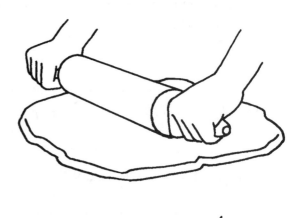

2. Cover the working surface with waxed paper. Roll out the clay into a ½" (1.25 cm) thick slab.

3. Use the ruler to measure off a 6" (15 cm) square. Ask an adult to use the sharp knife to cut out the square piece of clay.

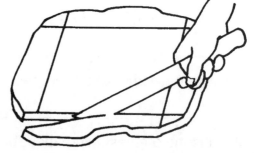

4. On one side of the clay, lightly carve in your name. Gently lift the tile from the waxed paper and turn it over.

5. With a little water on your fingers, smooth out the surface of your clay square.

The Enchanted Mule Section 3: Animal Tales

Spanish Tile (cont.)

6. Set the tile aside to dry completely (four or five hours).

7. Bake the clay in an oven according to the package directions. (Only adults should handle objects going in and out of the oven.)

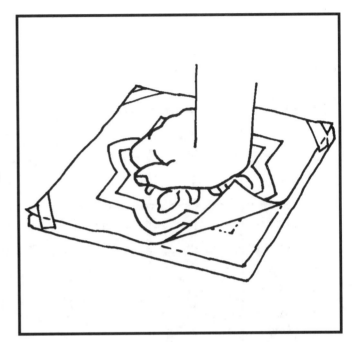

8. When the square tile has been baked and cooled, you will transfer the tile pattern from the graphite paper onto the tile. To do so, place the pattern over the tile. Gently but firmly, rub the graphite paper with your fist over the tile. Carefully lift the corner of the pattern up from the tile to see how much of the transfer is complete. You may need to go over the pattern with a pencil again while it is on the square tile. Continue this process until the entire pattern has been transferred.

9. Following the color key, paint the design with the three different colors of tempera or acrylic paints.

    ### color key:
    1 = white

    2 = dark red

    3 = dark blue

10. When the paint is dry, spray (or paint) the varnish to give the tile a shine.

Section 3: Animal Tales   The Enchanted Mule

Spanish Tile (cont.)

These are ½" (1.25 cm) squares.

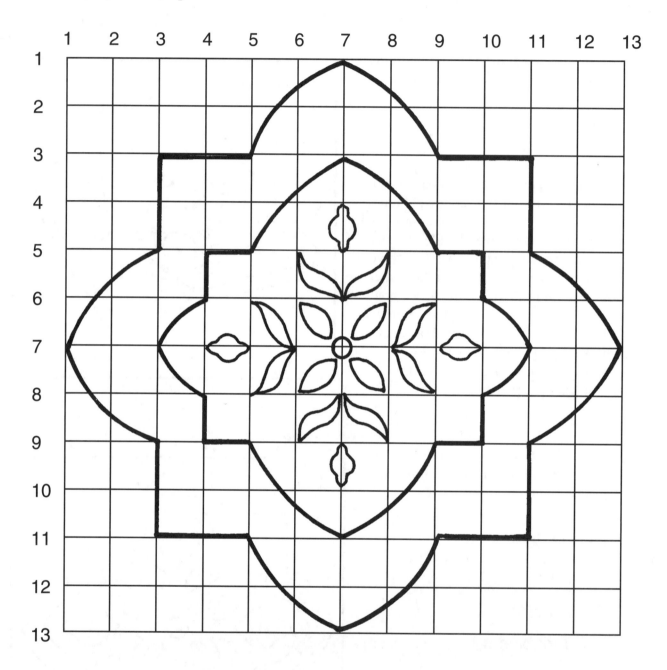

#464 Tales Around the World   © Teacher Created Materials, Inc.

Buffalo Woman

Native American, United States

Book: *Buffalo Woman* retold by Paul Goble (Simon & Schuster Children's, 1984)

Summary: There lives a young man who is a great hunter of buffalo. He feels a wonderful harmony with the buffalo and always gives thanks that the buffalo offer themselves to him and his tribe. One day he comes upon a buffalo cow at a stream. In the next moment, the cow turns into a beautiful maiden, and the man falls in love with her immediately. She is from the Buffalo Nation and is sent to be his wife. The two are to set an example to both peoples, showing a life of kindness toward one another. They have a son and name him Calf Boy.

The rest of his tribe does not like this woman or the boy, and they send them away. The young man follows his family, but Calf Boy tells his father that if he follows him to the herd, he will be killed. The man loves his family so much that when he gets to the buffalo herd, he risks his life with the Chief of the Buffalo Nation. He is forced to pick out his son and wife from the hundreds of buffalo. He does this successfully and then through a ceremony he also becomes a buffalo. The family lives happily together again. As a gift, the buffalo people give their flesh to the tribes of the plains to sustain their lives.

Discussion Questions:

- Just how good a hunter is this young man?
- How is Buffalo Woman different from the women of the tribe?
- Why do the people not like her and Calf Boy?
- What warning does Calf Boy continue to give his father?
- How does Calf Boy help his father when he reaches the Buffalo Nation?
- Describe the process of becoming a buffalo.

Journal Questions and Prompts:

- Would you become a buffalo to be with your spouse and child? Explain.
- Imagine that your family suddenly looked like everyone else and could not speak. How might you pick them out from the crowd?

Section 3: Animal Tales   *Buffalo Woman*

Buffalo or Bison?

The Plains Indians of North America had a special relationship with buffalo. Included in virtually every aspect of their lives, the buffalo provided the Plains Indians with a source for food, protective clothing, tepee covers, tools, utensils, fuel, and a variety of other items. The term buffalo, however, actually refers to another animal that lives in Asia and Africa! A North American "buffalo," as it is commonly known, is really a bison.

The American bison weighs about 2,000 pounds (900 kg) and stands more than 6 feet (1.9 m) high. The massive head and body are covered with long hair, and both sexes have horns. American bison can be very temperamental and ferocious, especially when people or other animals approach the herd. The bison became extinct due to their unfortunate encounters with humans. When white settlers first arrived in America, the grasslands from the Mississippi River to the Rocky Mountains were the home of some 30-million prairie bison. That number was reduced to about 500 by the end of the 19th century. Due to current ranches and refuges, there are about 45,000 bison in America today.

The true buffalo are the Asian water buffalo and African buffalo. Both species have horns and are deemed peaceful and docile creatures. These animals are widely used to help in farming activities such as rice cultivation. With their wide hooves and short legs, they are adept at swimming and walking in mud. Because they have relatively few sweat glands, they spend much of their time in water, cooling themselves.

Both buffalo and bison have been and continue to be a necessary force in the lives of many people.

After reading the information above, answer these questions.

1. How much does a bison weigh? _____
2. How many bison roamed the prairie at one time? _____
3. What two animals are true buffalo? _____
4. How was the bison helpful to the Plains Indians? _____
5. Why do buffalo need to cool themselves in water? _____
6. What physical feature do both bison and buffalo have in common? _____
7. How tall does a bison stand? _____
8. Which animal, bison or buffalo, is the more docile? _____

Buffalo Woman   Section 3: Animal Tales

Buffalo Hide

The Plains Indians of the United States depended on the buffalo (bison) for their existence. The buffalo provided clothing, food, robes, blankets, tools, rugs, fuel, and eating utensils. The Native Americans respected the buffalo and always gave thanks for their assistance in their way of life.

Oftentimes, stories would be recorded on buffalo skins. These stories were written in symbols known as pictographs (page 140).

Materials:

- large brown paper bag (1 per student)
- crayons
- light brown tempera paint
- bucket or sink full of water
- newspapers

Directions:

1. Cut along one seam of the paper bag to open the bag into a large piece of paper.

2. Using scissors or tearing (tearing looks more authentic), cut out a hide shape from the paper.

3. Using crayons and the pictograph samples on page 140, write a story on the bag. Be sure to press very hard onto the bag with the crayons.

4. In a bucket (or sink) of water placed on top of newspaper, dilute one cup (250 mL) brown tempera paint.

5. Lightly crumple the paper buffalo skin and immerse it in the tempera mixture.

6. Knead the hide gently to remove excess water.

7. Carefully open up the hide and lay it flat on newspapers to dry thoroughly.

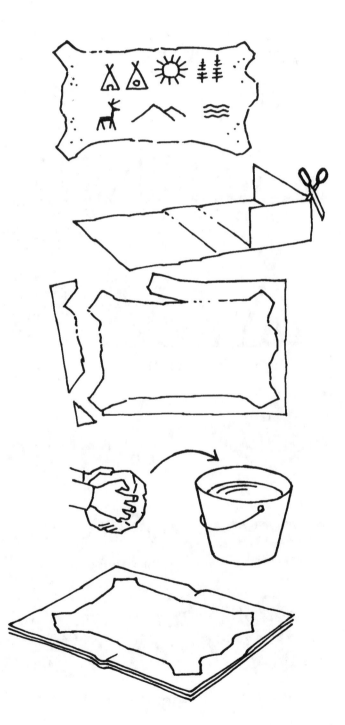

© Teacher Created Materials, Inc.   #464 *Tales Around the World*

Section 3: Animal Tales   *Buffalo Woman*

Buffalo Hide (cont.)

Section 3: Animal Tales

The Little White Dove

Panama

Book: "The Little White Dove" in *Stories from the Americas* collected and translated by Frank Henius (Charles Scribner's Sons, 1944)

Summary: A handsome young king comes upon a beautiful maiden along the bank of a river. The young king immediately falls in love and asks her to marry him. He tells the maiden to wait up in the tree for an escort from the palace and not to talk to anyone while he is away. He promises to return and marry her.

Later, an old, evil, ugly hag comes to the river to get some water. When she sees the reflection of the princess in the water, she thinks that it is her and begins admiring herself. The princess cannot help but laugh. The hag becomes angry, turns the maiden into a dove by pushing a dress pin into her head and then the dove/princess flies away. The hag takes her place in the tree. When the king returns, he is heartbroken, but he promises to keep his word to the woman in the tree (the hag) and marries her.

Several days later the dove flies back to the palace and inquires of the gardener about the king. Each day the gardener tries to catch the dove but to no avail. One day the king comes upon the dove and pulls the pin from the dove's head. The beautiful maiden is immediately transformed, the evil queen is put to death, and the king and his new queen live happily ever after.

Discussion Questions:

- How do the ministers feel about the king not being married?
- Why does the king wait so long to get married?
- Why does the king go back to the palace to get an escort for the maiden?
- Describe what happens each of the three times the hag comes to the stream.
- How does the gardener try to catch the dove?
- What trick finally catches her?
- Why is the king so enchanted with the dove?

Journal Questions and Prompts:

- The king and young maiden seem to fall in love instantly. Do you believe in "love at first sight" like the old saying says?
- Getting married is a big decision. Do you think the king and princess should have waited? Why or why not?
- Should the king have married the hag? Why or why not?

© Teacher Created Materials, Inc.   #464 Tales Around the World

Section 3: Animal Tales   The Little White Dove

True or False?

Read each statement. Decide if the sentence is true or false and circle your answer. On the back of this paper, write a reason why each one is true or false.

1. The young king sets out to find himself a wife.

    True   **False**

2. The young maiden takes her time to decide if she will marry the king.

    True   **False**

3. The maiden does not tell anyone what has happened.

    True   **False**

4. The hag thinks it is unfair that she is a servant when she is so beautiful.

    True   **False**

5. The hag puts the pieces of the broken vessels back together again.

    True   **False**

6. The hag pretends to caress the maiden's beautiful hair.

    True   **False**

7. The hag takes a pin from the maiden's hair and sticks it in her head.

    True   **False**

8. The king is heartbroken upon marrying the hag.

    True   **False**

9. Three gardeners tend the king's favorite garden.

    True   **False**

10. The dove begins talking to the gardener.

    True   **False**

11. The necklace of pearls finally lures the dove.

    True   **False**

12. The gardener pulls the pin from the dove's head.

    True   **False**

The Little White Dove Section 3: Animal Tales

Worry Doll

Panama is one of several Central American countries. Children in Central America have special dolls that have been used for many generations. These dolls are called Worry Dolls. Before going to bed at night, the children tell their troubles and worries to the tiny dolls and place them under their pillows. It is believed that while the children are asleep, the Worry Dolls solve all their problems! Children will often keep one doll for each worry.

Materials:

- wooden doll pin or straight clothespin (one per student)
- craft stick (one per student)
- yarn (medium to small width in variety of colors)
- scissors
- dark markers
- glue (Wood glue or carpenter's glue work best.)
- ruler
- masking tape (or glue gun, for adult use only)

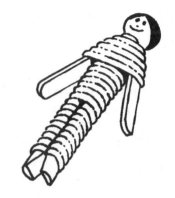

Directions:

1. Use a pencil to mark off the measurements on the craft stick (2¼" or 6.25 cm from both ends).

2. Carefully cut the stick with scissors along these two lines. You will not need the small middle piece.

3. Glue the two larger pieces (arms) along the sides of the clothespin at an angle.

4. Wrap a piece of masking tape around the "shoulders" of the doll and let it dry overnight. (If you are using a glue gun, you may proceed with the rest of the directions now. Remember that only an adult should handle a glue gun.)

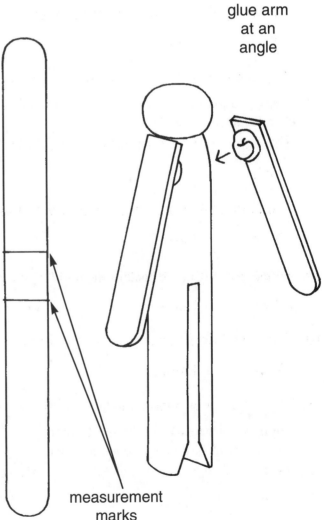

glue arm at an angle

measurement marks

© Teacher Created Materials, Inc. 143 #464 Tales Around the World

Section 3: Animal Tales   The Little White Dove

Worry Doll

5. Use a dark marker (brown or black) around the top of the clothespin to make hair. Add facial features and shoes, too.

6. Begin wrapping yarn around the doll. Start at the neck and work your way down to the waist of the doll. (The arms should be left uncovered.)

7. When you get to the legs, wrap yarn around each leg separately.

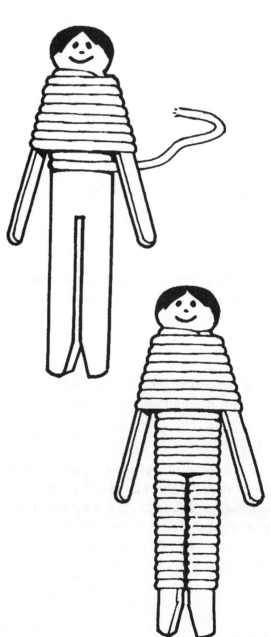

8. Tie the yarn off in the back of the doll.

9. You may want to add a different colored piece of yarn for a belt around the waist.

#464 Tales Around the World   144   © Teacher Created Materials, Inc.

Section 3: Culminating Activities

Terrific Titles

Titles of stories are very important. A good title will get the attention of a reader and tell a little bit about the story without giving away too much information. All the titles of the animal fairy tales meet those requirements.

Pretend you are an author and will be writing your own fairy tales with animal characters. Rewrite the titles of the stories you have just read by changing the animal name mentioned. Choose the title which is most interesting to you and write a brief summary about this possible fairy tale.

Original Title	Your New Title
Ti-Jean and the White Cat	Ti-Jean and the _____
Unanana and the Enormous One-Tusked Elephant	Unanana and the _____
The Enchanted Mule	The Enchanted _____
Buffalo Woman	_____ Woman
The Little White Dove	The Little White _____

New Title: _____

Author: _____

Story Summary:

_____
_____
_____
_____
_____
_____
_____
_____
_____

Section 3: Culminating Activities

Half and Half

In the tale of the *Buffalo Woman,* the son of the great hunter and buffalo maiden is called Calf Boy because he is half buffalo and half human. Throughout all literature, there are many tales of "half and half" creatures such as mermaids (half woman/half fish) and the Pegasus (half horse/half man).

If you could be half human and half animal, what animal would you choose? What special powers would you have as this creature? What is the magical story behind your becoming this creature? Where do you live?

For this activity you will create your unique "half and half" character by completing the Tell-All Table and drawing an illustration. Be creative and have fun!

Tell-All Table
What is your creature name?
What animal are you?
What is the story of your origin?
What are your magical powers?
Where do you live?
Who are your friends?
Who are your enemies?
What is wonderful about your life?
What is difficult about your life?

Section 3: Culminating Activities

Half and Half (cont.)

Draw and color a picture of your special half and half creature in the frame below.

Section 3: Culminating Activities

Animal Talk Show

Some of the animals in the fairy tales you have read are kind while others are evil. Some of them are actually human beings in disguise. If you could ask these animals some questions about their lives and thoughts, they would probably be more than happy to give you their opinions! Here is an opportunity to learn more about these special creatures. Working in a cooperative group of four, you will pretend to conduct a live television talk show with three of the five animals from the following stories:

Ti-Jean and the White Cat

Unanana and the Enormous One-Tusked Elephant

The Enchanted Mule

Buffalo Woman

The Little White Dove

Ready!

Talk with your group to decide which three animals you will be interviewing. One member of your group will need to be the talk-show host, and the other three students will assume the roles of the animals you choose.

Set!

1. Discuss each animal character with your group and as a team determine what are some interesting and important questions that should be asked of each.

2. The host should write these questions down and refer to them during the actual talk show.

3. Each "animal" should prepare for the show by thinking about his/her responses to these questions. The animal players can also go back and review the stories so that the details of the tales are fresh in their minds.

Action!

1. On the day of the talk show, each character can dress up in his or her respective role. To do so, use a simple prop or make a mask.

2. The show host should have a microphone prop.

3. Ask your teacher or adult leader to videotape the performance so that you can watch it later!

Section 3: Culminating Activities

Get to Know the Animals

In each of the fairy tales you have read in this section, a special animal is highlighted. One of these animals is a common household pet while others are more exotic or in danger of becoming extinct. Each animal is interesting and unique, and with a little research time, there is more information available for you to learn.

Work with a partner to complete the animal chart below. You will need to consult other information resources such as encyclopedias, animal books, and even books about the countries from which these animals originated.

Animal	Country of Origin	Size	Unique Features	Diet	Endangered List?	Location Today
white cat						
elephant						
mule						
buffalo (bison)						
dove						

Section 3: Culminating Activities

Animal Tales Crossword

Review your knowledge of the animal tales with this crossword puzzle.

Across

2. trusted a white cat to help him become a king
3. insisted upon building her hut in the middle of the road
5. is half human and half buffalo
7. country where a mule and poor stable hand trade places
8. hot cereal Unanana makes for her children

Down

1. beautiful homespun threads fly out of this nut
4. official title of the priest who rides upon the mule
6. true name for the American buffalo
9. small, white bird cursed by an evil hag
10. country of origin for *The Little White Dove*

Section 3: Culminating Activities

Animal Tales Research Ideas

Choose one of the tales you read in this section of the book. Complete a research project on the country from which the tale originates. Work with a partner to conduct the research and to write the report. Choose your topic from the ideas below and on the next page. If you have another idea, discuss it with your teacher and get his or her approval. You can get the information you need from the library (in encyclopedias, country books, and other reference books), computer online services, CD-ROM encyclopedias, and interviews with people from the country you are researching.

Note to the Teacher: Work sheets for this report and for a traditional country report can be found on pages 82–87. Alternatively, a report on an animal from a tale can be completed in lieu of a country report. Animal Report work sheets can be found on pages 153–154.

Canada *(Ti-Jean and the White Cat)*

- Canada's first people, the Inuit, and the eight main tribal groups today
- different immigrant waves to Canada, beginning with the Vikings
- Jacques Cartier
- Canadian Mounties
- popular organized sports such as lacrosse and ice hockey
- Alexander Graham Bell
- Dr. Frederick Banting
- Dr. Charles Best
- J. Armand Bombardier
- Alfred J. Russell
- Montreal

Zulu, South Africa *(Unanana and the Enormous One-Tusked Elephant)*

(**Note:** South Africa is not a single country but rather a region containing seven different countries.)

- traditional dress of the Zulu
- Bantu tribes and their influence on the Zulu
- the Zulu warrior Shaka
- the Zulu battle dance
- diamond mining industry
- gold mining industry
- traditional South African foods

Spain *(The Enchanted Mule)*

- legends of Don Quixote de la Mancha and Don Juan
- fandango
- Pablo Picasso
- Altamira, one of the world's best examples of prehistoric art
- Spanish Empire and some of its explorers

Section 3: Culminating Activities

Animal Tales Research Ideas (cont.)

Spain (*The Enchanted Mule*) (cont.)

- Spanish Inquisition
- running of the bulls
- traditional Spanish foods
- Father Junipero Serra and the many California missions he founded

Native American, United States (*Buffalo Woman*)

- different tribes in the plains region of the United States
- tepees
- importance of the buffalo (bison) for the Plains Indians
- Chief Black Kettle
- the Sioux Wars
- traditional arts of weaving and pottery
- horses
- Blackfoot
- Sioux
- Cheyenne
- Comanche

Panama (*The Little White Dove*)

- journeys through the Panamanian jungle during the California Gold Rush
- Panama Canal
- people living in Panama before the Europeans: Guaymi, Choco, and Cuna
- pollera, the traditional women's national costume, and the montuno, the men's costume
- rice, coffee, and banana industries
- how European explorers used Panama as a stopping place after they stole the gold and other treasures from the Inca people of South America
- Panama City
- rain forests
- Carnival

Animal Tale Research Ideas   Section 3: Culminating Activities

Animal Report

Name: _____

Animal: _____

Species: _____

Animal relatives: _____

Country where it originated: _____

Places it can be found today: _____

Size: _____

Coloring: _____

Temperament: _____

_____

_____

_____

Diet: _____

_____

_____

_____

How it gets its food: _____

_____

_____

_____

Sleep habits: _____

_____

_____

_____

Way it behaves toward fellow animals: _____

_____

_____

Section 3: Culminating Activities

Animal Tale Research Ideas

Animal Report (cont.)

Draw and color a picture of the animal in its natural habitat.

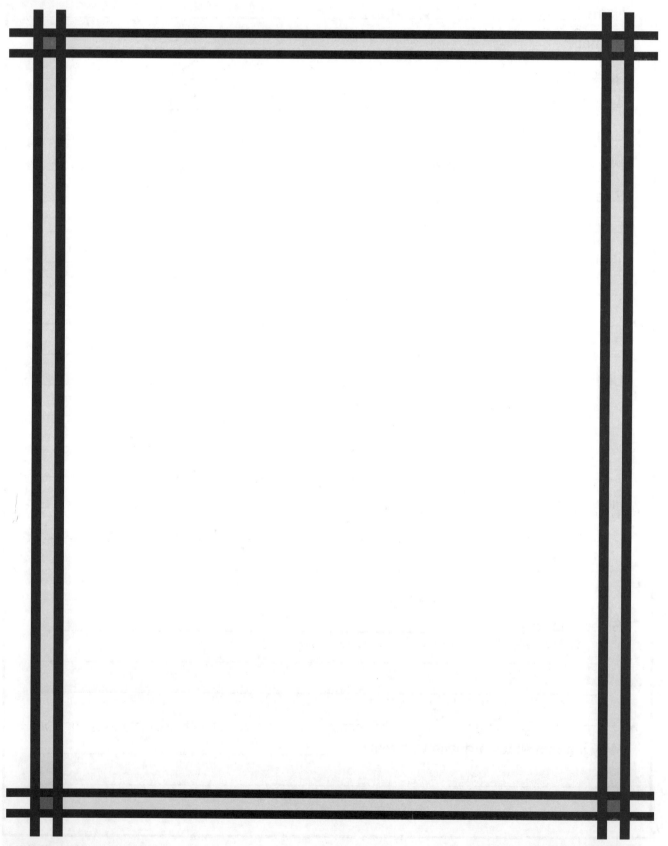

Section 3: Section Test

Animal Tales Test

I. **Matching:** Match each tale with the clue or action taken.

_____ 1. *Buffalo Woman*   A. Upon the advice of an animal, this man brings a toad back to a king.

_____ 2. *Ti-Jean and the White Cat*   B. Pedro trades places with this animal.

_____ 3. *Unanana and the Enormous One-Tusked Elephant*   C. This animal has a pin stuck in its head.

_____ 4. *The Enchanted Mule*   D. Her calf-boy helps his father.

_____ 5. *The Little White Dove*   E. This woman is very proud of her beautiful children.

II. **Name That Country:** Write the country of origin for each tale.

1. *Ti-Jean and the White Cat*
   _____

2. *Unanana and the Enormous One-Tusked Elephant*
   _____

3. *The Enchanted Mule*
   _____

4. *Buffalo Woman*
   _____

5. *The Little White Dove*
   _____

III. **Short Answer Essay:** Write your answers to these questions on the back of this paper.

1. Describe how Unanana saves her children and the other villagers from the stomach of the enormous, one-tusked elephant.

2. Tell about a day in Pedro's life as a mule.

3. Compare one of the characters in one of these stories to a character from **another** story you know (for example, *White Cat* and *Puss-in-Boots*).

© Teacher Created Materials, Inc.   #464 *Tales Around the World*

Section 4: Comparative Tales

Red Riding Hood

Germany

Book: *Red Riding Hood* retold by James Marshall (Dial Books for Young Readers, 1987)

Summary: There lives a sweet girl who is loved by all, especially her grandmother. Her grandmother gives her a red, hooded cloak one day, and the girl wears it so much that everyone calls her Red Riding Hood. One day her mother tells her to take some custard to her grandmother who is not feeling well. Her mother instructs Red Riding Hood not to loiter along the way.

As she walks down the path, Red Riding Hood comes upon a wicked wolf. She is not afraid of him and begins talking with him. The wolf tricks her into loitering off the path to pick some flowers for her grandmother. In the meantime, the wolf goes to the grandmother's cottage, eats her in one bite, and then disguises himself in her clothes in order to trick Red Riding Hood. When Red finally comes to the cottage, she notices that her grandmother looks different. She asks a few questions but then the wolf eats her up in one bite, too. The wolf is so full that he falls asleep and begins to snore loudly. A huntsman hears the snoring and goes to check on the grandmother. He quickly cuts open the wolf and out steps Red Riding Hood and her grandmother. The wolf dies, and Red Riding Hood promises never to wander off into the forest again.

Discussion Questions:

- How does the girl get her name?
- What is in the basket for her grandmother?
- Why does the wolf send Red Riding Hood off into the woods to pick flowers?
- What does Red say to the wolf?
- What lesson(s) does Red Riding Hood learn?

Journal Questions and Prompts:

- Apply the moral of this tale to today's life.
- What kinds of "wolves" do children need to watch out for today?
- What mistakes does Red Riding Hood make?
- What mistakes does the grandmother make?

Red Riding Hood Section 4: Comparative Tales

Clothing Connections

Even though it is not her real name, everyone calls her Red Riding Hood because of the red cloak that she wears. How would you like to be called a name that had to do with a type of clothing? Maybe you could be called "Little Jean Jacket," "Baseball Cap Boy," or "The High-Top Hopper."

Using one of the figures below, draw a picture of what you are wearing today. Be sure to include your socks, shoes, hat, jewelry, watch, coat, and every item you are wearing. On the back of this paper, write five different names for yourself, based on your clothing.

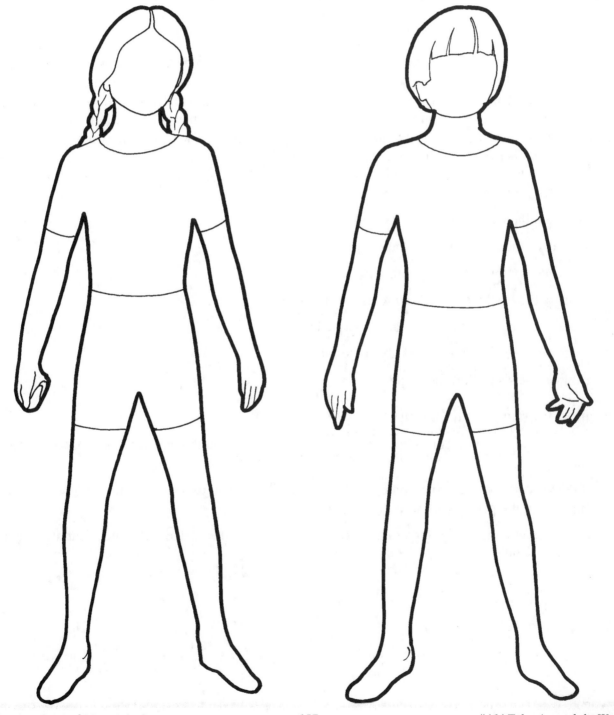

© Teacher Created Materials, Inc. #464 *Tales Around the World*

Section 4: Comparative Tales

Lon Po Po

China

Book: *Lon Po Po: A Red Riding Hood Story from China* translated by Ed Young (Putnam Publishing Group, 1989)

Summary: There lives a woman with three daughters. On their grandmother's birthday, the mother of the daughters sets out to visit her own mother, leaving her daughters alone with instructions not to open the door to strangers. At nightfall, an old wolf who lives nearby disguises himself as an old woman and comes to the house pretending to be the children's Po Po (grandmother).

The daughters are surprised, but they are so happy to see their Po Po that they let the wolf inside. The wolf turns out the lights, and they all go to bed. Each daughter asks the wolf questions about its appearance, and finally the eldest daughter realizes that their Po Po is really a wolf. She tricks the wolf by taking her sisters out to the gingko tree to get nuts. Three times they pretend to lift the wolf up to the tree but drop him on purpose. On the third time the wolf dies. The daughters rush into their house and tell their mother the tale when she returns the next day.

Discussion Questions:

- What are the names of the sisters, and who is the oldest?
- Why does their mother leave them home alone?
- What instructions does the mother leave the girls?
- What is the first question asked to the wolf in disguise?
- What does the wolf say is his tail? sharp claws?
- What does Shang tell the wolf about the gingko nuts?
- How do the sisters kill the wolf?

Journal Questions and Prompts:

- What would you do if someone came to your door whom you thought you knew but were not sure?
- If delivery or repair persons come to your door and want you to open it, what can you do to ensure that the persons are who they say they are?
- Is there anything else the girls might have done to protect themselves after they found out their Po Po was a wolf?

Lon Po Po Section 4: Comparative Tales

Babysitting Tips

Shang, the oldest daughter in the story, is left in charge of her two younger sisters while their mother is away. Her mother leaves her with the instruction "close the door tight at sunset and latch it well." Had her younger sisters not opened the door for the wolf, they would not have put themselves in danger.

Being left in charge of smaller children is a very big responsibility. It is important to be alert, to use your common sense, and to follow instructions left by the adult normally in charge.

Below are some safety tips for babysitters. Add some more to this list.

Babysitting Tips

1. Follow all instructions left by the adult.
2. Have phone numbers where the adult can be reached in case of an emergency.
3. Look through peepholes or windows to see who is at the door before deciding whether it is safe to open it.
4.
5.
6.

Write about your worst or best experience as a babysitter. If you have never been responsible for a younger child, write about your worst or best experience being babysat. Use the back of this paper if you need more room.

Section 4: Comparative Tales

Beauty and the Beast

France

Book: "Beauty and the Beast" from *Beauties and Beasts: The Oryx Multicultural Folktale Series* retold by Betsy Hearne (Oryx Press, 1993)

Summary: There lives a rich merchant who has three sons and three daughters. The children are all well educated and beautiful, but one daughter is especially kind and beautiful, so she is known to all as Beauty. The merchant falls upon hard times and loses his fortune. On one of his trips to seek money, he comes upon a castle in a terrible storm. He is cared for by the beings in the palace, and he is able to leave their care warm and fed. However, as he leaves the grounds, he picks a rose for Beauty. Suddenly a terrible beast appears and tells the man that he will only spare his life if he brings back one of his daughters to die in his place.

Beauty agrees to go back to the beast. She at first is frightened, but after time she grows to appreciate and love the beast for his inner quality of goodness, and she overlooks his exterior. She leaves the beast for eight days to tend to her ill father, but she promises to return. Her sisters, who are jealous of her beauty and new-found happiness, keep Beauty longer than eight days, and the beast begins to die of sadness. After their separation, Beauty realizes how much she has grown to love the beast for his good character, and she returns to the castle in time to save him from his death. The beast immediately transforms into a handsome young prince, and the two become married and live happily ever after.

Discussion Questions:

- What happens when the father comes to the castle?
- Why does the beast react so angrily toward the father?
- Why does Beauty decide to go back in her father's place?
- At what point does Beauty first begin to realize that the beast is not going to eat her?
- What kind of men do her sisters marry?
- How do they plan to take away her happiness?
- What happens to Beauty's sisters in the end?

Journal Questions and Prompts:

- If you were Beauty, would you have gone back to the castle in place of your father? Explain.
- Tell about a time when you offered to do something for someone else to help him or her.
- If someone offered to bring you one special gift, what would you ask for?

Beauty and the Beast Section 4: Comparative Tales

Telling Letters

An anagram is a form of poetry in which the title of the poem or subject is written in a column, and each letter of the title is a reference about the subject. Retell the story of *Beauty and the Beast* by using the anagram format.

B _____
E _____
A _____
U _____
T _____
Y _____
A _____
N _____
D _____
T _____
H _____
E _____
B _____
E _____
A _____
S _____
T _____

Section 4: Comparative Tales

The Lizard Husband

Indonesia

Book: "The Lizard Husband" from *Beauties and Beasts: The Oryx Multicultural Folktale Series* retold by Betsy Hearne (Oryx Press, 1993)

Summary: There is an old woman who raises a lizard as her child. When the lizard becomes fully grown, he asks her to go to the house with seven sisters to ask one of them to marry him. All the sisters say no, except the youngest. Kapapitoe (the youngest sister) takes special care of her new husband even though her other sisters make terrible fun of the couple and say that she can never go to the planting feast with a lizard.

As the growing season comes upon them, it is up to each sister to make a garden. The lizard helps his wife make a grand garden. He tells her to gather seven coconut shells. He sets the shells on the ground and orders them to make a house for him and his bride. The next day the house is built, and the shells turn into servants.

At the river, the lizard and his wife bathe, but the lizard sheds his skin and becomes a handsome man. When the couple go to the festival, all of the sisters are so jealous that they will not let Kapapitoe near her husband. The next day the handsome man wishes he and his wife could be far away. Suddenly they find themselves living in a beautiful house high upon a rock so that the other sisters cannot reach them. There they live happily ever after.

Discussion Questions:

- What does the lizard's "grandmother" take with her to the House of Lise?
- How does the oldest sister react to the request?
- What action do the sisters take toward the lizard to show their displeasure of him?
- What does Kapapitoe wear to the planting feast?
- How do the couple get away from the bothersome sisters?

Journal Questions and Prompts:

- Why do you think that Kapapitoe agrees to marry the lizard?
- What message does this story have about goodness and kindness reaping rewards?

Leapin' Lizards!

Not only is the lizard in this fairy tale special, lizards in real life are fascinating creatures, too. Did you know that there are over 3,000 known species of lizards? Lizards are found on every continent (except Antarctica) and in virtually every kind of habitat. Some lizards live in rainy areas, some in deserts and mountains, and some can swim in the ocean. The marine iguana of the Galapagos Islands swims in the ocean to feed on seaweed and can travel up to 65 feet (19.5 m) beneath the surface. Another kind of lizard can almost "fly." The Draco lizards of southeast Asia have sheets of skin attached to their long ribs and are capable of gliding through the air.

The lizard's skin is dry and scaly like a snake's, one of its close relatives. Like other reptiles, lizards are ectothermic, meaning cold-blooded. Ectothermic animals depend primarily on external heat sources, like direct sunlight or a heated rock, to regulate their body temperature.

The average size for lizards is 16 inches (40 cm), with the smallest being less than one inch (2.5 cm) and the largest species up to 10 feet (3 m) long.

Many lizards have a third eye located toward the back of the head. This eye acts as a light meter of sorts.

To protect themselves from enemies, lizards pull a clever trick by breaking off their tails. They do this voluntarily. The broken tail diverts the attention of the predator so the lizard can get away. New tails grow back shortly.

A lizard's sense of smell is very acute and important to its survival. There are two organs found inside the lizard's mouth (called Jacobsen's organs) which work with the forked tongue to detect different smells in the air. That is why you will see a lizard constantly flicking his tongue in and out.

Read the information above and then answer these questions.

1. How many types of lizards are there, and where can they be found?
   _____

2. What is special about the marine iguana and Draco lizard?
   _____

3. What does ectothermic mean?
   _____

4. Explain how a lizard protects itself from enemies.
   _____

5. Why do lizards constantly flick their tongues in and out?
   _____

Section 4: Comparative Tales

The Frog King

Germany

Book: "The Frog King" in *The Brothers Grimm: Popular Folk Tales* translated by Brian Alderson (Doubleday & Company, 1978)

Summary: There is a princess who loves nothing more than to play toss with her golden ball. She often sits at the well and tosses the ball into the air, but one day it falls into the well. She is very sad, but along comes a frog who says that he will retrieve the ball if she promises to be his playmate. The princess makes the promise, but in her heart knows that she will change her mind after he gets the ball. After the frog retrieves the ball, she runs off.

For three nights in a row, the frog comes to the castle and insists on eating from her plate, drinking from her cup, and sleeping in her bed. The king insists that his daughter keep her promise, even though the princess is very unhappy about this. On the third night after sleeping under her pillow, the frog turns into a handsome young king, and the two become the best of friends. Later in life they marry each other.

Discussion Questions:

- How do the princess and frog meet?
- What does the princess say she will give the frog?
- What does the frog want instead?
- Why does the princess think that the frog will not bother her again?
- How does the princess react when the frog first comes to the castle?
- What does the king do?
- Explain how the frog turned into a king.

Journal Questions and Prompts:

- What is your favorite toy? Why?
- Have you ever made a promise that you later regretted? How about one that you were later very glad you had made?
- If you were the frog king, would you still want to be friends with the princess after discovering that she only wants to be with you when you are the young king?

The Frog King   Section 4: Comparative Tales

Promises, Promises

In *The Frog King* the princess makes a promise to the frog, but even as she speaks the promise, she has no intention of keeping her word.

How important is it to keep a promise? Should you ever make a promise if you are not sure you can keep it? Work with a partner and read the following situations. Discuss with each other how you think the matters should be handled. Write your responses on the lines provided. If you need more space, use the back of this page. When you are finished, share your thoughts with the rest of the class.

1. You promised to help your best friend with her math homework on Friday night. Later, you are invited to a birthday party the same evening. What will you do?

2. You ask your mom to buy you a new puppy, and she agrees because you promise her that you will feed him, bathe him, and take him for walks. After the first two weeks, you are becoming tired of this new responsibility and do not want to do the chores anymore. What will you do?

3. You promise the new kid in class that you will play with him at recess. Your other friends do not like this child and ask you to play with them instead. What will you do?

4. You are babysitting your younger sibling while your parents are out. You promise them that you will not stay up late and watch television even though they will not be home. What will you do?

5. You promise your parents that you will never try drugs, alcohol, or cigarettes. Your best friends want you to try one of these with them. You have also promised your friends that you will always support them. What will you do?

Section 4: Comparative Tales

The Toad-Bridegroom

Korea

Book: "The Toad-Bridegroom" in *Favorite Folktales from Around the World* edited by Jane Yolen (Pantheon Books, 1988)

Summary: One season, a poor fisherman finds that he is not catching as many fish as usual. The lake where he fishes eventually dries up, and at the bottom he discovers a big toad. The fisherman thinks that the toad has eaten all the fish, and he becomes very angry. The toad tells the fisherman to take him home, and he will bring good fortune.

The fisherman and his wife grow to love the toad and raise him as their own son. One day the toad decides that he wants to marry one of the rich man's daughters. The rich man scoffs at the idea. Later that night, the toad uses his wits to trick the man into agreeing. The next day the rich man agrees and the youngest of his daughters marries the toad. Shortly after the marriage, the toad tells his wife to cut open his skin with scissors. She does and out steps a handsome young man. The man rises up to heaven, carrying his bride and parents with him.

Discussion Questions:

- How does the fisherman initially express his anger toward the toad?
- How does the fisherman's wife react to the toad?
- What happens to the toad's foster mother when she tells the rich man of the toad's request?
- How does the toad trick the rich man into agreeing that he should marry one of his daughters?
- How is the youngest daughter selected?
- What happens at the hunt when the toad goes along?

Journal Questions and Prompts:

- The happy ending in this tale takes the toad/man, his wife, and his parents to heaven. Is this a happy ending in your eyes? Explain.
- Imagine you had a toad for a brother or sister. What would life be like in your home?

The Toad-Bridegroom   Section 4: Comparative Tales

Frogs and Toads

Both frogs and toads are cold-blooded amphibians. Able to live in both water and on land, amphibians begin life in an aquatic stage where they have gills, which they lose as they develop into lungs. Frogs live near fresh-water areas while toads live in drier regions such as fields, gardens, and woodlands.

Toads and frogs look different, too. Frogs are colored dark green with a white belly. They have long legs for distance jumping, a large head, a short body, and no tail. The general colors of toads are brown, tan, gray, or black. Their skin is rough and often covered with warts. Toads are not jumpers like frogs but rather make short hops or even walk.

Both frogs and toads have unique features which help them to survive in nature. The toad has several poisonous glands all over its body and when attacked will produce a white substance that will either kill a predator or simply taste bad enough for the predator to leave the toad alone. Frogs are able to survive extremely cold temperatures for long periods of time with as much as 65 percent of their total body water turning into ice. As the weather gets warmer, the frog "thaws" back to its regular temperature.

Frogs and toads are found on every continent of the world except Antarctica.

Read the information about frogs and toads above and then answer these questions.

1. What does the word amphibian mean?

   _____

   _____

2. In what kinds of habitats do frogs and toads live?

   _____

   _____

3. Explain how frogs and toads look different from each other.

   _____

   _____

   _____

4. How does a toad protect itself from its enemies?

   _____

   _____

5. How can a frog survive extremely cold environments?

   _____

   _____

6. Where on the earth are frogs not found?

   _____

Section 4: Culminating Activities

Character Chart

In the six fairy tales you have read, there is a predominant leading character, and in five of them that character is a female. When reading several stories and learning about many different characters, it is sometimes difficult to keep track of all the facts. This character chart is a handy way to take notes on important information about the characters. You do not need to use complete sentences when completing this chart but rather write notes and ideas. (On the column labeled "Miscellaneous Note," write any thought, idea, or symbol that comes to mind when thinking about this character.) Try using this type of note-taking strategy for other areas of study, too.

Character	Story Title	Main Action Taken	Positive Quality	Less Positive Quality	Miscellaneous Note
Red Riding Hood					
Shang					
Beauty					
Kapapitoe					
princess					
fisherman					

Section 4: Culminating Activities

It's a Zoo Out There!

In four of the six stories that you read in this section, the male characters are some sort of animal at the beginning of the story and then later turn into handsome young men. How did these characters become animals in the first place? Were they born animals? Were they the victims of an evil enchantment from a witch or warlock? In the squares below, write your idea on why these characters began the stories as animals. Draw a small illustration of each animal character too.

Beast	Lizard Husband

Frog King	Toad-Bridegroom

© Teacher Created Materials, Inc. — #464 *Tales Around the World*

Section 4: Culminating Activities

Plot, Setting, and Character

All stories, no matter how long or short, have three components to them. These three parts give the story what it needs in order for the tale to be interesting. These three parts are plot, setting, and characters.

Plot: the why and how of the story; the problem and the solution

Setting: where and when the story takes place

Characters: people, animals, and living objects in the story

Compare and contrast the story parts from each story as directed on each of the three Venn diagrams (pages 170–171).

Setting: *Red Riding Hood* and *Lon Po Po*

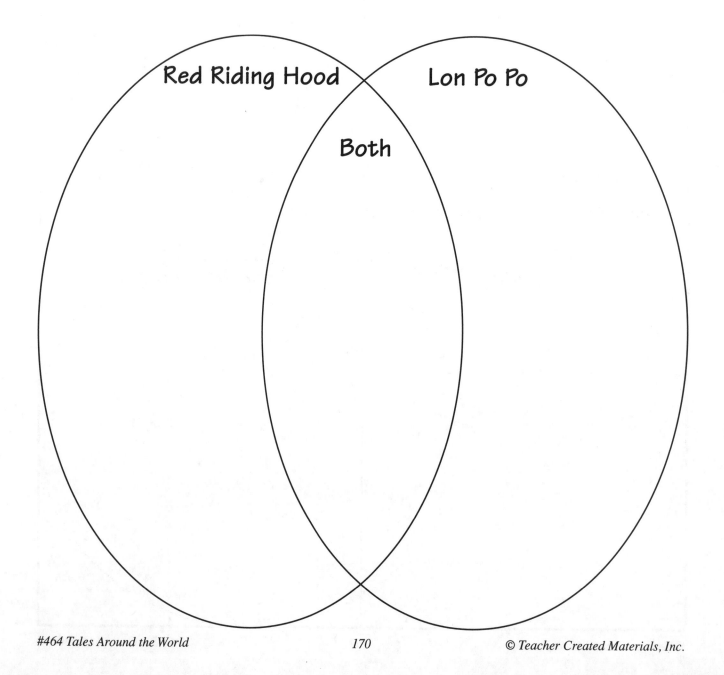

Plot, Setting, and Character *(cont.)*

Section 4: Culminating Activities

Plot: *The Frog King* and *The Toad-Bridegroom*

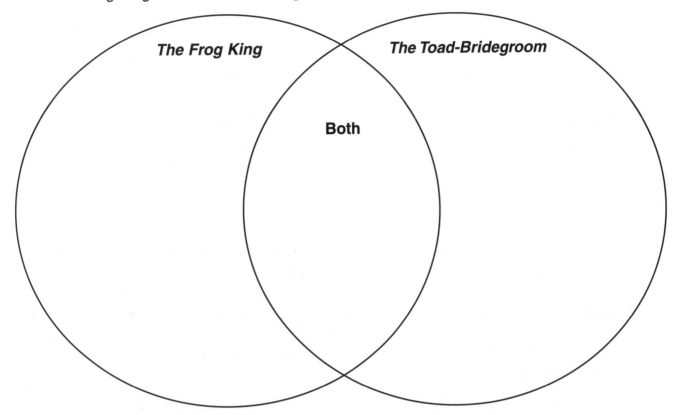

Character: *Beauty and the Beast* and *The Lizard Husband*

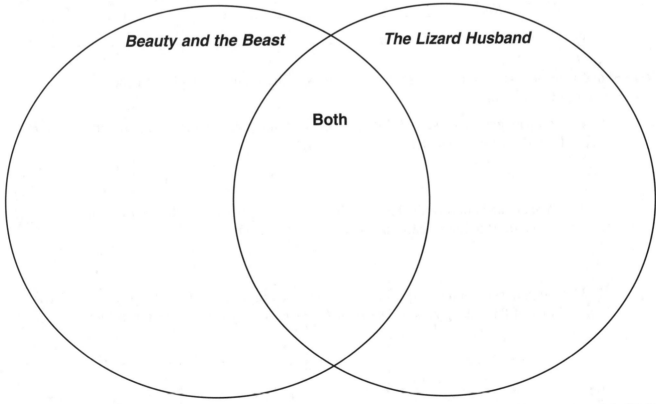

Section 4: Section Test

Comparative Tales Test

I. **Matching:** Match each fairy tale with the clue or action taken.

   _____ 1. *Red Riding Hood*   A. This character wanted to share everything with the princess.

   _____ 2. *Lon Po Po*   B. This character used shells to help build a house.

   _____ 3. *Beauty and the Beast*   C. The clothes that this character wore told the name of this person.

   _____ 4. *The Lizard Husband*   D. A fisherman blamed this character for eating up all of the fish.

   _____ 5. *The Frog King*   E. The gingko tree was important in this tale.

   _____ 6. *The Toad-Bridegroom*   F. A child with five siblings saved her father's life.

II. **Name That Country:** Write the country or origin for each fairy tale.

   1. *Red Riding Hood* _____
   2. *Lon Po Po* _____
   3. *Beauty and the Beast* _____
   4. *The Lizard Husband* _____
   5. *The Frog King* _____
   6. *The Toad-Bridegroom* _____

III. **Short Answer Essay:** Write full-sentence answers to these questions. Use the back of this paper if you need more room.

   1. Compare and contrast Red Riding Hood with the oldest daughter, Shang, in *Lon Po Po*. Provide at least three details.

   2. Compare and contrast the beast in *Beauty and the Beast* with the lizard from *The Lizard Husband*. Provide at least three details.

   3. Compare and contrast the princess' father (the king) in *The Frog King* with the rich father of three daughters in *The Toad-Bridegroom*. Provide at least three details.

The Paper Bag Princess

Book: *The Paper Bag Princess* by Robert N. Munsch (Firefly Books Limited, 1986)

Summary: Princess Elizabeth lives a happy life with all the finery and nice clothes she wants. She is very happy that she will be marrying Prince Ronald. However, one day a fierce dragon comes and smashes her castle, burns all her nice clothes, and carries off Prince Ronald. The only thing left to wear that is not burnt is a paper bag.

Princess Elizabeth sets off to find Prince Ronald. When she comes to the dragon's cave, he slams the door in her face. She knocks again, and this time she tricks the dragon by flattering him. She tricks him into using up all his fiery breath and tiring himself out. When the dragon collapses, she goes into the cave to find Prince Ronald. Prince Ronald looks at Princess Elizabeth and tells her to come back when her hair is combed and she is wearing nicer clothes. Princess Elizabeth tells Prince Ronald that he is a bum. The two do not get married, but she does live happily ever after.

Discussion Questions:

- What does the dragon do to Princess Elizabeth?
- How is she able to follow the dragon?
- What does the dragon say before he slams the door in her face?
- How does she trick the dragon the first time?
- How does she trick the dragon the second time?
- What is Prince Ronald's reaction to her when she enters the cave to save him?
- What does Princess Elizabeth say to Prince Ronald?

Journal Questions and Prompts:

- What do you think about the ending of this fairy tale?
- If you were Princess Elizabeth, what would have you said to Prince Ronald?
- What do you think happened to the princess after she left Ronald in the cave?

What Are They Doing Now?

In most traditional fairy tales, the evil witch (or other terrible character) dies, and the prince and princess get married and live happily ever after. In *The Paper Bag Princess*, the dragon does not die, the prince and princess do not get married, and the princess merrily trots off alone into the sunset. What do you think all these characters are doing now? Are they happy? Does the princess meet anyone new? Does the dragon learn his lesson, or is he still bothering local kingdoms? Does the princess go to the city and start a career? Use your imagination and give the details of the current lives of these three characters.

Princess Elizabeth

_____
_____
_____
_____
_____

Prince Ronald

_____
_____
_____
_____
_____

The Dragon

_____
_____
_____
_____
_____
_____

Section 5: Tales with a Twist

Sidney Rella and the Glass Sneaker

Book: *Sidney Rella and the Glass Sneaker* by Bernice Myers (Simon & Schuster Children's, 1985)

Summary: Sidney Rella is the youngest boy in the Rella house with two older brothers who are much larger and stronger than him. Every day after school, Sidney's brothers go to football practice, but Sidney has to stay home and do chores. When Sidney wants to try out for the football team, his older brothers laugh at him. As Sidney sits feeling so sad, a small man appears. This small man is his fairy godfather who comes to give him his wish.

The day of the big game, the fairy godfather turns Sidney's clothes into a sparkling football uniform with glass sneakers. He tells Sidney to be home by six o'clock or the uniform will disappear. Sidney makes many touchdowns, but during the last play of the game, the clock strikes six and his uniform disappears. Sidney runs through the goalposts in his underwear, and he loses one of the glass sneakers.

The next day the coach goes to every house in town and asks each boy to try on the sneaker to find the great football player. Sidney becomes one of the greatest football players in the country and then later he becomes the president of a large football corporation.

Discussion Questions:

- What do Sidney's parents do all day?
- What does Sidney's mother say about his doing all the chores?
- What does the fairy godfather think Sidney is wishing for at first?
- What items does the fairy godfather need for Sidney's first uniform?
- What kind of uniform is it?
- What does the coach do for Sidney the evening he finds him?
- What happens to Sidney after he stops playing football?

Journal Questions and Prompts:

- Instead of a glass sneaker, what kind of special shoe would you have given Sidney to play football? Be descriptive and include an illustration if you like.
- Imagine your fairy godmother or godfather granted you your dearest wish. What would the wish be, and what do you imagine happening?

Section 5: Tales with a Twist   *Sidney Rella and the Glass Sneaker*

Shoes Around the Globe

While Cinderella and Sidney have special glass shoes made for them, most of us buy our footwear at the shoe store. Like many other products, shoes are made in different parts of the world and then shipped to other countries to be sold.

Look to your shoes to learn an international story! Look on your shoes to discover where they were made (most will say) and then complete these instructions.

I. Individuals

1. Draw and color your shoe in this box. Cut it out.

2. Tape or tack your shoe design to the correct country on a classroom wall map of the world.

II. Whole Class

1. Observe the results of the shoe placements on the map. Discover which country exports the most shoes and the least. What do you notice about the locations of the shoe-producing countries?

2. Complete a graph to record the results of the class findings. You can make your own graph or use the one on page 177. (If more than 10 countries are represented, attach another section of grid lines to page 177 as needed.)

III. Small Groups

1. Get together with the other people in your class whose shoes came from the same country as yours.

2. Using the world map on page 178, plot out a route to get shoes from the country of origin to your country. Make your route realistic and take into account all the possible means of transportation.

3. Go to the library and conduct research on the country from which your shoe originated. Find out what other products are exported from that country.

Sidney Rella and the Glass Sneaker Section 5: Tales with a Twist

Shoes Around the Globe (cont.)

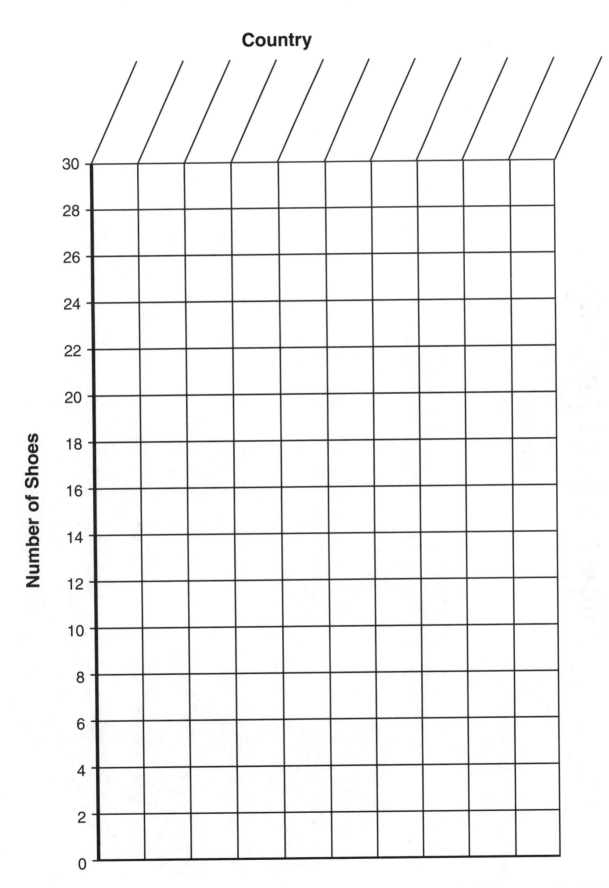

Section 5: Tales with a Twist — Sidney Rella and the Glass Sneaker

Shoes Around the Globe *(cont.)*

World Map

See page 176 for directions.

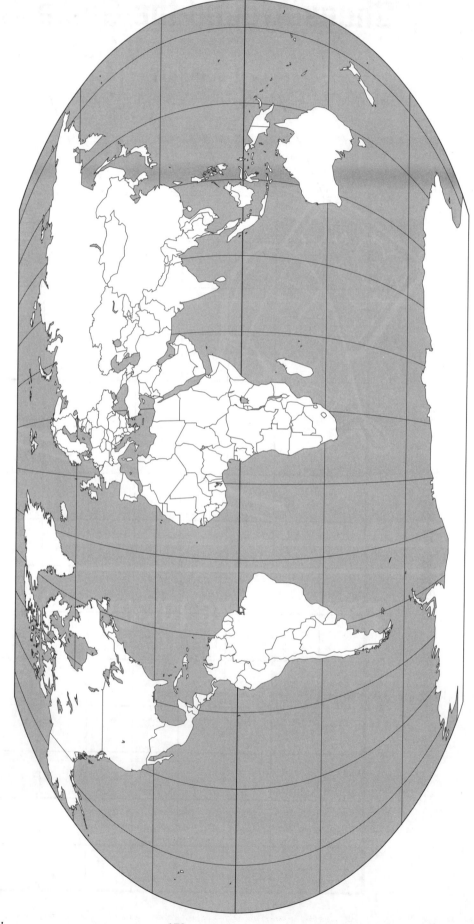

Section 5: Tales with a Twist

Sleeping Ugly

Book: *Sleeping Ugly* by Jane Yolen (Houghton Mifflin Co., 1995)

Summary: There lives a beautiful princess named Miserella. While she is very beautiful on the outside, she is very mean, cruel, and rude on the inside. One day while she is having a temper tantrum in the woods, she gets lost. She runs into an old fairy and rudely tells her to take her home. The fairy takes her instead to Plain Jane's cottage. Plain Jane is not a beautiful girl, but she is very kind.

The fairy likes Jane's manners, so she grants her three wishes. Princess Miserella is so angry at this that she throws two more tantrums. The fairy casts spells upon her, and Jane uses up her wishes to undo the spells. In a skirmish, the fairy casts a sleeping spell, and it touches all three of them. They end up sleeping for 100 years.

A poor prince comes by at this time and decides to practice his kissing on the fairy and Jane before waking up the beautiful Miserella. However, he falls in love with Jane, and the two live happily ever after. They keep the sleeping princess in their house for a conversation piece.

Discussion Questions:

- How does Princess Miserella treat dogs, cats, and cooks?
- Describe Plain Jane both inside and out.
- How does Miserella greet the fairy?
- What is Plain Jane's cottage like?
- What two spells does the fairy cast upon Miserella?
- What happens during the 100 years that the three are asleep?
- Why does Prince Jojo decide to practice his kissing first?
- What makes him change his mind about kissing Miserella?
- What happens to the fairy and Miserella?

Journal Questions and Prompts:

- What does the old saying "don't judge a book by its cover" mean to you?
- What is meant by the saying "pretty is as pretty does?"
- Tell about an experience when you thought someone was going to act in a certain way because of his or her physical appearance but instead that person acted differently.

Section 5: Tales with a Twist *Sleeping Ugly*

Three Wishes

If you were given three wishes, would you be willing to use them for another person, especially someone who treated you unkindly? Plain Jane was. In the fairy tale *Sleeping Ugly*, the fairy gives Plain Jane three wishes, and Plain Jane is such a kind girl that she uses up two of her wishes on the spoiled Princess Miserella. Fortunately, she has one wish left which helps to make her life an even happier one.

Respond to each of the questions below.

- There is an old saying which says "it is better to give than to receive." What does that saying mean to you?

  _____
  _____
  _____
  _____

- If you had three wishes but you could only use them to help somebody else, who would you like to help? Why?

  _____
  _____
  _____
  _____

- What would your three wishes be for this person?

  1. _____
  2. _____
  3. _____

- What would your three wishes be for yourself (if you cannot wish for more wishes or magical powers to give yourself more wishes)?

  1. _____
  2. _____
  3. _____

- Use the back of this paper to write about a time when you gave someone something and did not expect anything in return. How did you feel? How did the person feel? Why didn't you want anything back?

Section 5: Tales with a Twist

The True Story of the Three Little Pigs

Book: *The True Story of the Three Little Pigs* by Jon Scieszka (Scholastic, Inc., 1991)

Summary: This tale of the three little pigs is told from the wolf's perspective. He claims that he was framed for the crime of killing the pigs.

Alexander T. Wolf, as he calls himself, is supposedly baking a cake for his granny when he runs out of sugar. He decides to go to his neighbor's house to borrow some. Due to his terrible cold, he sneezes violently and beyond his control. The sneezing is the cause of his huffing and puffing. Since he does not want the dead pigs lying in the rubble of their houses to go to waste, he eats them.

At the third pig's house, built of bricks, the pig is impolite, says the wolf, and he begins to make fun of the wolf's granny. The wolf gets angry, and this is when the police arrive to see the wolf creating a scene. The news reporters change the story around to make it more exciting, and that, declares the wolf, is how he ends up in jail.

Discussion Questions:

- How does the wolf justify eating small, cute animals?
- How does he compare his eating habits to those of humans?
- What is the wolf making and for whom?
- Why does the wolf eat the first pig?
- What does the pig say to the wolf at the second house?
- What does the third pig say about the wolf's granny?
- Which is the smartest pig?
- Why did the news reporters change the story?

Journal Questions and Prompts:

- Explain your thoughts about animals eating other animals for food.
- Do you believe the wolf's story or the original story of *The Three Little Pigs*? Explain.
- Rewrite another familiar folk tale from the perspective of the "bad guy."

Section 5: Tales with a Twist

The True Story of the Three Little Pigs

True Stories

In *The True Story of the Three Little Pigs*, Alexander T. Wolf tells his side of the story. Mr. Wolf claims that he is innocent, and the reason he ends up in jail is because he is framed. He offers explanations for everything that happens in the story.

Whose side of the story do you believe? There is always more than one side to a story, depending on who is doing the telling. Choose a traditional fairy tale from below and write a short story from the perspective of one of the characters listed. (If you have your own idea for a story, ask your teacher if you can use that instead.) Use this page as your brainstorming page and the following page for your short story. When you are finished, share your "true story" with the rest of the class.

Cinderella: the prince, a stepsister, the fairy godmother

Hansel and Gretel: the father, the witch

Red Riding Hood: the wolf, the grandmother

Jack and the Beanstalk: the giant, the harp

The Three Bears: one of the bears

Fairy tale: _____

Character: _____

Character's summary of the story from his or her point of view:

_____
_____
_____

Character's explanation as to why the original story is so much more popular than his or hers:

_____
_____
_____

What the character has been doing since the story took place:

_____
_____
_____

#464 Tales Around the World
© Teacher Created Materials, Inc.

The True Story of the Three Little Pigs   Section 5: *Tales with a Twist*

True Stories (cont.)

The True Story of _____

by

_____

_____

_____

_____

_____

_____

_____

_____

_____

_____

_____

_____

_____

_____

_____

_____

The True Story of the Three Little Pigs

Section 5: Culminating Activities

What Are You Thinking?

Even though authors give characters dialogue and sometimes explain their thoughts, do you ever wonder what thoughts might go through their minds if they had minds of their own? Here is your chance to "mind read" the thoughts of the characters from the stories in this section.

Each character's head is drawn with a thought bubble. Read the scene from the story for that character and then complete the thought bubble with what that character's thoughts could be.

Character: Prince Ronald

Scene: right after the princess leaves

Character: third little pig

Scene: while the wolf is making a scene outside his house

Character: Plain Jane

Scene: right after the fairy gives her three wishes

Character: Princess Miserella

Scene: at the end of the story asleep in the living room

Section 5: Culminating Activities

What Are You Thinking? *(cont.)*

Character: Prince JoJo
Scene: just before kissing the old fairy

Character: Sidney Rella
Scene: running home after scoring a touchdown in his underwear

Character: football coach
Scene: after asking Sidney to try on the glass sneaker but before he knows Sidney is the football star

Character: dragon
Scene: right after Princess Elizabeth first knocks at his door

Section 5: Culminating Activities

What Are You Thinking? *(cont.)*

Character: first little pig
Scene: when he hears the wolf at his door

Character: Sydney's oldest brother
Scene: when he realizes the star football player is Sydney

Character: reporter
Scene: when he comes upon the wolf causing a scene

Character: old fairy
Scene: when Plain Jane undoes her magic with her wish

Section 5: Culminating Activities

Traditional Endings

In this section, the authors either took a traditional story or formula and changed the characters and endings, or they used satire. Satire is a type of humor that is usually based on sarcasm and wit. You already know the traditional endings of *The Three Little Pigs, Sleeping Beauty,* and *Cinderella*. What if *The Paper Bag Princess* was a traditional story, too? How would its ending be different from the stories you read?

For this activity, you will rewrite the ending to *The Paper Bag Princess* in a traditional tone. Write your story ending on page 188.

Before you begin rewriting the ending, take a moment to review how a traditional fairy tale ends. Take some notes before turning to the next page.

Traditional Fairy Tale Ending

1. happily ever after
2. prince (or male character) saves the day (or princess)
3. prince and princess (or female character) get married
4. evil character is destroyed or never heard from again

The Paper Bag Princess

Original ending: _____

_____

_____

_____

_____

_____

Possible traditional endings: _____

_____

_____

_____

Section 5: Culminating Activities

Traditional Endings (cont.)

The Traditional Version of *The Paper Bag Princess*

Section 5: Culminating Activities

Bake a Cake for Granny

According to the wolf in *The True Story of the Three Little Pigs,* the whole story is a misunderstanding, and he has been framed. Mr. Wolf claims that he was innocently baking his granny a cake and merely set off to borrow a cup of sugar when the fiasco began. Unfortunately for Granny, Mr. Wolf never got around to finishing the cake.

Whether you believe the wolf's side of the story or not, Granny still needs a cake. You and your baking buddies can help! You and your team will make and bake a cake and then decorate it for Granny's birthday. Invite Granny to your class to sample each of the birthday cakes and award the prize to the tastiest and/or most decorative. To complete the baking contest, ask another class to bring the punch and enjoy sampling all the cakes!

When finished, make and complete a graph after polling the classes to find out their taste preferences.

The recipes on pages 190–195 are for the cakes only. Your group will need to decide what kind of frosting and decorations will be used.

Note: Only adults should handle cakes going in and out of hot ovens.

Section 5: Culminating Activities

Bake a Cake for Granny (cont.)

Chocolate Cake

Ingredients:

- 2 cups (500 mL) cake flour
- ¾ cup (185 mL) cocoa
- ¾ cup (185 mL) shortening
- 1¼ tsp. (6.25 mL) baking soda
- 1 tsp. (5 mL) vanilla extract
- 1¾ cups (435 mL) sugar
- 1¼ cups (315 mL) milk
- 3 eggs
- 1 tsp. (5 mL) salt
- ½ tsp. (2.5 mL) double-acting baking powder

Preparation:

1. Preheat oven to 350° F (180° C).
2. In a large bowl measure all the ingredients.
3. With the mixer at a low speed, beat until the cake is well blended.
4. At a high speed, mix for five minutes.
5. Grease and flour two nine-inch (22.5 cm) round cake pans.
6. Pour the batter into the pans and bake for 30–35 minutes.
7. Cool the layers on a rack. Cool completely before frosting.

#464 Tales Around the World 190 © Teacher Created Materials, Inc.

Section 5: Culminating Activities

Bake a Cake for Granny *(cont.)*

Yellow Cake

Ingredients:

- 2¼ cups (565 mL) cake flour
- ¾ cup (185 mL) shortening
- 3 eggs
- 1 tsp. (5 mL) salt
- 1½ cups (375 mL) sugar
- ¾ cup (185 mL) milk
- 2½ tsp. (12.5 mL) double-acting baking powder
- 1 tsp. (5 mL) vanilla extract

Preparation:

1. Preheat oven to 375° F (190° C).
2. Grease and flour two nine-inch (22.5 cm) round cake pans.
3. In a large bowl, measure all the ingredients.
4. With the mixer at low speed, beat until everything is well blended.
5. At a high speed, mix for five minutes.
6. Pour the batter into cake pans, smoothing the top with a rubber spatula.
7. Bake the cake layers for 25 minutes or until a toothpick inserted deeply into the center comes out clean.
8. Cool in the pans on wire racks for 10 minutes.
9. Remove from the pans and cool completely on the racks.

© Teacher Created Materials, Inc. #464 Tales Around the World

Section 5: Culminating Activities

Bake a Cake for Granny *(cont.)*

Devil's Food Cake

Ingredients:
- 2 cups (500 mL) cake flour
- 1¼ cups (315 mL) buttermilk
- 3 eggs
- 1½ tsp. (7.5 mL) baking soda
- 1 tsp. (5 mL) vanilla extract
- 1½ cups (375 mL) sugar
- ½ cup (125 mL) shortening
- 3 squares unsweetened chocolate (melted)
- 1 tsp. (5 mL) salt
- ½ tsp. (2.5 mL) double-acting baking powder

Preparation:
1. Preheat the oven to 350° F (180° C).
2. Grease and flour two nine-inch (22.5 cm) round cake pans.
3. In a large bowl measure all the ingredients.
4. With the mixer at a low speed, beat until everything is well blended.
5. At a high speed, mix for five minutes.
6. Pour the batter into cake pans, smoothing the tops with a rubber spatula.
7. Bake the cake layers for 25 minutes or until a toothpick inserted deeply into the center comes out clean.
8. Cool pans on wire racks for 10 minutes.
9. Remove the cake from the pans and cool completely on the racks.

Section 5: Culminating Activities

Bake a Cake for Granny (cont.)

Spice Cake

Ingredients:

- 2 cups (500 mL) cake flour
- ¾ cup (185 mL) milk
- ½ cup (125 mL) shortening
- 2½ tbsp. (37.5 mL) double-acting baking powder
- 1 tsp. (5 mL) ground cinnamon
- ½ tsp. (2.5 mL) ground cloves
- ¾ cup (185 mL) sugar
- ½ cup (125 mL) packed brown sugar
- 2 eggs
- 1 tsp. (5 mL) salt
- 1 tsp. (5 mL) ground allspice
- ½ tsp. (2.5 mL) ground nutmeg

Preparation:

1. Preheat the oven to 350° F (180° C).
2. Grease and flour two nine-inch (20 cm) round cake pans.
3. In a large bowl with the mixer at a low speed, beat all ingredients together until well blended.
4. Beat three minutes at a high speed.
5. Pour the batter into pans.
6. Bake the cake layers for 25 minutes or until a toothpick inserted deeply into the center comes out clean.
7. Cool the pans on wire racks for 10 minutes.
8. Remove them from the pans and cool them completely on the racks.

Section 5: Culminating Activities

Bake a Cake for Granny (cont.)

German Gold Pound Cake

Ingredients:

- 2 cups (500 mL) sugar
- 3½ cups (875 mL) cake flour
- 6 egg yolks
- 2 tsp. (10 mL) vanilla extract
- 1 cup (250 mL) butter, softened
- 1 cup (250 mL) milk
- 1½ tsp. (7.5 mL) double-acting baking powder
- ¼ tsp. (1.25 mL) salt

Preparation:

1. Preheat the oven to 350° F (180° C).
2. Grease and flour a 10" (25 cm) Bundt pan or two nine-inch (22.5 cm) loaf pans.
3. In a large bowl with the mixer at a high speed, beat the sugar and butter until light and fluffy.
4. Add the flour and the rest of the ingredients. At a low speed, beat until well blended.
5. Beat at a high speed for four minutes, occasionally scraping the bowl.
6. Pour the batter into the Bundt pan and bake for one hour, or if using loaf pans bake for 45–50 minutes. The cake is done when a toothpick inserted in the center comes out clean.
7. Cool the cake in the pan(s) on a wire rack for 10 minutes.
8. Remove the cake from the pan and then cool it completely on the rack.

Section 5: Culminating Activities

Bake a Cake for Granny (cont.)

Deluxe Marble Cake

Ingredients:
- 2 squares unsweetened chocolate
- 1/4 cup (65 mL) water
- 1/2 cup (125 mL) butter, softened
- 3/4 cup (185 mL) evaporated milk
- 2 tsp. (10 mL) double-acting baking powder
- 1/2 tsp. (2.5 mL) salt
- 1 1/4 cups (315 mL) sugar
- 1 tsp. (5 mL) vanilla extract
- 2 cups (500 mL) all-purpose flour
- 3 eggs
- 1 tsp. (5 mL) orange extract
- 1/2 tsp. (2.5 mL) baking soda

Preparation:
1. Preheat the oven to 350° F (180° C).
2. Grease a nine-inch (22.5 cm) springform pan.
3. In a one-quart saucepan over a very low heat, melt the chocolate and 3/4 cup (185 mL) sugar with water.
4. Stir in the vanilla and let it cool.
5. Into a large bowl, measure 1 cup (250 mL) sugar and all the ingredients except the chocolate mixture.
6. Beat until well mixed with the mixer at a low speed, constantly scraping the side of the bowl with a plastic spatula.
7. At a high speed, beat for five minutes.
8. Remove 2 1/2 cups (625 mL) of the batter.
9. Beat the chocolate mixture into the remaining batter.
10. Alternate spooning plain and chocolate batters into the pan.
11. With a butter knife, cut through the batter a few times. This will swirl the flavors a bit.
12. Bake for 55 minutes. The top will appear to be cracked when the cake is ready.
13. Cool the cake in the pan on a wire rack for 10 minutes.
14. Remove the cake from the pan and cool it completely on the rack.

© Teacher Created Materials, Inc. #464 Tales Around the World

Section 5: Section Test

Tales-with-a-Twist Test

I. **Matching:** Match each fairy tale with the clue or action taken. (Some answers could have more than one letter choice.)

    A. *Sidney Rella and the Glass Sneaker*   C. *The Paper Bag Princess*
    B. *Sleeping Ugly*   D. *The True Story of the Three Little Pigs*

    _____ 1. This character uses up some wishes for another person.

    _____ 2. By using flattery, this character outwits a dragon.

    _____ 3. A cup of sugar and a few sneezes are important in this tale.

    _____ 4. A magical creature helps this character get a wish.

    _____ 5. Two older siblings make life miserable for this character.

    _____ 6. "Do not judge a book by its cover" is the lesson in this tale.

    _____ 7. This character wears some unusual clothes.

    _____ 8. This character claims to have been "framed."

II. **Short Answer Essay:** Write your responses in complete sentences. Use the back of this paper if you need more room.

    1. What is the twist in *The Paper Bag Princess*?

    2. Compare the fairy godfather in *Sidney Rella* to the fairy godmother in the traditional version of *Cinderella*.

    3. Explain the moral of the story of *Sleeping Ugly*.

    4. Do you agree or disagree with the wolf's story in *The True Story of the Three Little Pigs*? Explain your answer.

Culminating Activities

Name That Character

Name That Character is an enjoyable way for students to use their story comprehension skills. It is both an individual and group activity. Play the game upon completion of reading any section or group of tales.

Individual

Each student selects a favorite character from one of the tales the class has read. This character can be a lead or supporting character. Character selections can also be animals. The only requirement is that the character selected is one which all the other students have heard of and read about. Students then consider all the details about this character, such as how he or she looks, what he or she wears, his or her good or evil nature, and various personality qualities and specific actions that this character takes in the story. Each student then completes the character chart.

Group

Once all the students have completed their character charts, they are collected by the Game Runner (usually the teacher). Students use a piece of binder paper and number each line up to the same number of total students. The Game Runner then begins with the first character chart by telling the clues. Be sure that the name of the character is not given at this time! As the clues are read, students write down who they think the character is. After reading all the character charts, the Game Runner tells who each of the characters is. The student with the most right names wins.

Evaluation

Students can be evaluated by the descriptive and accurate information that is recorded on their own character charts. This game can be used in other language arts units as well.

Culminating Activities

Name That Character *(cont.)*

Character: _____

Title of Tale: _____

Lead Character?   Yes   No

Physical Qualities	Personality Traits	Things the Character Does

You could compare my character to _____ in the tale

_____.

#464 Tales Around the World   © Teacher Created Materials, Inc.

Culminating Activities

Letter to a Character

This activity can be done upon completion of one section or the entire book, depending on your preference. The following are three suggestions for variations of the letter-writing activity.

Write a Letter, Write a Response *(Individual Activity)*

Each student will choose a character from one of the tales read. He or she will write this character a letter telling a little about him or herself and then asking the character questions. (There is a letter-writing form provided on page 200, or the students can design their own stationery.)

Letters should indicate that the student has an acceptable level of comprehension of the story. When the first letter is finished, the student then assumes the role of this character and writes back in response, answering the questions posed in the first letter.

For an attractive bulletin-board display, students place the letters in envelopes, address them, and design their own stamps.

Write a Letter, Write a Response *(Group Activity)*

This version follows the same directions as above except for the response portion. Once all the original letters have been written and sealed in their envelopes, place them in a box. Decorating the box in the style of a mailbox is a nice touch. Students then randomly choose a letter from the mailbox. Each student writes a response to this letter as if he or she were that character. Students seal up their letters, and they are delivered to the original writers. Collect the letters and place them in a large class book.

Cross-Age Letter Writing *(Group Activity)*

Ask a lower grade level class to write letters to their favorite fairy tale characters. (Your older students may need to help their cross-age partners write these letters.) Write letters back in response. Primary-age students are especially appreciative of receiving a letter from a magical character.

Culminating Activities

Letter to a Character *(cont.)*

Date _____

Dear _____,

   I recently read about you in the tale _____. I thought the story was _____. The part I especially liked was _____
_____
_____.

I have a few questions that I would like to ask you.

_____
_____
_____
_____
_____
_____
_____
_____
_____

Sincerely,

_____

P.S. _____

Culminating Activities

Modern-Day Traditional Tales

After reading and listening to several traditional tales, your students will have developed a stronger sense of plot, setting, and character development for this genre of literature. Let them put this knowledge to work as they compose their own traditional tales with modern-day themes.

Review the fairy tale recipe on page 19. Refer to the pocket chart information (page 6) and discuss personality traits and repetition of character types found in traditional tales. Examine the setting pocket chart and make comparisons between traditional tale settings and modern-day places. For example, the king's court might be today's mall, or the dark forest could be a gang hangout. Begin brainstorming with your students to find these comparisons.

Students will begin writing their modern-day tales by completing the brainstorm storyboard provided on page 202. You may want your students to work in partner teams for this activity. Once students have completed the storyboard and you have conferenced with them (or reviewed their preliminary work), they may begin writing the actual tales.

In order to keep their stories in the same flavor as the many illustrated tales they read, the modern-day fairy tales should be illustrated and made into books. Provide construction paper with writing lines at the bottom. Students should design an interesting cover and either staple or bind the tales together. If you have access to a computer, encourage students to compose their writing with a word processing program and then cut and paste the print to their hand-drawn illustrations. If you have a multimedia student-authoring program (like *HyperStudio* or *Kids Studio*), students can create their tales in this format. When the modern tales are complete, your students can visit a primary class and read their stories aloud.

Culminating Activities   *Modern-Day Traditional Tales*

Brainstorm Storyboard

Before you begin writing your modern-day tale, you will need to spend some time brainstorming ideas and designing your story plot. Write your ideas on this storyboard and refer to it often once you begin writing the tale. Write down any ideas you have, and do not worry if they do not make sense at first. The brainstorm storyboard is like a bank to keep track of all your creative ideas.

Plot (Write down possible modern-day problems and solutions.)

Problem   **Solution**

_____   _____

_____   _____

_____   _____

_____   _____

Setting (There is usually one main location where the action unfolds along with several other less significant places.)

Main Places   **Sub-Places**

_____   _____

_____   _____

_____   _____

Characters (First consider all the potential "good guys and gals" for your tale. Write down their names, occupations, and any other details about them that come to mind. Do the same for potential "bad guys and gals.")

Hero/Heroine   **Character Details**

_____   _____

_____   _____

_____   _____

Villain/Villainess   **Character Details**

_____   _____

_____   _____

_____   _____

Culminating Activities

Mock Trial

Conducting a mock trial is a terrific way for students to apply their reading comprehension skills in an integrated and cross-curricular approach. Not only must students be familiar with details of the story (plot development, character analysis, and story structure, to name a few), but they also learn about the judicial process, utilize dramatization and public speaking skills, and employ high-level critical-thinking skills. There is a significant amount of preparation involved before actually conducting the trial, so be sure to plan accordingly. If you will be following the guidelines provided, plan for approximately three weeks of preparation before the actual trial date.

Choosing the Tale

While this activity would work with any of the tales mentioned in this book, feel free to choose any tale that your students are interested in and familiar with. You should choose a story with a fairly obvious "crime," for example:

Tale: *Jack and the Beanstalk*
Crime: breaking and entering, stealing, murder
Defendant: Jack
Plaintiff: giant's wife and the people of fairy-tale land

Tale: *The Three Bears*
Crime: breaking and entering, stealing, trespassing, property damage
Defendant: Goldilocks
Plaintiff: the Bear Family

Tale: *Unanana and the Enormous One-Tusked Elephant*
Crime: assaulting the elephant
Defendant: Unanana
Plaintiff: Animal Protection Society

After you (or the class) have chosen the tale, review the story for details. Determine what the crime(s) committed is, who is being accused, and who is doing the accusing.

Judicial Information

Before assigning roles to the students, spend some time discussing basic judicial items. Some of these should include the following:

- terminology (prosecution, defense, argument, rebuttal, verdict, etc.)
- unanimous voting by the jury
- idea of "innocent until proven guilty"
- evidence and proof
- "guilty beyond a shadow of a doubt"
- punishment fitting the crime
- "due process"
- the jobs and roles of people involved in a trial

Culminating Activities

Mock Trial (cont.)

Assigning Roles

Each student in the class will be able to participate in the mock trial. Depending upon the tale you are using, there will be a variety of parts. The list below is a basic summary of trial roles:

1. Judge
2. Defense Attorney
3. Assistant to Defense Attorney
4. Prosecuting Attorney (District Attorney)
5. Assistant to Prosecuting Attorney (Assistant District Attorney)
6. Bailiff
7. Court Reporter
8. Jury Members (12)
9. Defendant
10. Plaintiff

The above roles total 21 students. There also need to be various witnesses (eyewitnesses, character witnesses, etc.) and professional "experts." For example, in the case of Jack vs. The People of Fairy-tale Land, an eyewitness for the prosecution could be the golden harp. A character witness on behalf of the defense could be the old man who sold Jack the beans. Character witnesses can be characters from other tales, as well. A character witness for Jack might be Gretel from *Hansel and Gretel*. Speaking from personal experience, Gretel could state that Jack was acting only out of self-defense.

When assigning witnesses and experts, be sure to assign each individual to either the prosecution or the defense team. These teams will later be working together to develop and build their case. If you have a relatively small class, enlist the help of a neighboring class to participate as jury members. Since many of the students will want the same part, ask each member of the class to write down his or her top three choices for the trial parts they would like to play. Collect their preferences and assign parts according to how you see fit.

Student Preparation

Depending on the age and ability level of your class, students should do the majority of preparation for the trial themselves. They will be accountable for whatever responsibilities their respective roles require (page 206). The attorneys will have the most work to do in advance while the advance preparation for jury members is minimal. Provide the students an outline of the trial schedule and procedures (page 207) and assist them in developing case strategies. If the character witnesses and professional "experts" need some help, assist them in preparing their statements, too. Encourage parents to help their children, too. Parental involvement in this activity will create interesting conversations at home.

Classroom and Time Management

It is important to provide time for prosecution and defense teams to work together in class. Jury members and the other courtroom jobs (judge, bailiff, court reporter) do not need nearly as much preparation as do the other students. A relevant and challenging activity for these students involves using a student tradebook series which focuses on fictional courtroom cases. Published titles include *You Be the Jury; You Be the Jury: Courtroom II; You Be the Jury: Courtroom III; You Be the Detective;* and *Who Dunnit?*

Culminating Activities

Mock Trial (cont.)

All of the books are written by Marvin Miller and published by Scholastic, Inc. These books provide a short synopsis of various cases, present evidence and arguments for each, utilize courtroom terminology, and then ask the readers to vote to determine guilt or innocence. These are excellent activities in problem solving, critical thinking, and using persuasion.

To get ready for the trial, also assign one of the jurors to be the Head Juror. During classroom trial preparation time, the jury and other courtroom individuals will meet in one area of the room. The Head Juror will then read the case aloud, show pictures of the evidence, and lead the discussion among the group. Using these books allows the students to become familiar and comfortable with the "round table" forum and debating strategies that will later be used for the actual mock trial.

Dramatization

To help make this simulation even more interesting, encourage your students to "dress the part." Attorneys should dress nicely (perhaps borrow a tie from Dad or a blazer from Mom) and feel free to use briefcases that they have borrowed from parents or other adults. Borrow a black graduation gown or choir robe for the judge. The bailiff can wear a toy badge and sport a toy holster and toy handcuffs. (It is best not to include a toy gun in the bailiff's ensemble. Imagination will suffice.) Character witnesses should also wear costumes. Costumes need not be elaborate or expensive. A simple prop will be sufficient to help the students feel more in character.

If possible, conduct the trial in a place other than your classroom to create an official mood. Use the school library, stage, or, if at all possible, an actual courtroom. Depending on the court system where you live, there are often one or more courtrooms that are not in use on certain days. Arranging a field trip to the courthouse and conducting the trial in an actual courtroom will provide an exciting experience for your students!

Give your students tips on public speaking and dramatization. Remind them that the mock trial is very much like acting in a play.

Tips and Other Suggestions

Early in the preparation stages for the trial, invite a legal professional to come to your class as a guest to speak to your class about what actually occurs in a courtroom and the preparation involved. This experience is not only helpful for preparation of the mock trial but also serves as a way for students to learn about career choices. Also invite parents to visit and to share their jury-duty experiences.

Be sure to videotape the mock trial for students to view at a later time. Invite parents and grandparents to attend. After conducting the trial one time, invite other classes to watch a second time and ask them to take a collective vote on the verdict (most students are happy to do the trial again!). Pass out certificates to each member of the class for their participation in the trial (page 208).

As a follow-up writing activity, students should write their thoughts and feelings about their respective roles in the mock trial. Were their jobs like they expected them to be? Would they want the same roles again or different ones? What are their true, personal opinions of the verdict, aside from the roles they played? How did this experience affect their impressions of the real judicial system?

After students have written their responses, hold a classroom discussion to debrief. The students are sure to have many opinions.

Culminating Activities   *Mock Trial*

Mock Trial Roles

Role	Responsibility
Judge	Preside over entire trial. Follow schedule. Announce verdict reached by the jury. Issue punishment or release of defendant.
Head Juror	Direct all debates and conversations in juror's room during deliberations. Announce the verdict.
Juror	Listen objectively to both cases from the prosecution and defense. Listen to arguments offered by other jurors during deliberations. Make an informed decision.
Bailiff	Escort the defendant into the courtroom. Announce the entrance of the judge ("All rise: the Honorable Judge_____is now presiding.") Swear in each witness. (Do you promise to tell the truth, the whole truth, and nothing but the truth?)
Court Reporter	Using the "stenographer" machine (or whatever prop is used), record all that is said during the trial. Since you will not actually be typing every word, you will need to listen well so that you can repeat any information that is requested.
Defense Attorney	Represent the defendant and work toward establishing his/her innocence. Prepare a competent case using a variety of resources. Present the closing statement for your side.
Assistant Defense Attorney	Assist in all matters pertaining to the case for the defense. Present the opening statement for your side.
Prosecuting Attorney	Represent the plaintiff and work toward proving his/her accusations. Prepare a competent case using a variety of resources. Present the closing statement for your side.
Assistant Prosecuting Attorney	Assist in all matters pertaining to the case for the plaintiff. Present the opening statement for your side.
Character Witness	Work closely with the attorney for the side you represent. Understand clearly what your perspective is so your comments during the trial appear to be "natural."
Professional Expert	Work closely with the attorney for the side you represent. Understand clearly what your perspective is so your comments during the trial appear to be "natural."

Mock Trial Procedures and Schedule

I. Bailiff escorts defendant to defense table and announces the judge.

II. Judge calls court to order.

III. Opening Statements
 A. Prosecution
 B. Defense

IV. Prosecution Case
 A. Plaintiff called to stand and questioned.
 B. Witnesses and experts called to stand and questioned.
 (Defense may cross-examine each witness before he or she leaves the stand.)

V. Defense Case
 A. Defendant called to stand and questioned.
 B. Witnesses and experts called to stand and questioned.
 (Prosecution may cross-examine each witness before he or she leaves the stand).

VI. Summations
 A. Defense
 B. Prosecution

VII. Jury Charged
 Jury retires to the jurors' room. Head juror leads discussion and the group comes to consensus on the verdict. Jury returns to courtroom.

VIII. Verdict
 A. Head juror passes card with verdict written on it to the bailiff who gives it to the judge.
 B. Head juror announces verdict to the court.
 C. Judge dispenses punishment or releases defendant and adjourns court.

Culminating Activities   *Mock Trial*

This Certificate Is for Recognition of Outstanding Merit, Creativity, and Fine Judicial Skills in the Mock Trial of

Case Name

Name

Trial Role

Teacher   **Date**

Principal

Culminating Activities

International Food Faire

By hosting an International Food Faire, the students can celebrate the diversity of cultures by learning about and experiencing different foods from around the world. Each student is responsible for researching a recipe from a country from one of the stories read, making that dish, and sharing it at the International Food Faire. Here are some tips on organizing this exciting and taste-tantalizing event.

Ready!

On small strips of paper write down the names of the traditional tales read and their countries of origin. Fold and drop the strips into a container and allow each student to draw a strip to determine who will be responsible for what country.

Set!

Students will then conduct research and learn about the various foods from the country they chose. Once they have determined what recipe they will bring, each student will complete a recipe card for his or her dish (page 210). The card should include illustrations to show the preparation and final product.

Go!

A few days prior to the International Food Faire, students can make from construction paper country flags to hang around the room. Offer extra credit to the students who bring in audio cassettes featuring music from their country (most public libraries have a large selection for checkout). Play the tapes during the event for background music. Serve small portions of the food items so that students may have a taste from as many dishes as possible. Encourage the class to try several of the items even if the dish may look unusual or unfamiliar. Remind students that this is an opportunity to learn about other cultures, and it is important to keep an open mind.

Tips

1. Photocopy the recipe cards and compile them into an international cookbook for each student.
2. Invite parents. (Not only will there be plenty of food, but their attendance will also provide an opportunity for students to share their other work from this unit, and the extra helping hands will be needed!)
3. You may want to provide guidelines for the types of dishes brought to the event in order to create a more balanced meal. For example, divide your class in thirds and ask each group to bring a main dish, side dish, and dessert, respectively.
4. Ask some parents to bring in hot plates to help keep warm dishes at a desirable temperature. If possible, obtain a microwave oven to use in class. For items which need to be refrigerated, make an arrangement with the cafeteria to keep dishes in their large refrigerators. (Space in the staff fridge is hard to come by!)
5. Find out if any students have a particular food allergy. Remind those students to read the recipe cards to discover ingredients used.
6. For students who may have extreme difficulty in obtaining a recipe for their country, ask them to bring paper plates, utensils, napkins, or drinks.

Culminating Activities

International Food Faire (cont.)

Recipe: _____

Country: _____   Tale: _____

Ingredients:

_____   _____
_____   _____
_____   _____
_____   _____
_____   _____

How to Prepare:

_____
_____
_____
_____
_____
_____
_____
_____
_____
_____
_____
_____

From the Kitchen of _____
                                                                               name

Culminating Activities

Curious Castle Facts

When we think of traditional tales, certain images come to mind. One such image is that of the magical castle. Virtually every fairy tale and many folk tales include this large, fantastic, and stately building. Depending on the country in which the tale is told, the castle may have a different name, but regardless of the name, the castle is an important place in traditional tales for both the heroes and the villains.

While there are many make-believe castles in traditional tales, there have been and still are many real castles all around the world. Read the castle facts to learn more about these mysterious and wondrous structures.

Did you know . . . ?

- During the Middle Ages (700–1500 A.D.) there were thousands of castles in western Europe.
- Castles were a symbol of power, authority, and defense. Castles were built to protect the people who lived in them.
- Castles were mostly built on or near natural defenses such as cliffs and coastlines.
- A ditch could be dug around the finished castle with river water diverted to it. These water-filled ditches, called moats, made castles much harder to attack.
- Many of the first castles ever built were made from wood. A wooden tower was built on top of a mound and encircled by a timber fence.
- Wooden castles burned and rotted easily, so builders began using stone.
- Even though every castle built is unique, most castles were designed around one tall tower. These stone towers are called keeps.
- Castle walls are often 12 feet (3.6 m) thick.

Now that you know some interesting castle facts, team up with a partner to do some research on one of these famous castles.

- Neuschwantein Castle in Germany
- Castle at Penafiel in Spain
- Kronborg Castle of Denmark
- Lusignan Castle in France
- Palace at Chambord, France (Francois I)
- Castle Beaumaris of Britain
- Glamis Castle in Scotland
- Hedingham Castle in Essex (England)

Culminating Activities

Castle Building

Work with a partner or small group to design and build your own castle. Is your castle going to be dark and gloomy, or will it be bright and magical? Anything is possible, so let your imagination take you wherever you would like.

For extra credit, write a short fairy tale that takes place in your castle. The class can also hold a contest to determine which castle is the scariest, most beautiful, most majestic, most inspiring, most realistic, and so forth.

Materials:

- cardboard
- empty cardboard boxes (such as tea-bag boxes, oatmeal cylinders, jewelry boxes, soap boxes, and various sizes of food boxes)
- sharp craft knife (for adult use only)
- tape
- rulers
- glue
- plastic straws
- needles and thread
- dime (one per castle)
- tagboard (or cardstock)
- paint
- paintbrushes

Directions:

Note: If this project is done in class, it will probably take four or five lesson blocks to finish. These instructions lend themselves to a generic castle. Feel free to be creative and design your own unique castle, adding banners, different buildings, scenery, and whatever else you desire to make your castle special.

Making the Gatehouse

The gatehouse is the entrance to the castle. It houses the drawbridge and is the living quarters for the guards and/or constable.

1. Cut out a rectangle of cardboard. Divide it into four equal sections with your ruler. On one section on the end, draw a thin line (approximately ¼" or .6 cm) for a tab. Score all four lines with the scissors.

2. Make battlements by cutting evenly spaced, square notches along one of the long edges of the rectangle.

3. Draw and cut a door into the bottom of the first and third panels of the rectangle. Draw a line inside of a rectangle and cut to make double doors which open.

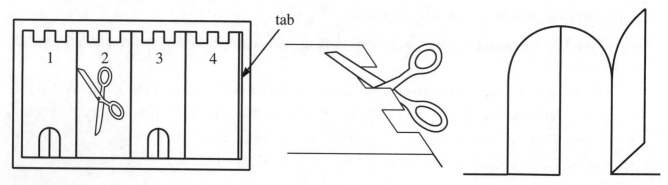

Castle Building (cont.)

4. Pierce a small hole in the left-hand side of panel #2. Pierce another in the right-hand side of panel #4. The holes must be the same distance from the bottom edge. Make the holes big enough for a straw to fit through.

5. Add glue to the inside edge of panel 1 and glue it to the tab. Fold the rectangle into the tower shape. You may want to secure the tower with tape. Push the straw through both holes.

6. Make a drawbridge from a small piece of cardboard. Use tape to attach it to the door on panel 3.

7. Thread the needle. Be sure to knot both loose ends of the thread. Push the threaded needle through one of the drawbridge's outer corners and then up through the front wall of the gatehouse.

8. Lower the drawbridge flat. Tape a dime to the bottom of the drawbridge for weight. Gently pull the thread straight and tape the rest of the thread to the straw. Make one more drawbridge "chain" in the same way.

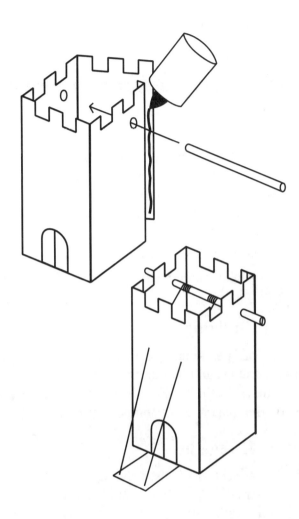

Making the Towers

1. You can use a cylinder cardboard shape (like a box of oats) and cover it with construction paper.

2. Add battlements to the tower by cutting along the top of the construction paper.

Alternative: You can make towers without the cylinders, too. Cut out a rectangle piece from the tagboard (or cardstock). Glue (and/or tape) the roll and cut out square battlements along the top. (You will need to make at least four towers.)

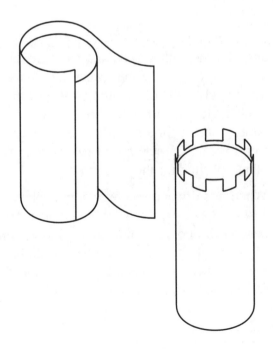

Culminating Activities

Castle Building (cont.)

Making the Walls

1. Place the four towers on the table in the square size you want your castle to be. Measure the distance between the towers. Remember that the gatehouse will fit in the middle of one castle wall, so account for this in your measurements.

2. The distance measured between the towers will be the length of the wall piece. Using your ruler, measure and cut out the four cardboard pieces. (The pieces should be approximately two inches or five cm shorter than the towers when standing between them.)

3. Cut square battlements along one edge of each wall piece.

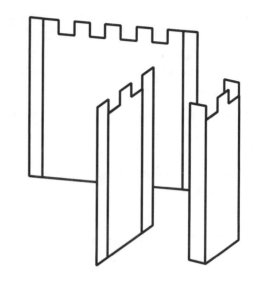

Interior Buildings

The interior open area of castles hosted a variety of smaller buildings. Some of these buildings included stables and buildings for weapon and food storage. This area often included a courtyard with a fountain and foliage. Decide which buildings you want to include in your interior area and using construction paper, cover and decorate the outside of the boxes to create the buildings.

Putting It Together

1. To connect the walls to the towers, cut strips of construction paper one inch (2.5 cm) in width. The length will depend on the height of your walls.

2. Place one tower and one wall piece at a right angle to each other. Take the construction-paper strip and fold it over the corner that is made. Then apply a liberal amount of glue to the strip. Go back to the corner and press down. Hold the paper in place for a minute to set. Repeat this step for each corner and the gatehouse. Allow plenty of time for the castle to dry.

3. When it is dry and secure, you may paint the castle. Spray paint or tempera paints work the best on cardboard. Paint small windows and arches on the towers. Add your finishing touches such as banners, figurines, a moat, foliage, and whatever else you would like.

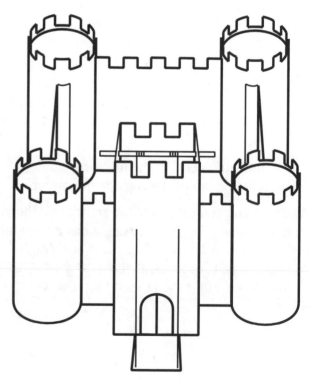

Culminating Activities

Traditional Tale Q & A

This is an enjoyable, cooperative, learning-based game which employs all levels of Bloom's Taxonomy skills. The dynamics of the game create a situation which fosters interdependence among students, and all students are engaged at all times. Play Q & A as an assessment activity or just for fun upon completion of this unit of study. The game can also be played at the end of each section to help review for the section test. There are a number of ways to play the game, and as you run through Q & A a few times, you will probably want to customize the game to best suit your needs and the needs of your students.

Materials:

- tagboard
- 25 self-adhesive pockets (the kind formerly used in library books)
- 25 colored circle stickers (5 each of 5 different colors)
- 25 index cards
- 6 rulers or 1' (30 cm) sticks (suggestion: paint stirrers)
- 6 differently colored oval shapes with a 10" (25 cm) diameter
- colored markers (to match the colored stickers)

Game Board Directions:

1. Place the pocket cards on the tagboard to form five rows of five. Glue the backs to the tagboard.

2. Determine which color each row will be.

3. Starting with the first row (horizontally), place one color of the sticker circles on the lower, front part of the pocket card. Continue placing stickers on all five of the top row.

4. Repeat the process with the other rows, using a different color each time.

5. Starting with the top row again, use a marker in the same color as the stickers to write the number 10 on each of the cards.

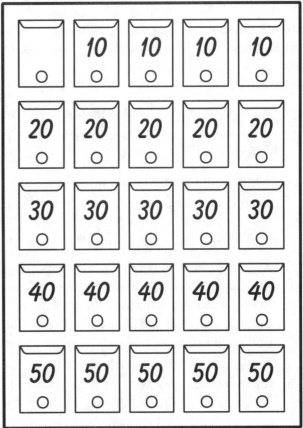

6. Do the same procedure for the next four rows, using matching ink markers for the respective dots. Write the numbers as illustrated.

7. Laminate the board with the pockets to maintain durability. Use a razor blade to cut open the pockets after laminating. (Only adults should handle the blade.)

© Teacher Created Materials, Inc.   #464 Tales Around the World

Culminating Activities

Traditional Tale Q & A *(cont.)*

Game Sticks Directions:

1. Write on each of the colored oval shapes in large type: Q & A.
2. Laminate the shapes for durability.
3. Tape or glue the shapes to a stick or ruler to make a sign.

Game Cards Directions:

1. The questions for Q & A range from easy to challenging. For example, 10-point questions are at the knowledge level of Bloom's Taxonomy and begin "Who," "When," or "What," while 50-point questions adhere to the synthesis and evaluation levels, asking students to modify, judge, classify, and make value judgements.
2. With the card held lengthwise, write the point value at the top.
3. On the back of the card, write the question at the top and the answer at the bottom.
4. Place the cards in their appropriate pocket slots with the point values showing.

Object of Game:

The object of Q & A is to be the team with the most points at the end of the game. Teams take turns answering the questions, with each member of each team also having a turn to speak. The game is finished when all the cards have been answered.

How to Play:

1. Arrange the students into six groups of five each or whatever works for your class.
2. Place the game sticks at each table.
3. On the board write down the six different colors for each group for scorekeeping purposes.
4. Begin with one group and rotate in a clockwise fashion.
5. Each team member will have the opportunity to hold the game stick. Even though team members collaborate on the answer and decisions that need to be made, only the person holding the game stick is allowed to speak for the group.
6. The game stick is then rotated clockwise after each team's turn.
7. The game-show host or hostess will ask that team to decide which color and point value they wish to try. The host then reads the card aloud for the whole class to hear. Give the team about one minute to discuss possible answers. While the team is thinking, the other teams should also be doing the same, as they may have an opportunity to answer this question at a later time.
8. The game stick holder will then answer the question. If the question is correct, that team receives the points, and the game then moves on to the next team. If the team does not answer the question correctly, then the next team in the rotation has a chance to steal the points. If the next team answers the previous question correctly, they get the points for that card and then may also choose another card to answer. If the second team cannot answer the "steal" question, then the card simply goes back into its place and the team is still allowed to choose a question.
9. This procedure continues throughout the course of the game until all the cards have been answered.

Culminating Activities

Traditional Tale Q & A *(cont.)*

Rules and Guidelines

1. Only the person holding the game stick may speak for the group.

2. All responses to questions must be discussed with the entire group before answering. If the game-stick holder speaks before collaboration, then the team loses its turn.

3. The majority of the team must agree on the response before it is presented to the host.

4. Teams may only respond when it is their turn.

Some Helpful Hints

1. The questions may be created by the teacher or by the students.

2. You may want to provide the option of bonus cards. Behind one or two cards, place a bonus card which provides another question and opportunity for points.

3. Play the game in a Jeopardy™ style where the host reads the answer and the students must come up with the possible question.

4. To promote good listening skills, the host should only read the question two times. This encourages the students to repeat the question to each other.

5. If you will be offering prizes for the winners, be sure to offer a prize to the teams who worked well cooperatively. Competition is fun and necessary but use every opportunity to affirm successful teamwork experiences.

Culminating Activities

Traditional Tale Q & A *(cont.)*

Bloom's Verbs

Knowledge		Comprehension		Application	
name	recall	explain	paraphrase	transfer	apply
list	draw	summarize	review	compute	show
define	count	interpret	demonstrate	produce	change
march	identify	predict	conclude	choose	paint
label	sequence	tell	generalize	use	select
describe	quote	discuss	locate	demonstrate	prepare
recite	write	restate	identify	interview	dramatize
tell	find	illustrate	report	draw	imitate

Analysis		Synthesis		Evaluation	
differentiate	compare	create	produce	judge	predict
contrast	outline	design	compose	select	rate
deduce	characterize	propose	invent	prove	choose
classify	separate	organize	pretend	decide	evaluate
debate	analyze	construct	originate	appraise	conclude
research	discriminate	develop	integrate	rank	assess
distinguish	examine	plan	rewrite	criticize	justify
relate	diagram	makeup	perform	prioritize	argue

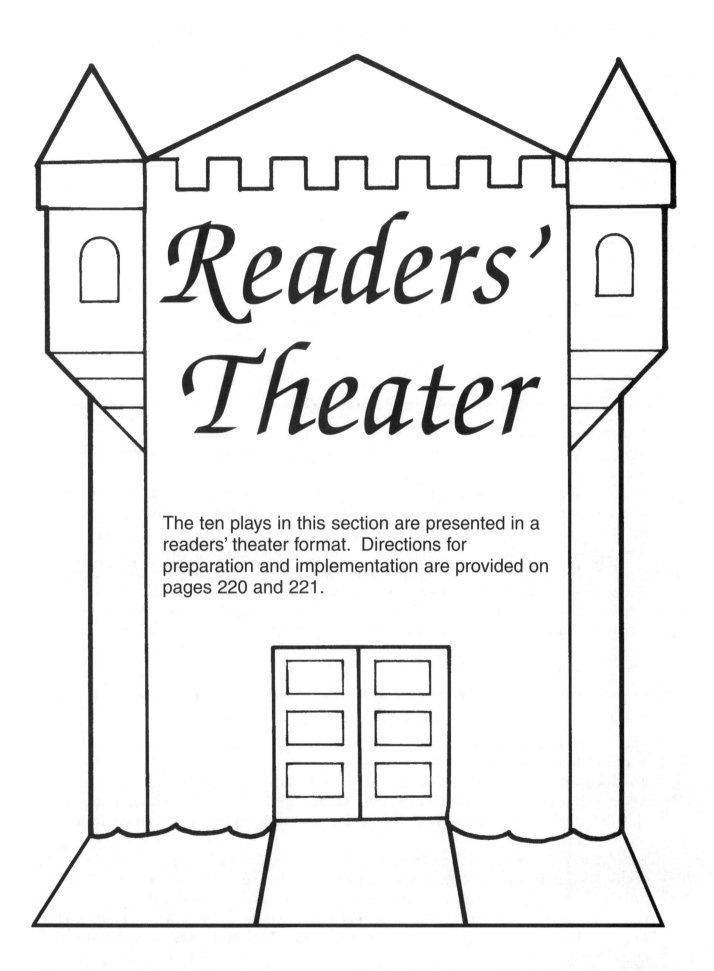

Readers' Theater

The ten plays in this section are presented in a readers' theater format. Directions for preparation and implementation are provided on pages 220 and 221.

Introduction to Readers' Theater

Readers' theater is the oral interpretation of literature presented by expressive readers to an audience listening with imagination. Traditionally, no costumes, props, or elaborate staging (as in a play) are employed. It is the text that is featured.

Using readers' theater in the classroom brings literature alive and makes it memorable. Reading, speaking, and listening are integrated in a purposeful context, and the benefits to your language-arts program are many. Students are actively involved with literature and motivated to read and reread. Their enjoyment and interest are stimulated. Their imaginations are invoked. Reading fluency and comprehension increase. Self-esteem soars, and students of all abilities succeed.

Because readers' theater requires no special equipment or costs and teacher preparation is minimal, it is easy to implement.

Preparation

- Have a script for each reader, plus one for yourself. If you plan to make sets of the entire section, reproduce pages 222–312. Have each student write his or her name on the cover sheet (page 222).
- Mount scripts in sturdy file folders for the readers' handling ease.

Implementation

- Distribute the scripts.
- Read through the selection several times with the students so they are familiar with the piece as a whole.
- Have students select their parts. (Students tend to choose parts appropriate to their own reading level and interests, and generally they get more involved than when the teacher assigns the parts.)
- Readers mark their scripts, highlighting their lines and their interpretations (their actions). (**Note:** Scripts have been designed with plenty of space on a page for students to take notes.)
- Begin rehearsal. It is important to allow plenty of time for this rehearsal phase, several days or even a week. Students will be eager and their interest and motivation will be high. Do not be surprised if they want to keep on working after the time is up or during recess. While they are practicing, reading, and rereading the selection, they are also building reading and oral competency, reinforcing sight words, expanding their vocabulary, and increasing their comprehension.

Rehearsal Phase

- Students are practicing reading with expression and fluency.
- They are working on entrances, introductions, and exits. (These elements add to the mood of the piece and the characterizations.)
- The readers are getting feedback from each other and/or small "test" audiences, perfecting their pronunciation, their voice quality and delivery, and their performance skills. (A video camera is an excellent tool in this process. It allows students to see and hear themselves. They are their own best critics!)
- Finally, the readers are ready to perform. They have mastered all the usual problems: wiggly bodies, noisy pages, scripts blocking readers' faces, voices too soft to be heard at the back of the room, and the inevitable giggles. Self-esteem is soaring and excitement is high.
- Gather the audiences around: classmates, other classes, assemblies, parents, and so forth. Do not forget the video camera! Performances can be taped throughout the school year and played at Open House.

Introduction to Readers' Theater (cont.)

The Benefits of Readers' Theater

- ❏ Reading, listening, and speaking are integrated in a purposeful context.

- ❏ Literature comes alive in the classroom, and enjoyment and interest are stimulated.

- ❏ Students are actively involved with learning and setting their own high standards.

- ❏ Attentive listening is promoted.

- ❏ Imagination is activated.

- ❏ Students are motivated to read and reread selections.

- ❏ Repetition and involvement foster reading competency.

- ❏ Comprehension increases as students develop an understanding of the characters and their relationships and learn to recognize the mood and message of a selection.

- ❏ Oral communication and presentation skills are developed.

- ❏ Personal and social growth are fostered through cooperative interaction.

- ❏ Students at all ability levels can succeed.

- ❏ Standard and high quality American English are modeled.

- ❏ ESL students are motivated and helped.

- ❏ Positive self-esteem is developed by the participants.

- ❏ Immediate student progress and attitude improvement are attainable.

Readers' Theater

Table of Contents

The Four Musicians. 223

Lazy Jack 235

A Cat Is a Cat Is a Cat. 242

The Woodcutter and the Pine 248

The Cat and the Parrot. 255

The Honey Gatherer's Three Sons. 265

Coyote Rings the Bell 274

Beetle and Paca 283

The Weary Spirits of Lanai 291

Baba Yaga Bony-Legs 302

This book belongs to

The Four Musicians

A Folk Tale from Germany

(Scripted for Seven Readers)

Germany has a long and rich history of storytelling. Fortunately, in the early 1800s the Brothers Grimm wrote down and collected hundreds of these folk tales, many of which are now classics in Western culture, such as *Hansel and Gretel*, *Snow White*, and *Rapunzel*. *The Four Musicians* was also first recorded by the Grimm Brothers. It is a humorous tale in which the unassuming heroes triumph over evil. Like many popular German tales, it is full of drama and suspense.

The Four Musicians

Cast of Characters

Narrator

Donkey

Dog

Cat

Rooster

Robber 1

Robber 2

Stage Setup:

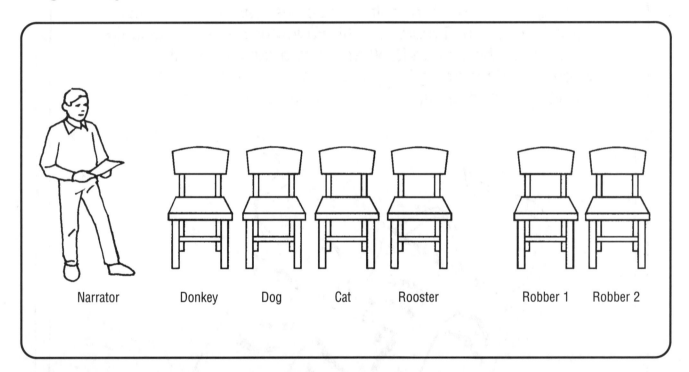

Entrance:

The Narrator enters and introduces the tale.

All other readers (except the ROBBERS) enter the performing area. They take their positions and introduce themselves and the parts they will be reading.

The Robbers sneak into the performing area. They take their positions and introduce themselves and the parts they will be reading.

All readers open their scripts, and the tale begins.

The Four Musicians (cont.)

Donkey: There once was a donkey who worked faithfully for his master for many, many years. But, with old age, the donkey's strength began to fail, and his daily loads were more than he could bear.

Narrator: His master decided the donkey was of no use anymore and planned to put an end to him, but the donkey's long ears heard of this, and he promptly hobbled away.

Donkey: I will go to Bremen-town. My body may be weak, but my voice is still strong. Hee-Haw! I'll become a musician and make my music in the streets.

Narrator: The donkey had traveled a short distance when he spied something by the roadside. It was a large hound, flopped in a heap and panting deeply, gasping for air.

Donkey: What makes you pant so, my dear friend?

Dog: I have run away. For many years I guarded my master's house and helped him in the hunt, but now I am too old. My master was going to do me in. Alas, what else could I do? I had to run away.

The Four Musicians *(cont.)*

Donkey: Come with me, good hound. I am going to Bremen-town. We shall earn our living there being musicians.

Narrator: The dog and the donkey walked on together.

Cat: Soon they came to a cat sitting in the middle of the road, looking as dismal as three wet days.

Donkey: Pray tell, good lady, what is the matter?

Cat: I fear my life shall end quite soon. My teeth are blunt, and my bones are stiff. Nowadays, I prefer to sit by the fire and purr instead of chasing silly mice about. My mistress calls me useless and this morning threatened to drown me.

Donkey: No, no this should not be. Come with us to Bremen-town and make music in the streets. Certainly you can still serenade.

Cat: Hmm, purr-haps, well yes.

Narrator: And so, the cat, the dog, and the donkey walked on down the road until they came to a farmyard.

The Four Musicians *(cont.)*

Rooster: A rooster flew up onto the gate and crowed loudly as could be, Cock-a-doodle-doo!

Donkey: Bravo! What a voice!

Rooster: Oh that. I was only predicting fine weather for our washing-day. But my mistress doesn't care anymore. In fact, she ordered the cook to add me to the broth being prepared for the guests arriving next Sunday.

Donkey: Heaven forbid! You'd better come with us. We're off to Bremen-town to be musicians. What grand concerts we four will make!

Rooster: Indeed! Cock-a-doodle-doo!

Narrator: Bremen, however, was far away. The four travelers could not reach it in a single day. When night fell, they found themselves in a thick woods. Searching for a safe place to sleep, they found shelter under a great oak tree.

Donkey: The donkey . . .

Dog: . . . and the dog

The Four Musicians (cont.)

Donkey: . . . rested on a bed of leaves amid the crooked roots of the tree.

Cat: The cat climbed up to a comfortable (well, almost comfortable) branch.

Rooster: The rooster flew to the topmost twig of the great oak tree. The safest place to be. From his high perch he could look out over the countryside. There! In the distance, there's a light. It must be a house.

Donkey: If that be so, let us get up and go there. I am not used to sleeping in the woods. The sooner we change for the better, the more pleased I will be.

Dog: Grrreat! I bet I can get a few bones with a bit of meat.

Cat: . . . and a saucer of milk.

Rooster: . . . and a few table scraps for me. Cockle-dee.

Narrator: The rooster led the way. When they neared the cottage, the donkey, being the tallest, went to look in the lighted window.

The Four Musicians (cont.)

Dog: Well? What do you see?

Donkey: What do I see? I see that this is a robbers' house! There are swords and pistols on the walls. Great chests of money and plunder lie about on the floor, and the robbers are sitting at a table loaded with eatables and drinkables. They are making themselves quite comfortable and merry.

Dog: We surely could do with some of those eatables!

Rooster: Indeed, but what about the robbers?

Narrator: The companions huddled together and at last hit upon a plan.

Donkey: The donkey stood on his hind legs with his forefeet on the windowsill.

Dog: The dog teetered on the donkey's shoulders.

Cat: The cat climbed up onto the dog.

Rooster: And the rooster perched on the head of the cat.

The Four Musicians (cont.)

Narrator: When all were ready they began their music. (all speaking at the same time)

Donkey: Hee-Haw! Hee-Haw! Hee-Haw!

Dog: Bow-Wow-Wow! Bow-Wow!

Cat: Meow! Meow! Meeooow!

Rooster: Cock-a-doodle-doo! Cock-a-doodle-doo!

Narrator: Then the four musicians burst through the window with a dreadful clatter and tumbled into the room!

Robber 1: The robbers thought a pack of goblins had come to devour them!

Robber 2: They fled into the woods . . .

Robber 1: . . . too frightened even to look back.

Narrator: And our four companions feasted on the eatables until they could feast no more. Stuffed and tired, they blew out the candles, ready for bed.

The Four Musicians *(cont.)*

Donkey: The donkey nestled down on some loose straw in the front yard.

Dog: Yawning, the dog stretched out on a mat just inside the door.

Cat: The cat curled up on the hearth, enjoying the warmth from the embers and ashes.

Rooster: And the rooster perched on the ridge of the roof just beside the chimney. He ruffled his feathers and closed his eyes.

Narrator: All were soon fast asleep.

Robber 1: Just after midnight the robbers came creeping back to the house.

Robber 2: No lights were burning. Everything seemed quiet and peaceful.

Robber 1: Perhaps we made a mistake.

Robber 2: Maybe we were too hasty and ran away without reason.

Robber 1: You wait here at the edge of the woods. I will go to see.

The Four Musicians (cont.)

Narrator: The robber quietly crept up to the house and slipped into the kitchen.

Robber 1: He fumbled around in the dark until he found a candle and a match on the mantle above the fireplace.

Cat: By now the cat was awake. She stood on the hearth, watching.

Robber 1: The robber saw her shining eyes. He thought they were hot coals left from the fire, so he reached down to light his match.

Cat: The cat was having no part of that! She flew into his face, hissing and scratching and spitting!

Robber 1: Yeooow! The frightened robber ran toward the door.

Dog: But, the dog was crouched and waiting. He bit the robber's leg.

Robber: Ooow-Ooow! The robber staggered through the door and out into the front yard.

Donkey: The donkey heard him coming and readied his hind legs. Thwack! He kicked the robber into the air.

The Four Musicians (cont.)

Rooster: The rooster flapped wildly on the rooftop, screeching, Cock-a-doodle-doo! Cock-a-doodle-doo!

Robber 1: Thud. The robber landed back down on the ground. He scrambled to his feet.

Narrator: And those feet did not stop running until they were deep in the heart of the woods.

Robber 2: The other robber finally caught up with him.

Robber 1: We cannot go back!

Robber 2: Not anymore?

Robber 1: Not anymore! A gruesome witch waits in the kitchen. I felt her breath and long claws on my face. A dreadful demon guards the door, a demon who gobbles legs. Stomping about the yards there's a fearsome giant with a huge wooden club, and he sent me flying. And, dancing wildly on the rooftop is a greedy goblin, shouting, "Chuck him up to me! Chuck him up to me!"

Robber 2: Tell me no more! Tell me no more!

The Four Musicians (cont.)

Narrator: From that day forward the robbers never returned.

Donkey: The four musicians found themselves with a cozy cottage . . .

Dog: . . . and grrr-eat amounts of food.

Rooster: Ease and comfort filled their days . . .

Cat: . . . purr-fectly fitting their old age.

Narrator: And that is the end of our tale.

Lazy Jack

A Folk Tale from England

(Scripted for Eight Readers)

In English folklore, "Jack tales" are a popular tradition. Jack is usually a country bumpkin who, despite all odds, succeeds in the end. In this tale Lazy Jack stumbles happily along while following his mother's advice a bit too literally.

Lazy Jack

Cast of Characters

Lazy Jack
Mother
Neighboring Farmer
Cowkeeper
Baker
Butcher
Rich Man
Rich Man's Daughter

Stage Setup:

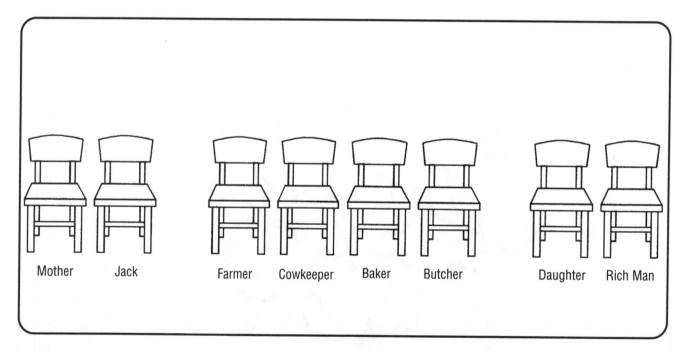

Entrance:

Lazy Jack is already in position, lounging in his chair. He introduces the folk tale and then introduces himself and the part he will be reading.

All other readers enter the performing area single file and take their places. They each introduce themselves and the parts they will be reading.

All open their scripts, and the tale begins.

Lazy Jack (cont.)

Jack: Once there was a boy named Jack.

Mother: Everyone called him Lazy Jack.

Jack: In the summers he basked in the sunshine. In the winters he snoozed in front of the hearth, warming his feet at the fire.

Mother: All year around, year after year, his poor old mother did all the work. At last she could bear no more! Lazy Jack! We are poor. If you do not begin to earn your porridge, I will turn you out!

Jack: Well, this roused Jack.

Farmer: Monday, he went to work for a neighboring farmer. At the end of the day, the farmer paid him a penny for his work.

Jack: Jack was delighted! He'd never had a penny before! He didn't know what to do with it, so he lost his penny while crossing a brook on the way home.

Lazy Jack (cont.)

Mother: Foolish lad! You should have put it in your pocket.

Jack: I'll do so another time, Mother.

Cowkeeper: Tuesday, Jack went to work for a cowkeeper. The cowkeeper paid him a jar of milk at the end of the day.

Jack: Jack put the jar of milk into the large pocket of his jacket. The milk spilled out, every drop, long before he ever reached home.

Mother: Silly sod! You should have carried it on your head.

Jack: I'll do so another time, Mother.

Cowkeeper: Wednesday, Jack returned to work for the cowkeeper. This time the cowkeeper paid him a cream cheese.

Jack: Jack put the cream cheese on his head. By the time he arrived home, chunks of cheese had crumbled away, and what remained was melted and matted into his hair.

Mother: Noodle-noggin! You should have carried it carefully in your hands!

Lazy Jack (cont.)

Jack: I'll do so another time, Mother.

Baker: Thursday, Lazy Jack went to work for the baker. The baker paid him only a large tomcat for his labors.

Jack: Jack began walking home. He carefully carried the cat in his hands. But he was quickly covered with so many scratches, he had to let the tomcat go.

Mother: Porridge-brains! You should have tied a string around its neck and dragged it along behind you.

Butcher: On Friday, Jack went to work for the butcher. At the end of the day, the butcher rewarded Jack with the handsome present of a shoulder of mutton.

Jack: Jack tied a string around the mutton and dragged it home through the dirt. By the time he got home, the meat was completely spoiled.

Mother: Ninnyhammer! You should have carried it on your shoulder!

Jack: I'll do so another time, Mother.

Lazy Jack (cont.)

Cowkeeper: Saturday, Jack worked for the cowkeeper and was paid a donkey for his trouble.

Jack: Jack, though strong, had difficulty hoisting the donkey onto his shoulder. But at last, he started trudging slowly home.

Rich Man: On the road to Jack's house, there lived a rich man and his only daughter.

Daughter: The beautiful daughter was deaf and mute and had never laughed in her life. The doctors said she would only recover if someone could make her laugh. Many tried.

Rich Man: None succeeded. In despair, the father finally offered his daughter in marriage to the first man to make her laugh.

Daughter: Now, the daughter just happened to be looking out the window . . .

Jack: . . . when Jack trudged by with a struggling donkey upon his shoulder, its legs sticking up and kicking the air.

Daughter: She burst into gales of laughter!

Lazy Jack (cont.)

Rich Man: The overjoyed father kept his promise.

Daughter: His daughter and Jack were wed.

Jack: And, that's how Jack ended up with a rich wife and a large house, where he and his bride lived happily ever after.

Mother: And, so did his mother, of course!

A Cat Is a Cat Is a Cat

A Folk Tale from Vietnam

(Scripted for Six Readers)

In the tradition of an anecdotal folk tale (a commonplace event with a universal theme), this realistic tale is built upon a proverb. A man who has fallen in love with a cat receives sage advice from one of his guests.

A Cat Is a Cat Is a Cat

Cast of Characters
Narrator
Man
Cat
Guest 1
Guest 2
Wise Man

Stage Setup:

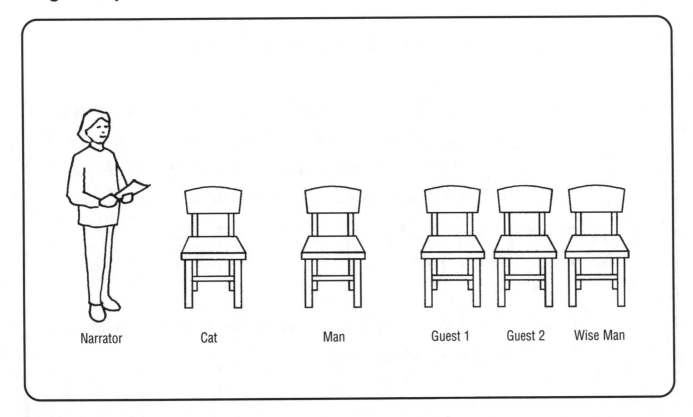

Entrance:

All readers except the cat enter the performance area in single file and take their places. The Narrator introduces the tale and then the characters introduce themselves and the parts they will be reading.

The cat meanders in, proud and elegant. When in place, he or she introduces him- or her-self and the part.

All open their scripts, and the tale begins.

A Cat Is a Cat Is a Cat (cont.)

Man: There once was a man who had a cat.

Cat: Or rather, a cat chose to arrive at his house one day.

Narrator: But this was not just any cat. This was an extraordinary cat. She walked with the pride of an empress. Her fur shimmered black, white, and burnished gold, like silk in the setting sun. And, her eyes, oh, her eyes . . .

Cat: Never was anything more beautiful than this cat.

Man: The man fell in love, at once! Each day he thought and thought and thought, unable to work, unable to eat. What should he call his clever, proud, and lovely cat? At night he tossed and turned. The name must be perfect.

Narrator: At last it struck him.

Man: Heaven! Yes, of course, I'll call her Heaven. What could be more perfect?

Narrator: The man, very pleased with this decision, invited his friends over for a grand dinner. After dinner he would tell them Heaven's name.

A Cat Is a Cat Is a Cat (cont.)

Guest 1: Well, what is it? What have you chosen for her?

Guest 2: Yes, what is it?

Guest 1: How do you call her?

Man: Heaven.

Guests: Heaven?

Guest 1: How can you call her Heaven?

Man: Ah, heaven is the best, the top. What could be more perfect than heaven?

Narrator: One of the guests, a thin wise man, scratched his beard and stared dreamily at the bamboo ceiling.

Wise Man: Hmm, Heaven, Heaven . . . but a cloud! A cloud can darken heaven's face.

Man: A cloud? This is true, a cloud could cover heaven. Well, let me think . . . Cloud then! Yes, I will call my cat Cloud. (All nod in agreement, except the wise man.)

A Cat Is a Cat Is a Cat (cont.)

Wise Man: Hmmm . . . but what about wind?

Guests: What about wind?

Wise Man: Ah, wind can chase the clouds away.

Guests: That's true, that's true.

Man: All right! I like it! I will call my cat Wind.
(All nod, except the wise man.)

Cat: Just at this moment, the lovely cat strolled through a patch of sun on the porch.

Guests: Here, Wind! Come here, Wind!
(The wise man's hand shoots out, his fingers spread wide, halting their voices.)

Wise Man: No, no, no. (He shakes his head sadly.) What about a wall?

Guests: What about a wall?

A Cat Is a Cat Is a Cat *(cont.)*

Wise Man: Ah, a wall can stop the wind.

Man: Wall, I'll call her Wall!
(All nod, except the wise man.)

Wise Man: Of course . . . there's always a mouse. A mouse can nibble through a wall.

Man: Mouse? I'll call her, Mouse! My dear little Mousie.

Wise Man: Ah, but . . . everyone knows who can catch a mouse.

Man: All right! All right! All right! I'll call my cat Cat!

Narrator: After all . . .

All: . . . a cat is a cat is a cat!

The End

The Woodcutter and the Pine

A Folk Tale from Japan

(Scripted for Six Readers)

Japanese folk tales traditionally embody the ideals and customs of the culture. This is the tale of a gentle woodcutter who would hurt nothing, not even a tree. It reflects respect for nature. Incidentally, it is said in Japan that a pine tree brings good fortune.

The Woodcutter and the Pine

Cast of Characters

Narrator 1

Narrator 2

Narrator 3

Woodcutter

Pine Tree

Neighbor

Stage Setup:

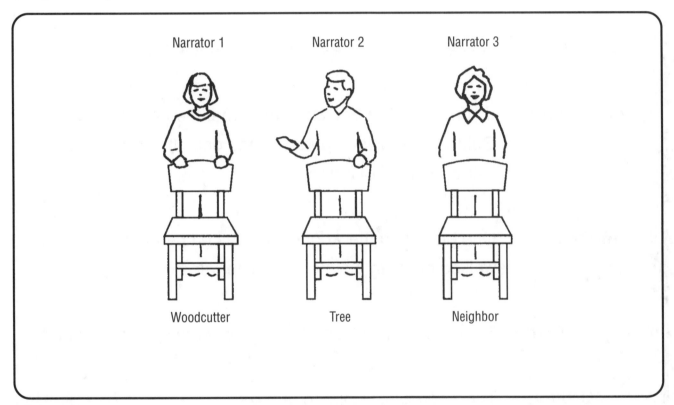

Entrance:

Narrator 2 and the Pine Tree are already in their positions. Narrator 2 introduces the folk tale and then they both introduce themselves and the parts they will be reading.

Narrator 1 and the Woodcutter enter from one side of the performing area. They take their positions and introduce themselves and the parts they will be reading.

Narrator 3 and the Neighbor enter from the other side of the performing area. (The Neighbor enters as if sneaking on.) They take their positions and introduce themselves and the parts they will be reading.

All open their scripts, and the story begins.

The Woodcutter and the Pine *(cont.)*

Narrator 1: Once there was a woodcutter. He was very poor.

Woodcutter: I have no money and very little to eat.

Narrator 1: This woodcutter was good and very kind. He would not hurt anyone or anything.

Woodcutter: Not even a tree.

Narrator 1: He gathered only dead branches that fell to the ground.

Woodcutter: If you tear a live branch from a tree, the tree will bleed. Golden sap will drip and drip and drip. It is the sap that is the lifeblood of a tree.

Narrator 1: One day when the woodcutter was gathering firewood, he walked beneath a stately old pine tree.

Tree: Sticky, sticky is my sap, for my tender twigs are snapped.

Narrator: The woodcutter stopped, amazed.

Woodcutter: What? What is this? What do I hear?

The Woodcutter and the Pine (cont.)

Narrator 1: He looked up into the old pine tree.

Narrator 2: Someone had ripped three branches from the tree, and sap poured from the wounds.

Woodcutter: These tender twigs I will wrap and in that way stop the sap.

Narrator 1: The woodcutter tore three strips of cloth from his own clothing. Gently, he wrapped each branch, carefully bandaging the old pine tree.

Narrator 2: As he finished wrapping the third and final branch, many tiny gold and silver things rained down from the tree.

Woodcutter: What? What is this? What do I see?

Narrator 1: He bent and fingered the shiny things.

Woodcutter: It's money! Lots of it!

Narrator 1: In fact, the surprised woodcutter was almost buried in ancient gold and silver coins. Coins so ancient that they were not round but oblong in shape.

The Woodcutter and the Pine (cont.)

Woodcutter: Thank you, thank you, venerable tree.

Narrator 1: The smiling woodcutter scooped and scooped the shiny coins into his wood-gathering baskets and trudged home.

Narrator 3: His neighbor in the village was also a woodcutter, but he was not nice. He was not kind. In fact, it was he who tore the branches from the tree. He saw the woodcutter with his glittering load.

Neighbor: Where did you get all that money? Look how nice and bright it is!

Narrator 1: The woodcutter held up the money so his neighbor could see.

Woodcutter: It's from a tree, an old pine tree.

Neighbor: The big one at the far edge of the forest?

Woodcutter: Yes, that's the one.

The Woodcutter and the Pine (cont.)

Narrator 3: The bad woodcutter disappeared as fast as he could into the forest.

Narrator 2: He emerged at the far edge under the old pine tree.

Tree: Sticky, sticky is my blood. Touch me, and you'll receive a flood.

Neighbor: Yes! Yes! Just what I want, a flood of golden things.

Narrator 3: He reached up and broke off another branch.

Narrator 2: The pine tree suddenly showered him with a glistening, golden shower. But it was not coins. It was sap, sticky, sticky sap.

Narrator 3: The bad woodcutter was covered. Sticky sap was in his hair and on his arms and legs. It was so sticky he could not move.

Neighbor: Help! Help!

All: No one came.

The Woodcutter and the Pine (cont.)

Narrator 3: He was trapped. One day passed. Two days passed.

Narrator 2: At the close of the third day, the sap began to soften. It softened just enough so that the bad woodcutter could drag himself home.

Tree: Three days for three branches.

Narrator 3: After that, the bad woodcutter never broke another living branch from a tree.

The Cat and the Parrot

A Folk Tale from India

(Scripted for Ten Readers)

This classic tale of greed is from India, though various versions are found all around the world. This particular tale is an example of a cumulative folk tale. Its story builds upon repeated refrains.

The Cat and the Parrot

Cast of Characters

Narrator 1

The Cat

Narrator 2

Parrot

Narrator 3

Old Woman

Old Man

King

Land Crabs (2 readers)

Stage Setup:

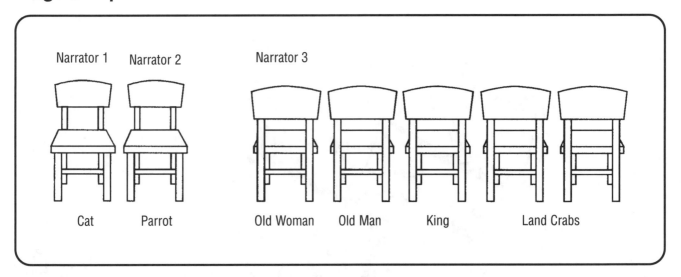

Entrance:

The Narrators enter from the side of the performing area. Narrator 1 introduces the folk tale. The Narrators introduce themselves and the parts they will be reading and then take their positions.

The Old Woman, the Old Man, the King, and the Land Crabs enter from the other side of the performing area. They introduce themselves and the parts they will be reading, and they take their positions (with their backs to the audience).

The Cat and the Parrot enter through the audience. They walk side by side, showing their friendship. They introduce themselves and the parts they are reading. They take their positions.

All readers open their scripts, and the tale begins.

The Cat and the Parrot (cont.)

Narrator 1: There was once a cat and a parrot who were very good friends. One day they agreed to take turns inviting each other for dinner. It was the cat's turn first, but the cat, being a very greedy cat, did not like to share.

Cat: All I shall give the parrot is a pint of milk, one small slice of fish, and a bit of rice which he may cook for himself.

Narrator 2: The parrot, being a very polite parrot, did not complain, but he did not have a very good time. Next it was the parrot's turn.

Parrot: Ah yes, I shall offer a fine and elegant meal. This will teach my friend, the cat, how entertaining should be done. I'll roast meat, brew a pot of tea, and fill a basket with juicy fruits. Best of all, I'll bake 500 little spicy cakes — a laundry basket full! 498 for the cat, and two little cakes for me.

Narrator 1: The greedy cat arrived, never bothering to say hello. He sat and immediately gobbled down everything set before him, including the 498 little spicy cakes.

The Cat and the Parrot *(cont.)*

Cat: I'm hungry. What else have you to eat?

Parrot: Only these two little spicy cakes I saved for myself, but you may have them, if you please.

Narrator 1: The cat gulped down the last two little cakes and looked around for more.

Parrot: I'm sorry, there's nothing more — unless you want to eat me. Ha, ha!

Narrator 1: The cat licked his chops and then . . .

Cat: (The Cat winks and licks his lips.)

All: Slip! Slop! Gobble! Down went the parrot!

Parrot: (The Parrot bows his head.)

Narrator 3: An old woman who happened to be standing nearby saw all this. She scolded the cat.

Old Woman: (The Old Woman turns to face the audience.) You naughty cat, how dreadful of you to eat your friend the parrot.

The Cat and the Parrot (cont.)

Cat: Friend? Indeed! What's a parrot to me? I've a good mind to eat you, too. (The Cat winks and licks his lips.)

Narrator 1: And then—

All: Slip! Slop! Gobble! Down went the old woman. (The Old Woman bows her head.)

Narrator 3: The cat strolled down the road and soon he met an old man with a donkey. The old man tugged and tugged, urging his stubborn donkey to hurry up. Then he saw the cat.

Old Man: (The Old Man turns to face the audience.) Get out of my way, cat! Don't you see I'm in a hurry. I fear my donkey might kick you.

Cat: Kick me! Indeed! What's a donkey to me?

I've eaten 500 spicy cakes.

I've eaten my friend the parrot.

I've eaten an old woman.

And I've a good mind to eat you, too.

Cat: (The Cat winks and licks his lips.)

The Cat and the Parrot *(cont.)*

Narrator 1: And then—

All: Slip! Slop! Gobble! Down went the old man and his donkey.

Old Man: (The Old Man bows his head.)

Narrator 1: The cat walked further on down the road where he met a royal procession.

Narrator 3: The king was at the head, proudly escorting his new bride. Behind him, his men-at-arms marched in single file, and behind them were ever so many elephants paraded two by two. The king, just married, was feeling rather kind. He smiled at the cat.

King: (The King turns to face the audience.) Please, pussy cat, step aside. I don't want my elephants to trample you.

Cat: Trample me? Indeed!

I've eaten 500 spicy cakes.

I've eaten my friend the parrot.

I've eaten an old woman.

I've eaten an old man and his donkey.

And I've a good mind to eat you, too.

(The Cat winks and licks his lips.)

The Cat and the Parrot (cont.)

Narrator 1: And then—

All: Slip! Slop! Gobble! Down went the king, down went the queen, down went his men-at-arms, and down went the elephants two by two!

King: (The King bows his head.)

Narrator 1: The cat walked on but much more slowly. His belly was very fat, and he really was quite full.

Cat: (The Cat pats his very fat belly.)

Narrator 3: But, then he met two land crabs scuttling across the road.

Land Crabs: (The Land Crabs turn to face the audience.) Get out of our way, Cat, or we will nip you.

Cat: Nip me? Indeed!

I've eaten 500 little spicy cakes.

I've eaten my friend the parrot.

I've eaten an old woman.

I've eaten an old man and his donkey.

I've eaten a king, a queen, his men-at-arms and ever so many elephants.

And now I'm going to eat you, too.

The Cat and the Parrot (cont.)

Narrator 1: And then—

All: Slip! Slop! Gobble! Down went the Land Crabs.

Land Crabs: (The Land Crabs bow their heads. Slowly, they raise their heads again and pretend to look around.)

Narrator 3: Down inside the cat, the land crabs began to look around. It was dark and rather crowded.

King: (The King raises his head and pantomimes patting his bride's head.) The unhappy king sat in a corner, holding his bride who had fainted. His men-at-arms scrambled about, treading upon each other's toes. And the elephants tried ever so hard to line up two by two.

Narrator 3: In the opposite corner . . .

Old Woman: (The Old Woman raises her head.) . . . sat the old woman, feeling very grumpy.

Narrator 3: Next to her . . .

Old Man: (The Old Man raises his head.) . . . the old man stood, still tugging his stubborn donkey.

The Cat and the Parrot (cont.)

Narrator 3: And, in the middle of them all was a great pile of 500 little spicy cakes! And, on top of the pile . . .

Parrot: (The Parrot raises his head.) . . . perched the parrot, his colorful feathers dull and droopy.

Narrator 3: The Land Crabs snapped their claws.

Land Crabs: Let's get to work! Snip, snap.

Narrator 3: They cut a hole in the side of the cat.

Land Crabs: Snip, snap, snip, snap.

Narrator 3: And when the hole was big enough . . .

Land Crabs: (The Land Crabs stand up as if squeezing through a hole and then shake themselves a little when they are free.) . . . out scuttled the land crabs.

King: (The King stands up, pretending to be holding his bride, who is getting very heavy.) And out staggered the king, carrying his bride in his arms.

Narrator 3: Out marched his men-at-arms in a single file. And out paraded ever so many elephants, tramping two by two.

The Cat and the Parrot (cont.)

Man: (The Old Man stands up, pretending to pull his donkey.) Out came the old man, still urging his stubborn donkey to hurry up.

Old Woman: (The Old Woman stands up, shaking her finger at the cat.) Out strolled the old woman, who stopped to scold the cat.

Parrot: (The Parrot stands up and pantomimes nibbling a cake.) Out hopped the parrot with his two little spicy cakes.

Narrator 2: Which was all he had wanted in the first place.

Narrator 1: And the poor old cat spent that day and the next sewing up the hole in his side.

Cat: (The Cat pantomimes sewing up his side.)

All: Stitch, stitch, stitch.

The Honey Gatherer's Three Sons

A Folk Tale from Central Africa

(Scripted for Ten Readers)

All the African cultures have a rich and varied tradition of storytelling. This is a tale told to Congolese children by the elders of the village. It teaches the importance of cooperation.

The Honey Gatherer's Three Sons

Cast of Characters

Narrator 1
Honey Gatherer
Narrator 2
Hear
Narrator 3
Follow
Narrator 4
Piece
Bees (2 readers)

(The Bees' part may also be used as audience participation.)

Stage Setup:

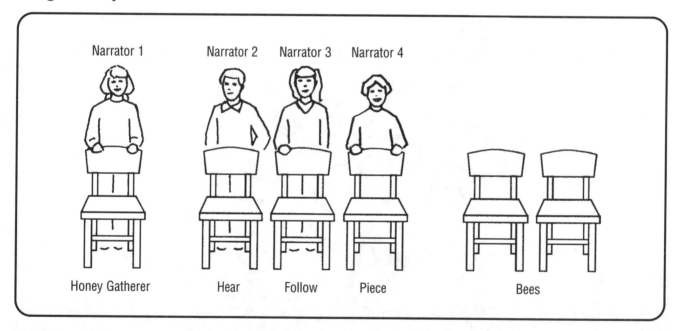

Entrance:

All readers (except the Bees) enter the performance area single file. They take their positions. The Honey Gatherer introduces the folk tale. All the characters introduce themselves and the parts they will be reading.

The Bees then enter buzzing. They make their way through the audience and then they take their positions and introduce themselves and their parts.

All readers open their scripts and the story begins.

The Honey Gatherer's Three Sons (cont.)

Narrator 1: A honey gatherer had three sons. They were all born at the same moment in time and were all equal in every way.

Narrator 2: Except that each son had a surprising power and was so named.

Hear: I was named Hear-It-However-Faint-the-Sound.

Follow: I was named Follow-It-However-Great-the-Distance.

Piece: I am Piece-It-Together-However-Small-the-Pieces.

Narrator 2: Their names were so long their friends just called them . . .

Hear: . . . Hear . . .

Follow: . . . Follow . . .

Piece: . . . and Piece.

Narrator 1: One day the honey gatherer went deep into the forest. He walked further and further from the village until he came to a tree that was as high as a hill.

Bees: Buzzzzzzzzzzzzz.

The Honey Gatherer's Three Sons (cont.)

Honey Gatherer: That tree must be full of honey.

Narrator 1: So the honey gatherer climbed up into the tree. Higher and higher he climbed.

Honey Gatherer: Suddenly a branch broke . . .

All: Crack!

Narrator 1: . . . and he fell to the ground . . .

Honey Gatherer: . . . and broke into ten pieces. (The honey gatherer slumps in the chair as if he has fallen.)

Narrator 2: Hear was sitting by the hut in the village.

Hear: Oh no! Father just fell from a tree. Hurry! We must help him.

Narrator 3: His brother, Follow, said . . .

Follow: Follow me, I will lead the way.

Narrator 3: They followed their father's tracks deep into the forest until they came upon his body lying in ten pieces.

The Honey Gatherer's Three Sons (cont.)

Piece: I will fix him . . .

Narrator 4: . . . said Piece, and he put all ten pieces together and carefully fastened them up.

Honey Gatherer: (sitting up again) And the father walked home while the sons carried his honey.

Narrator 1: The next day the honey gatherer again went out to look for honey.

Narrator 2: His sons sat at home.

Narrator 3: Each one bragged.

Narrator 4: Each thought he was more important than the others.

Hear: Without me you would not have heard Father.

Follow: Without me you would not have found Father.

Piece: Without me you would not have put Father back together again.

The Honey Gatherer's Three Sons (cont.)

Narrator 1: Meanwhile, the old honey gatherer walked deeper and deeper into the forest until he came to a tree as high as the clouds.

Bees: Buzzzzzzzzzzzzzzzzz. The bees buzzed in and out.

Honey Gatherer: That tree must be full of honey.

Narrator 1: So the honey gatherer climbed up and up into the tree until he could almost touch the clouds.

Honey Gatherer: Suddenly a branch broke.

All: Crack!

Narrator 1: He fell to the ground . . .

Honey Gatherer: . . . and broke into 100 pieces. (He slumps in the chair as if he has fallen.)

Narrator 2: His sons were still sitting at home, bragging about their powers when Hear said . . .

Hear: Father has just fallen!

The Honey Gatherer's Three Sons (cont.)

Narrator 3: Follow reluctantly set out to follow the footprints. At last they found the 100 pieces on the ground. He said . . .

Follow: See how important I am. I have found Father for you.

Narrator 4: Piece grudgingly put the honey gatherer together, saying . . .

Piece: I and I alone have fixed Father.

Honey Gatherer: (sitting up again) And, the father walked home while the sons carried his honey.

Narrator 1: On the third day the honey gatherer again set out to look for honey. This time he went further than ever before into the forest. There he found a tree that reached to the stars.

Bees: Buzzzzzzzzzzzzzzzzz. The bees buzzed in and out.

Honey Gatherer: That tree must be full of honey.

Narrator 1: So the honey gatherer climbed up and up into the tree. Higher and higher he climbed until he could almost touch the stars.

The Honey Gatherer's Three Sons (cont.)

Honey Gatherer: Suddenly a branch broke.

All: Crack!

Narrator 1: He fell to the ground . . .

Honey Gatherer: . . . .and broke into 1,000 pieces. (The Honey Gatherer slumps in the chair as if he has fallen.)

Narrator 2: Hear heard the fall.

Hear: I will not tell my brothers.

Narrator 3: When their father did not return, Follow knew there must have been an accident.

Follow: I will not show my brothers the way.

Narrator 4: Piece would not ask his brothers for help.

Piece: They will think they are more important than me.

Narrator 1: And, so the old honey gatherer still lies in 1,000 pieces . . .

Narrator 2: . . . while his selfish sons still argue . . .

The Honey Gatherer's Three Sons (cont.)

Narrator 3: . . . about who is the best.

Narrator 4: The truth is . . .

Honey Gatherer: (The Honey Gatherer sits up again.)

All: . . . we all need each other.

Coyote Rings the Bell

A Folk Tale from Mexico

(Scripted for Five Readers)

In Mexican folklore, Coyote often plays the trickster; however, he does not always succeed. In this tale he meets his match.

Coyote Rings the Bell

Cast of Characters

Narrator 1

Narrator 2

Hare

Narrator 3

Coyote

Stage Setup:

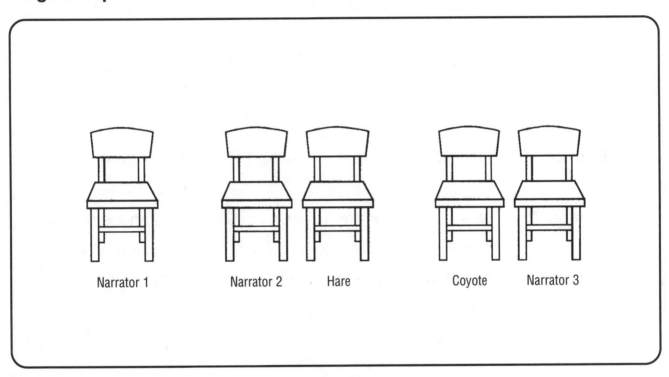

| Narrator 1 | Narrator 2 | Hare | Coyote | Narrator 3 |

Entrance:

Narrator 1 enters the performance area. Standing in the center, he introduces the folk tale and then himself and the part he will be reading. Narrator 1 then takes his position.

Narrator 2 and Hare enter the performance area and appear to be chatting. They take their positions and introduce themselves and the parts they will be reading.

Narrator 3 and Coyote enter from the opposite side of the performing area. They appear to be looking off in the distance, trying to spy Hare. They take their positions and introduce themselves and the parts they will be reading.

All readers open their scripts, and the story begins.

Coyote Rings the Bell (cont.)

Narrator 1: Coyote and Hare were rivals since time began.

Narrator 2: Coyote was fast, strong, and crafty.

Coyote: (Coyote steams his claws and polishes them on his chest.)

Narrator 3: Hare was fast, clever, and tricky.

Hare: (Hare hooks his thumbs under his armpits and sticks out his chest.)

Narrator 1: Whenever they met, each tried to outwit the other.

Narrator 2: One day after Hare finished munching a grand lunch of carrots, jicama, and tomatillos, he stretched out in the shade of a large tree for his afternoon siesta. He watched the leaves dance in the soft breeze until he fell fast asleep.

Hare: (Hare bows his head as if sleeping.)

Narrator 1: Now that same afternoon it just so happened that Coyote was on the prowl. Coyote was grumpy. Coyote was hungry.

Narrator 3: When he spied Hare sleeping under the tree, he crept closer and closer, ever so quietly, closer and closer until . . .

Coyote Rings the Bell (cont.)

All: Pounce!

Narrator 3: Plop! He landed with all four of his paws right on top of Hare.

Coyote: At last I have you! Now you are mine, Hare. My, you are round. My, you are fat. What a nice lunch you must have had. And mmm, what a nice lunch you will be for me.

Narrator 3: Coyote licked his lips.

Narrator 2: Hare thought fast.

Hare: Si, amigo. I had a fine meal indeed. Too fine a meal for a poor old hare such as me. I am old, amigo, old and tough, dry and stringy. So old that you might as well eat me, for I haven't long to live anyway.

Narrator 3: Coyote sat down on top of Hare and licked his lips again.

Narrator 2: Coyote was heavy. Hare had trouble breathing.

Hare: (gasping for air) Si, Coyote, you might as well eat me, unless of course, you would prefer something a bit more tender.

Coyote Rings the Bell (cont.)

Coyote: More tender? But what could be more tender than a nice, fat hare?

Hare: Why, little hares, of course!

Narrator 3: Coyote's ears perked up.

Hare: Lots of juicy little hares that play on this hill.

Narrator 3: Coyote glanced all around. His eyes narrowed.

Coyote: I am too smart for you, Hare. I know there are no little hares here.

Hare: No, not now. They are all in school.

Coyote: Mmm, little hares so soft and juicy. Tell me, amigo, where is this school?

Narrator 2: Hare squirmed under Coyote's weight.

Hare: The schoolhouse is not far from here. But you have only to wait until I ring the bell. Then all the little juicy hares come running out to play.

Coyote Rings the Bell (cont.)

Coyote: Bell? What bell?

Hare: The one I ring when the sun arches down and touches the tops of the trees on that far hill.

Narrator 3: Now Coyote had a plan.

Coyote: And where might this bell be?

Hare: It's right up there in this tree.
(Hare points overhead.)

Narrator 3: Coyote looked up. He turned his head this way. He turned his head that way, trying to see. At last he spied something large and round hanging from a branch high in the tree.

Coyote: And all those tender, soft, juicy, sweet, little hares come running when you ring that bell?

Hare: Si, but I can't ring the bell yet. It is too early.

Coyote: But if you did ring the bell now, would they come?

Hare: Certainly, but it is too early, amigo.

Narrator 3: Coyote grinned his friendliest grin.

Coyote Rings the Bell (cont.)

Coyote: Hare, old friend, I am not very hungry just now. I'm afraid I would not enjoy you if I ate you, and what a waste that would be.

Narrator 3: Coyote stood up and removed each of his paws from on top of Hare.

Narrator 2: Hare stretched himself slowly, keeping one eye on Coyote all the time.

Coyote: Poor old Hare. You must be stiff. Why don't you take a nice long walk and loosen up? A very long walk. Don't worry about the bell. I will ring it for you.

Hare: A little run would feel good. But remember, do not ring the bell before the sun touches the tops of those trees.

Coyote: No, no, of course not. But wait! You must tell me how to ring the bell. I don't see a rope to pull.

Hare: There is no rope. Just shake the tree. Shake it as hard as you can, and all the tender little hares will come running out to play.

Narrator 3: Coyote smiled. Coyote grinned. Coyote licked his lips again.

Coyote Rings the Bell (cont.)

Coyote: Don't worry, Hare, I'll shake it good and hard. Now be off with you, old friend.

Narrator 2: Hare was off in a flash. He paused when he was a safe distance away and called back.

Hare: Don't forget, wait until the sun touches the trees.

Coyote: Of course, Hare, I will wait.

Narrator 3: But, as soon as Hare was out of sight, Coyote leaned against the tree and shook it hard.

Narrator 1: Nothing happened.

Narrator 3: So he shook and shook, harder and harder, with all his might.

Narrator 1: Still no bell rang.

Narrator 3: Coyote backed up several yards and charged into the tree, giving it a most violent shake.

All: Kerplop!

Narrator 1: Down came the thing that was large and round and hanging high in the tree.

Coyote Rings the Bell (cont.)

Narrator 3: It landed on Coyote's head!

Narrator 1: Suddenly the air was thick with hornets.

All: Buzzzzzzzz! Buzzzzzzzz!

Narrator 1: Angry hornets. Furious hornets. Coyote had knocked down their nest. To teach him a lesson, they stung Coyote from the tip of his nose to the end of his tail.

Narrator 3: And Coyote howled and yowled all the way home to his den.

Narrator 2: There he licked his stings instead of eating tender, juicy, little hares.

Beetle and Paca

A Folk Tale from Brazil

(Scripted for Four Readers)

This tale of wits tells how Brazilian beetles came to be as beautiful as jewels. The folk tale comes from the Amazon region where the beetles are, in fact, worn as jewelry.

Beetle and Paca

Cast of Characters

Narrator

Beetle

Parrot

Paca

Stage Setup:

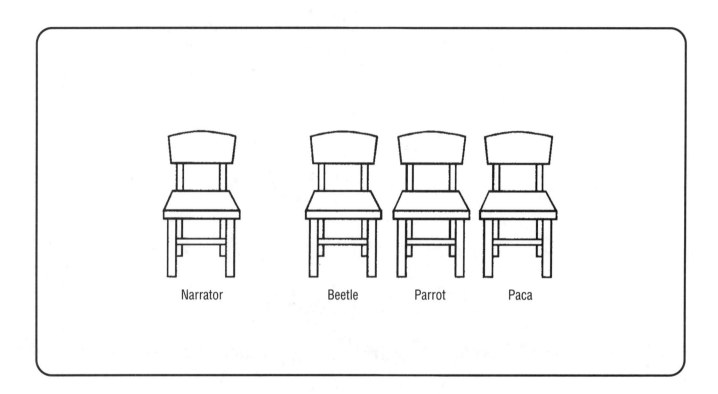

Entrance:

The Narrator enters the performance area. He introduces the folk tale. He introduces himself and the part he will be reading. He takes his position.

Beetle and Parrot enter together. They introduce themselves and the parts they will be reading and then they take their places.

Paca comes running in. He circles around the performers and then takes his place and introduces himself and the part he will be reading.

All open their scripts, and the tale begins.

Beetle and Paca (cont.)

Beetle: In the lush jungles along the Amazon River, there are beetles with green and gold coats that sparkle like jewels. In the patchy sun their emerald backs glisten as if dusted with gold.

Narrator: But, these beetles were not always so. In other times, long ago, their coats were a dullish shade of brown.

Beetle: On one of those days . . .

Narrator: . . . in fact, the last of those days . . .

Beetle: . . . one of those little brown beetles was crawling along the riverbank. Bit by bit he made his way beside the great Amazon River.

Narrator: Overhead, a bright green parrot preened on a jungle vine.

Parrot: Good day, Beetle.

Narrator: This, of course, was in the days when all living things could speak to one another.

Beetle and Paca (cont.)

Beetle: A good day to you, friend Parrot. You are looking quite fine today.

Narrator: Just then a paca came charging out of the bushes. He was running so fast, he barely stopped before landing in the river.

Paca: (panting) Good day, Parrot. Good day, Beetle. What are you two doing on this bright and lovely morning?

Parrot: Just resting.

Beetle: Not me. I'm on a journey.

Paca: A journey? Ha, ha! Listen to that, Parrot! Old slowpoke here is going on a journey. Why old Beetle creeps so slowly no one can even tell he's moving, and he's going on a journey? Ha, ha! Watch this!

Narrator: With that, Paca dashed back and forth along the riverbank, showing off his amazing speed.

Paca: See, Beetle! That's the kind of speed you need for a journey.

Beetle and Paca (cont.)

Parrot: You're boastful today, friend Paca. Why don't you and our friend Beetle have a race? Both of you go as fast as you can to that big tree at the next bend in the river. The one who gets there first wins. The prize shall be a fine new coat of the winner's choice.

Paca: A race? A fine new coat? Bravo! I am sure to win! Friend Parrot, I want a coat just like Jaguar's. Golden yellow with sleek black spots. And a tail! Yes! I want a tail, long and twitchy like Jaguar's.

Narrator: As everyone knows, a paca's tail is so short it is almost no tail at all, and his fur is dull brown with faded white spots. No wonder he envied Jaguar.

Beetle: If I should win, friend Parrot, I should like a coat as green as the sunlight on your emerald feather and splashed with gold from your yellow head.

Parrot: So be it.

Beetle and Paca: Ready.

Beetle and Paca (cont.)

Parrot: Go!

Narrator: The race began.

Paca: I'm off! Good-bye, Beetle.

Narrator: Paca called back over his shoulder, but after running a few steps, he slowed down.

Paca: Why should I hurry? A race with old slowpoke Beetle is the same as no race at all!

Narrator: Paca stopped for a drink of cool water from the river. Then he trotted along at a comfortable pace to the big tree at the next bend.

Paca: Beetle was there, sunning himself on the tree trunk!

Beetle: Where have you been, Paca? What a slowpoke you are! What took you so long?

Paca: How did you get here before me, Beetle? How did you run so fast?

Beetle and Paca (cont.)

Beetle: I did not run, Paca.

Paca: Well, you certainly could not crawl that fast!

Beetle: I did not crawl, Paca.

Paca: Did you swim, Beetle? But how could you swim as fast as I can run?

Beetle: I did not swim either, Paca, yet I got here first.

Paca: It must be a trick. You tricked me.

Beetle: It's not a trick, Paca. I flew! Have you forgotten that beetles can fly?

Parrot: Remember, Paca, I did not say whether you had to run or to crawl or to swim. All I said was you must both go.

Beetle: Yes, go as fast as you can! And I did! I reached the tree first, Paca. So, I guess the new coat is mine.

Beetle and Paca (cont.)

Paca: Paca hung his head.

Narrator: So proud of his own running, Paca, indeed, had forgotten that beetles can fly.

Paca: Paca walked off into the bushes, wearing his same old brown coat with faded little white spots.

Beetle: Come back, Paca. Admire my emerald-green coat. Count its thousands of specks of gold, each shining like a tiny sun. Come back, Paca.

Paca: But Paca did not come back.

Narrator: And to this day, Paca's coat is drab with small white spots, not at all like Jaguar's. Nor is his tail. It is still almost no tail at all.

Beetle: While Beetle wears a coat that sparkles like a jewel in the sun.

The End

The Weary Spirits of Lanai

A Folk Tale from Hawaii

(Scripted for Seven Readers)

Polynesian folklores are rich with legends of creation and how things came to be. This tale tells how the island of Lanai became a paradise.

The Weary Spirits of Lanai

Cast of Characters

Narrator

King

Ka-ulu

Queen

First Evil Spirit

Second Evil Spirit

Third Evil Spirit

Stage Setup:

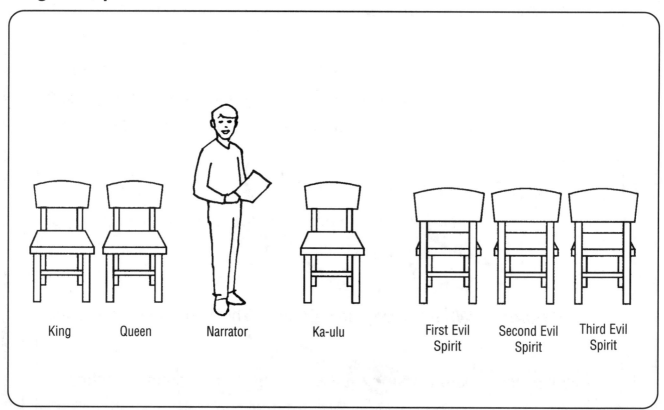

Entrance:

The Narrator enters the performance area. Standing in the center he introduces the folk tale and then himself and the part he will be reading. The Narrator takes his position.

All other readers enter singly, take their positions, and introduce themselves and the parts they will be reading. (After the Spirits introduce themselves, they sit with their backs to the audience.)

All readers open their scripts, and the tale begins.

The Weary Spirits of Lanai *(cont.)*

Narrator: Long, long ago the island of Maui was ruled by a great chief king. So great was this king, his people composed songs in his honor.

King: While other kings waged war, the Maui king ordered his men to plant great groves of breadfruit trees so his people always had plenty to eat and shelter from the hot sun.

Ka-ulu: The king and queen had a son named Ka-ulu. Ka-ulu grew up full of mischief, caring for nothing but his own fun. Time after time he led his companions racing through newly planted sweet potatoes, crushing young banana shoots, and trampling tender taro plantings.

Narrator: One day when Ka-ulu and his companions arrived at their favorite clearing, they found workers there, digging and planting.

Ka-ulu: What are you doing here? This is our playing ground.

Narrator: The workmen answered, "We are planting another breadfruit grove. Your father the king ordered it."

Ka-ulu: Breadfruit! Breadfruit! That's all he cares about!

The Weary Spirits of Lanai (cont.)

Narrator: That night in the dark, Ka-ulu slipped out and uprooted all the new breadfruit cuttings in the clearing.

King: When the king heard of the damage, he ordered his guards to find the culprit. To plant a breadfruit tree brings honor, but to destroy one brings death.

Ka-ulu: Ka-ulu was brought before the king.

Queen: The queen pleaded. No, my husband! Not death for our only son.

King: He shall be banished then, banished to the desolate island of Lanai.

Queen: But there are only evil spirits on Lanai. Surely our son will die.

King: Since Ka-ulu is interested only in tricks, let him try his trickery on the spirits.

Queen: The queen wept.

Ka-ulu: Don't worry, Mother. I shall find a way to outwit the spirits and make up the wrongs I have done. When you see a signal fire burning on the shore of Lanai, you'll know I have succeeded.

The Weary Spirits of Lanai (cont.)

Narrator: The king's canoe-men left Ka-ulu on the forsaken shore of Lanai. Ka-ulu stared across the lonely sea to his distant home on Maui. At his feet lay his water gourd, his food calabash, and a sleeping mat.

Ka-ulu: When Ka-ulu picked up his sleeping mat, it unrolled. A bundle wrapped in damp ti leaves fell out. Inside the bundle were taro and breadfruit plantings.

Queen: His mother had hidden them there.

Ka-ulu: Ka-ulu picked them up gently. He found a dry cave far up the beach and stowed his belongings there. Then he went inland to plant his taro and breadfruit.

Narrator: While returning, Ka-ulu met four of the dreaded evil spirits. Their pale, unwinking eyes studied him greedily.

First Evil Spirit: (turning to face the audience) Welcome to our island. Have you found a place to sleep tonight?

Ka-ulu: I have, thank you. I shall sleep in that pitch of thick green vines.

First Evil Spirit: The spirits looked at each other and smiled, knowing what vicious thorns grew on those vines.

The Weary Spirits of Lanai (cont.)

Narrator: That night, safe in his warm dry cave, Ka-ulu heard sharp cries from the spirits as they tramped through the thorny vines, searching for him.

First Evil Spirit: In the morning the spirits greeted Ka-ulu crossly. Did you sleep well?

Ka-ulu: Very well, thank you. I heard some cries in the night but not enough to disturb me. Sea birds, no doubt. Tonight I shall sleep in that tall tree, away from the water.

Narrator: Snug in his cave that night, Ka-ulu heard shouts and blows as the spirits struck at the tall tree, searching for him.

First Evil Spirit: The next morning they greeted him sullenly. Sleep well?

Ka-ulu: Very well, thank you. The tree rocked and the wind howled but not enough to disturb me. Tonight I shall try that little cave down where the surf breaks.

Narrator: That night Ka-ulu could not even hear the spirits as they thrashed about in the big surf, looking in all the caves.

The Weary Spirits of Lanai (cont.)

First Evil Spirit: The next morning, soaked in seawater, the spirits spoke no greeting at all.

Ka-ulu: Such a restful sleep I had. The best I've had so far, and that is fortunate since I have important work to do today. I must cultivate my breadfruit.

First Evil Spirit: The spirits jeered. No breadfruit grows on this island.

Ka-ulu: It grows here now. I planted it the day I arrived. When it bears fruit, I shall eat tasty breadfruit baked in the coals.

First Evil Spirit: Show us where it grows! This is our island. The breadfruit belongs to us!

Ka-ulu: Not so. No one shares the breadfruit unless he shares the work.

First Evil Spirit: Then show us what to do.

Narrator: From dawn to dusk, Ka-ulu kept the spirits busy clearing, weeding, and digging around his breadfruit plantings. The evening star shone down on a well-cultivated breadfruit grove, four weary spirits, and a cheerful Ka-ulu.

The Weary Spirits of Lanai (cont.)

Second Evil Spirit: (turning to face the audience) The next morning there were eight spirits instead of four. We heard about your breadfruit. We have come for our share.

Ka-ulu: Sorry. No work in the breadfruit grove today. There is too much to do in the taro patch.

Second Evil Spirit: Taro patch? There is no taro patch on this island.

Ka-ulu: There is now. I planted it the day I arrived. When my taro roots are ready for pulling, I shall eat freshly pounded poi.

Second Evil Spirit: This is our island! The taro belongs to us! Show us where it grows.

First Evil Spirit: Not so! No one shares the taro unless he shares the work!

Narrator: From dawn to dusk Ka-ulu kept the eight spirits busy building terraces, carrying water, and flooding the young taro plants. The rising moon shone down on a well-flooded taro patch, eight weary spirits, and a smiling Ka-ulu.

The Weary Spirits of Lanai (cont.)

Third Evil Spirit: (turning to face the audience) The following morning there were twelve spirits. We heard about your taro. We have come for our share.

Ka-ulu: Sorry. No work in the taro patch today. Too much to be done on the fishpond.

Third Evil Spirit: There is no fishpond on this island. Who needs a fishpond with a sea full of fish?

Ka-ulu: No one if you are willing to wait for the right season, the right weather, and a day when the fish are biting. But with my own fishpond, I shall have fresh-caught fish whenever I choose.

Third Evil Spirit: This is our island! The fish belong to us!

Narrator: Each of the last four spirits picked up a stone and moved towards Ka-ulu.

First and Second Evil Spirits: Not so! No one shares the fish unless he shares the work!

Ka-ulu: Gather more stones like the ones in your hands. Bigger ones. Heavier ones.

The Weary Spirits of Lanai (cont.)

Narrator: From dawn to dusk, Ka-ulu kept the twelve spirits busy gathering stones, passing them along the line, building the walls of the fishpond. The evening breeze swept over a well-built fishpond, twelve weary spirits, and a satisfied Ka-ulu. So the day passed, and the barren island of Lanai became a green paradise.

First Evil Spirit: The spirits had never been so well fed, nor so weary. We finish one job, and Ka-ulu comes up with another.

Second Evil Spirit: Before he came we didn't have to work at all. How much longer does this go on?

Third Evil Spirit: Be patient a little longer. The crops are flourishing. Soon we can do away with Ka-ulu and have all the food for ourselves.

Narrator: Ka-ulu, hiding in the darkness, grinned. Next morning he called the spirits together.

Ka-ulu: The dry season is coming. We must build a watercourse to bring water to our fields, or our crops will surely die. High in the mountains there is a stream. If we start today, clearing the stream bed and building walls, we can have the job done in three months. Hurry! Get digging sticks and meet me back here right away.

The Weary Spirits of Lanai *(cont.)*

All Spirits: Three months? Three more months?

Narrator: Scowling, the twelve evil spirits went off for digging sticks while Ka-ulu walked along the beach, gathering and piling driftwood.

Ka-ulu: Ten minutes passed. Fifteen. Twenty. Then came a great splashing!

Third Evil Spirit: All twelve evil spirits were swimming away from Lanai . . .

All Spirits: . . . as fast as they could swim.

Ka-ulu: Chuckling, Ka-ulu gathered more firewood, enough wood to build a great signal fire . . .

Queen: . . . a signal fire that could be seen from the Maui shore, where the queen waited for a sign from her son.

Baba Yaga Bony-Legs

A Folk Tale from Russia

(Scripted for Seven Readers)

Folklores from Russia are rich with peasants, tzars, dark forests, trying times, and clever solutions. This folklore features a Russian witch, Baba Yaga. Witches appear in folk tales from many cultures, but none are as colorful and distinctive as the Russian Baba Yaga.

Baba Yaga Bony-Legs

Cast of Characters

Narrator
Stepmother
Girl
Gate
Baba Yaga
Cat
Dog

Stage Setup:

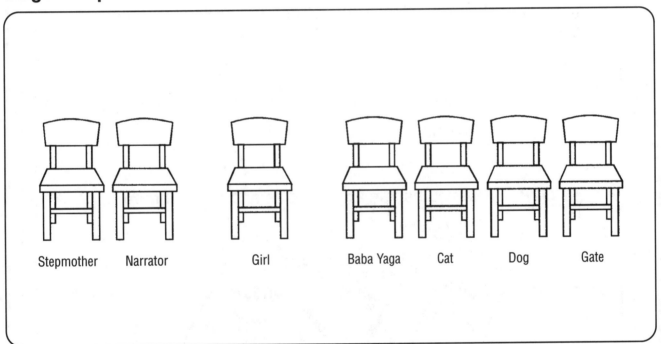

Entrance:

The Narrator enters the performance area. Standing in the center, he or she introduces the folk tale and then him- or herself and the part he or she will be reading. The Narrator takes his or her position.

All other readers enter singly and then introduce themselves and the parts they will be reading.

All readers open their scripts, and the tale begins.

Baba Yaga Bony-Legs (cont.)

Narrator: Long ago, in a small cottage next to a deep, dark forest, there lived a young girl with her father and new stepmother.

Stepmother: The stepmother did not like the girl very much and decided to get rid of her.

Narrator: So when the girl's father was away one day, the stepmother sent her to visit Baba Yaga Bony-Legs, the old witch who lived deep in the forest.

Stepmother: Go to my sister who lives in the woods and ask for a needle and thread. Bring it back, and I shall sew you a new shift.

Girl: But you have many needles and much thread, Stepmother.

Stepmother: Never mind. Do as I say, and be sure to tell my sister that I sent you.

Girl: The girl knew her stepmother was up to no good. Only wolves and baba yagas (who are witches) lived in the woods. She didn't know what to do.

Baba Yaga Bony-Legs (cont.)

Stepmother: For the journey, the stepmother gave her a piece of stale bread and a bone with a little meat left on it.

Girl: The girl wrapped the scraps of food in her handkerchief and set off into the woods. She walked and walked deeper and deeper into the dark forest. At long last she came to a small clearing.

Narrator: A thick stand of birch trees guarded the clearing.

Girl: Their branches clawed the girl's hair as she made her way through them.

Narrator: In the middle of the clearing, Baba Yaga's hut was perched on two large chicken legs. The hut circled around and around, around and around, and no one could enter. A fence of bones surrounded the hut.

Gate: A fence of bones with a staring gate — a staring gate that creaked loudly when the girl opened it, announcing her arrival.

Girl: Stop, little hut. Stop with your back to the forest and your face to me.

Narrator: The hut stopped turning.

Baba Yaga Bony-Legs (cont.)

Girl: The girl stepped inside . . .

Baba Yaga: . . . and there was Baba Yaga Bony-Legs, the old witch herself!

Narrator: She was huge with long, bony legs and arms. She sat at her loom with her head facing the door and her feet in either corner of the hut. Her wild hair rubbed the ceiling. Her mouth was full of gnashing iron teeth.

Baba Yaga: What do you want? And who sent you?

Girl: Your sister sent me to ask for a needle and thread.

Baba Yaga: My sister sent you? Excellent! Sit down and weave, my dear, while I fetch a needle and thread.

Girl: The girl sat down at the loom, too frightened to weave.

Narrator: With the loom not clacking, she could hear Baba Yaga talking to her servant-maid outside.

Baba Yaga: Go and heat the bath. Then get my niece washed and clean. I shall eat her for breakfast.

Baba Yaga Bony-Legs (cont.)

Narrator: When Baba Yaga left, the girl called the servant-maid. She offered her handkerchief as a gift.

Girl: Please, please, dear friend, wet the wood for the fire so that it will not burn. And bring the water for the bath in a leaky sieve.

Narrator: Baba Yaga waited awhile and then returned.

Baba Yaga: Are you weaving, Niece? Are you weaving, my dear?

Girl: Yes, Auntie, I'm weaving.

Narrator: Clackety-clack, clackety-clack went the loom.

Cat: Baba Yaga's scrawny cat came into the room.

Girl: Oh please, dear cat, is there no way of escaping here?

Narrator: She gave the cat her piece of bread.

Baba Yaga: Are you weaving, dear Niece? Are you weaving?

Girl: Yes, Auntie.

Baba Yaga Bony-Legs (cont.)

Baba Yaga: Good, my dear. I'll be right back.

Cat: Take that towel and Baba Yaga's comb and run from here, or she will gnash you between her iron teeth. Run as fast as you can. She will follow you, but if she gets near, throw down the towel and then the comb.

Narrator: Before slipping out the door of the hut, the girl grabbed the bottle of oil that was standing next to Baba Yaga's lamp.

Girl: Thank you, dear cat, thank you.

Cat: The cat sat down at the loom, clackety-clack, clackety-clack. Unaccustomed to weaving, he made a dreadful mess of it all.

Dog: When the girl stepped down into the yard, a snarling dog came lunging at her. Its bared teeth were all yellow and pointed.

Girl: She gave the dog her last scrap of food, the bone with a little meat left on it.

Dog: The dog wagged his tail and let her pass.

Baba Yaga Bony-Legs (cont.)

Girl: She tiptoed to the fence and poured oil on the creaky hinges of the gate.

Gate: The gate let her slip through silently.

Narrator: But when she reached the stand of birch trees, they caught her in their branches. They held her tightly. They would let her go no further.

Girl: Quickly she pulled a ribbon from her hair and tied up a branch.

Narrator: Immediately, all the birch trees lifted their branches together and let her pass.

Girl: Then she ran and ran and ran!

Narrator: In the meantime, Baba Yaga heard the loom clacking, and she didn't hurry back into her hut.

Baba Yaga: Are you weaving, dear Niece? Are you weaving?

Cat: Yes, Auntie, I'm weaving.

Baba Yaga Bony-Legs (cont.)

Narrator: The cat tried to disguise his voice but . . .

Baba Yaga: . . . in burst Baba Yaga. You stupid cat! You let her go! Why didn't you scratch her eyes out?

Cat: I have served you long. I have served you well. But never have you given me anything to eat. She gave me a piece of bread.

Narrator: Baba Yaga stormed out into the yard and pounced on the dog.

Baba Yaga: Why didn't you bark and bite and growl! You worthless cur!

Dog: I have served you long and well, but you've never even given me a burnt crust. She gave me a bone with meat!

Baba Yaga: And gate! Why didn't you creak? I should stomp you into splinters!

Gate: She oiled my hinges, Baba Yaga. You have never so much as put a drop of water on them.

Baba Yaga: Baba Yaga Bony-Legs was furious. She jumped into her iron kettle and grabbed her broom.

Baba Yaga Bony-Legs (cont.)

Narrator: The kettle flew, thumpety-bump, thumpety-bump, along the ground, making a frightful sound. All the while, Baba Yaga swept away the traces of her flight with the broom.

Girl: Deep in the forest, the girl heard the dreadful sounds of Baba Yaga coming after her. She put her ear to the ground. Baba Yaga was now close at hand. She flung down the towel, as the cat had told her.

Narrator: The towel became a wide, wide river.

Baba Yaga: Up came Baba Yaga to the river. She gnashed her teeth in spite. Then she went home to fetch her oxen and drove them to the river. They drank up every drop.

Narrator: Back in her kettle, Baba Yaga continued her chase.

Girl: But the girl stopped running long enough to put her ear to the ground once again. Oh no, Baba Yaga must have crossed the river. She was near! The girl threw down the comb.

Narrator: Instantly, a forest sprang up, a thick forest with thousands and thousands of trees so close together nothing could possibly pass through.

Baba Yaga Bony-Legs (cont.)

Baba Yaga: Baba Yaga sharpened her iron teeth. Chomp! She bit through a tree and cast it aside. Chomp. Chomp. Another and another.

Narrator: But the trees were too many and the minutes too few.

Baba Yaga: Baba Yaga gave up . . .

Girl: . . . just as the girl ran out of the woods and into the waiting arms of her father. She told him all that had happened.

Narrator: By the end of the story, the stepmother had vanished into the woods and was never seen again.

Girl: And the girl and her father lived peacefully ever after.

Bibliography

- **Africa**
    Aardema, Verna. *Once Upon a Time Tales from Africa.* Knopf, 1994
    Arnott, Kathleen. *African Myths and Legends.* OUP, 1990
    Macmillan, Terry Berger. *Black Fairy Tales.* Child Group, 1974
    Norman, Floyd. *Afro-Classic Tales.* Vignette, 1992
    Pitcher, Fiana. *The Mischief Maker.* Interlink Publishing, 1990
    Poland, Marguerite. *The Wood-Ash Stars.* Interlink Publishing, 1990

- **Armenia**
    Bider, Djemma. *A Drop of Honey.* S & S Trade, 1989
    Hogrogian, Nonny. *The Contest.* Green Willow, 1976

- **Asia**
    Conger, David. *Many Lands, Many Stories.* CE Tuttle, 1987

- **Australia**
    Troughton, Joanna. *Whale's Canoe: A Folktale from Australia.* P. Bedrick Books, 1993

- **Brazil**
    Lippert, Margaret. *The Sea Serpent's Daughter: A Brazilian Legend.* Troll, 1993

- **Celt**
    Guard, David. *Deirdre: A Celtic Legend.* Tricycle Press, 1993
    Jacobs, Joseph. *Celtic Fairy Tales.* Dover, 1968

- **China**
    Carpenter, Francis. *Tales of a Chinese Grandmother.* Amereon Ltd., 1937
    Chang, Monica. *The Mouse Bride: A Chinese Folktale.* Northland AZ, 1992
    Chin, Yin-Lien. *Traditional Chinese Folktales.* M. E. Sharpe, 1989
    Ching, Emily. *Fairy Tales: Chinese Children's Stories.* Wonder Kids, 1988
    Wilson, Barbara. *Wishbones: A Folktale from China.* Macmillan Children's Group, 1993

- **Egypt**
    Amoss, Bertha. *Tales of Ancient Egypt.* More Than Card, 1989
    Mike, Jan. *Gift of the Nile: An Ancient Egyptian Legend.* Troll, 1992

- **England**
    De la Mare, Walter. *The Three Sillies.* Creative Education, 1991
    Parker, Ed. *Jack and the Beanstalk.* Troll, 1979
    Pyle, Howard. *King Arthur and the Magic Sword.* Dial Books, 1990

- **France**
    Da Riff, Andrea. *Puss in Boots.* Troll, 1979
    Picard, Barbara. *French Legends, Tales and Fairy Stories.* OUP, 1992

- **Germany**
    Cooney, Barbara. *Snow White and Rose Red.* Delacorte, 1991
    Crikshank, C. *Grimm's Fairy Tales.* Puffin Books, 1985
    Levine, Arthur. *The Boardwalk Princess.* William Morrow, 1993
    McDonell, Janet. *Snow White and the Seven Dwarves: A Classic Tale.* Child's World, 1988
    Mikkel, Eric. *The Four Gallant Sisters.* Harvey Holt and Co., 1992
    Ross, Tony. *Mrs. Goat and Her Seven Little Kids.* Atheneum, 1990

- **Greece**
    Lines, Kathleen. *The Faber Book of Greek Legends.* Faber and Faber, 1986

Bibliography (cont.)

- **Haiti**
  Wolkstein, Diane. *The Magic Orange Tree and Other Haitian Folktales.* Schocken, 1987

- **Hawaii**
  Aguiar, Elithe. *Legends of Hawaii as Told by Lani Goose.* Lani Goose Publishing, 1986
  Williams, Julie. *Maui Goes Fishing.* UH Press, 1991

- **India**
  Carlson, Jeanne. *A King, a Hunter and a Golden Goose.* Dharma Publishing, 1987
  Jacobs, Joseph. *Indian Fairy Tales.* Dover, 1969
  Troughton, Joanna. *The Wizard Punchkin: A Folk Tale from India.* P. Bedrick Books, 1988

- **Ireland**
  Dunn, Patricia. *Children's Book of Irish Fairy Tales.* Dufour, 1987
  Leamy, Edmund. *Irish Fairy Stories for Children.* Dufour, 1992
  Lynch, Patricia. *Tales of Irish Enchantment.* Dufour, 1986
  Smith, Phillip. *Irish Fairy Tales.* Dover, 1993

- **Israel**
  Freeman, Florence. *It Happened in Chelm: A Story of the Legendary Town of Fools.* Shapolsky Publishing, 1990
  Ganz, Yaffa. *Savta Simcha and the Seven Splendid Gifts.* Feldheim, 1987
  Ganz, Yaffa. *Tali's Slippers, Tova's Shoes.* Mesorah Publishing, 1990
  Sanfield, Steve. *The Feather Merchants and Other Tales of the Fools of Chelm.* William Morrow, 1993

- **Italy**
  Cossi, Olga. *Orlanda and the Contest of Thieves.* Pelican, 1989
  Fox, Paula. *Amzat and His Brothers: Three Italian Folktales.* Orchard Books, 1993

- **Japan**
  Ozaki, Yei T. *The Japanese Fairy Book.* CE Tuttle, 1970
  Quackenbush, Hiroko. *The Runaway Riceball.* Kodansha, 1993
  Sakad, Florence. *Japanese Children's Favorite Stories.* CE Tuttle, 1958
  San Souci, Robert D. *The Samurai's Daughter.* Dial Books, 1992
  Smith, Phillip. *Japanese Fairy Tales.* Dover, 1992

- **Korea**
  Adams, Edward. *Blindman's Daughter.* CE Tuttle, 1981
  Carpenter, Frances. *Tales of a Korean Grandmother.* CE Tuttle, 1972
  Hyun, Peter. *Korea's Favorite Tales and Lyrics.* CE Tuttle, 1986
  Vorhees, Duance and Mark Mueller. *The Woodcutter and the Heavenly Maiden.* Hollym International, 1990

- **Latin America**
  Palacios, Argentina. *The Hummingbird King: A Guatemalan Legend.* Troll, 1993
  Reasoner, Charles. *Llama's Secret: A Peruvian Legend.* Troll, 1993

- **Mexico**
  Brenner, Anita. *The Boy Who Could Do Anything and Other Mexican Folk Tales.* Shoe String, 1992
  dePaola, Tomie. *The Lady of Guadalupe.* Holiday, 1980
  Kimmel, Eric. *The Witch's Face: A Mexican Tale.* Holiday, 1993
  Roland, Donna. *More of Grandfather's Stories from Mexico.* Open My World, 1986

Bibliography (cont.)

- **Mongolia**
  Khurelblat, B. and Narain. *Folk Tales of Mongolia.* Apartment Books, 1992

- **Native American**
  Harrington, John. *Indian Tales from Picuris Pueblo.* Ancient City Press, 1989
  Hausman, Geralk. *Ghost Walk: Native American Tales of the Spirit.* Mariposa Print Publishing, 1991
  Katz, William. *Proudly Red and Black: Tales of Native and African Americans.* Macmillan Children's Books, 1993
  Lacupa, Michael. *Antelope Woman: An Apache Folktale.* Northland, 1992

- **Norway**
  Bender, Robert. *The Three Billy Goats Gruff.* Harvey Holt and Co., 1993
  Kimmel, Eric. *Boots and His Brothers: A Tale from Norway.* Holiday, 1992
  Mills, Lauren. *Tatterhood and the Hobgoblins: A Norwegian Folktale.* Little, Brown & Company, 1993

- **Puerto Rico**
  Grand-Bernier, Carmen. *Juan Bobo: Four Silly Tales from Puerto Rico.* HarperCollins, 1994
  Mora, Francisco. *The Tiger and the Rabbit: A Puerto Rican Folk Tale.* Childrens, 1991
  Pitre, Felix. *Juan Bobo and the Pig: A Puerto Rican Folk Tale.* Dutton Children's Books, 1993

- **Russia**
  Mikolaycak, Charles. *Babushka: An Old Russian Folk Tale.* Holiday, 1984
  Phillip, Neil. *Fairy Tales from Eastern Europe.* Houghton Mifflin, 1991
  San Souci, Robert D. *The Tsar's Promise.* Putnam Publishing Group, 1992

- **South America**
  Alexander, Ellen. *Llama and the Great Flood: A Folk Tale from Peru.* HarperCollins, 1989
  Brusca, Maria. *The Cook and the King.* Harvey Holt and Co., 1993
  Finger, Charles. *Tales from the Silver Lands.* Doubleday, 1965
  Skivington, Janice. *The Girl from the Sky.* Children's, 1992

- **Turkey**
  Walker, Barbara. *A Treasury of Turkish Folktales for Children.* Texas Technical University Press, 1967
  Yolen, Jane. *Little Mouse and Elephant.* HarperCollins, 1994

- **Ukraine**
  Kismaric, Carole. *The Rumor of Pavel and Paali: A Ukranian Folktale.* HarperCollins, 1988

- **Multicultural Arts and Crafts**
  Berliner, Nancy Zeng. *Chinese Folk Art.* Little, Brown & Company, 1986
  Bossert, Helmuth. *Folk Art of Asia, Africa, Australia and the Americas.* Rizzoli, 1990
  Dockstader, Frederick. *Indian Art in America: The Arts and Crafts of the North American Indian.* New York Graphic Society, 1966
  Hamlyn, Paul. *African Art.* Hamlyn, 1968
  Harvey, Marian. *Crafts of Mexico.* Macmillan, 1973
  Saint-Gilles, Amaury. *Mingei: Japan's Enduring Folk Arts.* Heian International, Inc., 1983

Country and Continent Index

Africa
Africa	*The Honey Gatherer's Three Sons, The Ox of the Wonderful Horns*
Egypt	*The Egyptian Cinderella*
South Africa	*Unanana and the Enormous One-Tusked Elephant*

Asia
China	*Fa Mulan, Lon Po Po, Yeh-Shen*
India	*The Cat and the Parrot, Sir Buzz*
Indonesia	*The Lizard Husband*
Israel	*Seven Clever Brothers*
Japan	*Momotaro: The Peach Warrior, The Woodcutter and the Pine*
Korea	*The Toad-Bridegroom*
Russia	*Baba Yaga Bony-Legs, The Tale of Sadko the Minstrel, Vasilisa the Beautiful*
Vietnam	*The Brocaded Slipper, A Cat Is a Cat Is a Cat*

Central America
Mexico	*Coyote Rings the Bell, Legend of the Poinsettia*
Panama	*The Little White Dove*

Europe
England	*Lazy Jack*
France	*Beauty and the Beast*
Germany	*The Frog King, The Four Musicians, Red Riding Hood*
Italy	*The Canary Prince*
Poland	*The Jolly Tailor Who Became King*
Portugal	*Hearth Cat*
Scotland	*Kate Crackernuts*
Spain	*The Enchanted Mule, The Little Seven-Colored Horse*

North America
Bahamas	*The House in the Sky*
Canada	*Ti-Jean and the White Cat*
Hawaii	*The Weary Spirits of Lanai*
United States	*Buffalo Woman, Poor Turkey Girl*

South America
Brazil	*Beetle and Paca*

Answer Key

Page 22
Part 1
1. dog
2. monkey
3. pheasant

Part 2
1. seven centuries
2. saburau, meaning service
3. 1156 A.D.
4. illiterate, rural landowners who farmed in between battles
5. a strong military system with great leaders
6. strict code of ethics, "the way of the warrior"

Page 47
1. Moscow
2. Volga River
3. Lena River
4. Volga River
5. Ob River
6. Sea of Okhotsk
7. Iran
8. Novosibirsk
9. Irkutsk
10. Arctic Ocean

Page 51
1. Mungalo's mother gives him little clay oxen toys.
2. Mungalo's father gives him the great white ox.
3. Mungalo and the great ox leave the village.
4. The ox tells Mungalo the magic of his horns.
5. The ox beats the fierce bull in a fight.
6. Mungalo finds a village with no real food.
7. The singer turns out to be a thief, and he takes the horns.
8. Mungalo is treated like royalty in this village.
9. The chief's daughter becomes fond of Mungalo and agrees to marry him.
10. Mungalo and his wife return to his father's village and settle there.

Page 71
1. self, samurai dog, monkey, and pheasant
2. Sir Buzz
3. God
4. Each brother learns a magical trait he shares.
5. The tailor has the magic.
6. fairies
7. St. Nikolai and Princess Volkova
8. the ox and his horns
9. The princess gets the magic.
10. the memory or spirit of the maiden of Yueh or Mulan's own determination and sense of honor

Page 76
1. F
2. K
3. D
4. A
5. J
6. B
7. C
8. I
9. H
10. E
11. L
12. G

Pages 88–89
I
1. H
2. K
3. A
4. L
5. D
6. I
7. G
8. B
9. E
10. C
11. F
12. J

II
1. Japan
2. India
3. Mexico
4. Israel
5. Poland
6. Scotland
7. Russia
8. Africa
9. Italy
10. Bahamas
11. China
12. Spain

III
Responses will vary. Accept any reasonable answers.

IV
Drawings will vary. Accept any scene from one of the twelve tales.

Page 93
1. north
2. Crete
3. Libya
4. Cairo
5. Nile River
6. for commerce, travel, and the fertile land
7. Turkey
8. Athens
9. east
10. north to south

Answer Key (cont.)

Page 96
1. a. white, twilight
   b. red, sunrise
   c. black, nightfall
2. any three: clean yard, sweep floor, cook supper, pick out the peas and black grains from wheat, clean the poppy seeds
3. a. hen's legs
   b. skulls
   c. hands
4. Drawings will vary.

Page 103
1. Chief Wu and Yeh-Shen's mother both die.
2. Yeh-Shen's stepmother uses her coat to trick the fish.
3. Yeh-Shen's tears in the pond make an old man appear.
4. Yeh-Shen talks to the bones of her dead fish.
5. The fish creates a beautiful blue gown and golden, fish-like, magical shoes for Yeh-Shen to wear to the festival.
6. Yeh-Shen loses a shoe when running home.
7. A merchant finds the shoe and gives it to the king of the island.
8. Many women try on the shoe, but it will not fit.
9. In the middle of the night, Yeh-Shen goes to the pavilion and takes the shoe.
10. The king follows her home and has her try on the shoe.
11. The king and Yeh-Shen are married.
12. Her stepmother and stepsister are crushed to death in their cave.

Page 106
1. Meleagris and Agriocharis
2. snood, wattle
3. North America and Mexico
4. acorns, seeds, berries, and insects
5. lays 11 to 20 eggs; sits on them until hatch, up to 28 days

Page 112
Part 1
1. fish bones
2. falcon
3. fish bones
4. turkeys
5. fish
6. doll

Part 2
Answers will vary.

Page 113
1. falcon
2. fish bones (*Yeh-Shen*)
3. fish bones (*The Brocaded Slipper*)
4. fish
5. doll
6. turkeys
7. turkeys
8. fish bones (*The Brocaded Slipper*)
9. doll

Page 119

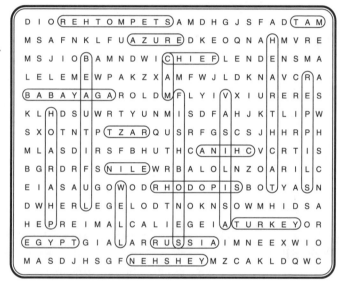

Page 122
I.
1. C
2. F
3. E
4. D
5. A
6. B

II.
1. China
2. Russia
3. Vietnam
4. Portugal
5. Egypt
6. Zuni Tribe, North America

III. Answers should reflect the ideas stated here.
1. The Pharaoh says that Rhodopis' eyes are as green as the Nile, her hair as feathery as papyrus, and her skin the pink of a lotus flower. This makes her truly Egyptian.

Answer Key (cont.)

2. Baba Yaga's hut is in the middle of the dark forest. It stands on hen's legs. The wall around the hut is made of human bones, and on its top are skulls. The gate in the wall has hinges of human feet.
3. Give credit for reasonable answers and logical use of examples.

Page 138
1. about 2,000 pounds (900 kg)
2. 30 million
3. Asian water buffalo and the African buffalo
4. provided tools, hides for clothing and tepee covers, food, fuel, utensils, and more
5. They have few sweat glands.
6. horns
7. about 6 feet (1.9 m)
8. buffalo

Page 142
1. False
2. False
3. True
4. False
5. False
6. True
7. False
8. True
9. False
10. True
11. True
12. False

Page 150
Across
2. Ti-Jean (no hyphen)
3. Unanana
5. Calf-Boy
7. Spain
8. porridge

Down
1. walnut
4. Archbishop
6. bison
9. dove
10. Panama

Page 155
I.
1. D
2. A
3. E
4. B
5. C

II.
1. Canada
2. Zulu, South Africa
3. Spain
4. Native American, USA
5. Panama

III. Answers will vary. Accept all reasonable responses.
1. When the elephant eats Unanana, she tells all the people inside to begin dancing, giving the elephant a bellyache. Using a knife, she cuts a doorway on the side of the elephant for everyone to pass through.
2. Pedro soon discovers that he no longer has freedom. He has a difficult time walking on all fours, and it is hard to support the weight of the large priest. Pedro tries to go back to his mother and wife to say good-bye, and he creates a scene in their house. When Pedro sits down, the priest slides off his back. He chases other priests who he feels are not treating his priest properly.
3. Accept all reasonable and supported comparisons.

Page 163
1. There are 3,000 types of lizards found in every continent except Antarctica and in every habitat.
2. The marine iguana swims in the ocean. The Draco glides through the air.
3. It means cold-blooded.
4. To protect themselves from enemies, lizards pull a clever trick by breaking off their tails.
5. A lizard's sense of smell is very acute and important to its survival. There are two organs found inside the lizard's mouth (called Jacobsen's organs) which work with the forked tongue to detect different smells in the air. That is why lizards constantly flick their tongues in and out.

Page 167
1. Amphibians are animals which can live in both water and on land.
2. Frogs live near fresh-water places while toads live in drier regions such as fields, gardens, and woodlands.

Answer Key (cont.)

3. Frogs are colored a dark green with a white belly. Frogs have long legs for distance jumping, a large head, short body, and no tail. The general colors of toads are brown, tan, gray, or black. Their skin is rough and often covered with warts.

4. The toad has several poisonous glands all over its body and when attacked will produce a white substance that will either kill a predator or simply taste bad enough for the predator to leave the toad alone.

5. Frogs are able to survive extremely cold temperature for long periods of time with as much as sixty-five percent of their total body water turning to ice. As the weather gets warmer, the frog "thaws" back to its regular temperature.

6. Frogs are not found in Antarctica.

Page 172

I.
1. C
2. E
3. F
4. B
5. A
6. D

II.
1. Germany
2. China
3. France
4. Indonesia
5. Germany
6. Korea

III. Accept all reasonable answers.

1. Shang (Lon Po Po) is smart, brave, and clever, but she disobeys her mother's wishes. Red Riding Hood is kind and not especially bright, and she also disobeys her mother. Shang outsmarts the wolf, and Red Riding Hood is eaten, although she is later rescued.

2. The beast is outwardly mean and inwardly kind. He is one of six children. At first he lives in isolation, but later he finds true love and gets married. The Lizard is helpful, magical, and lives with an old woman. He is one of seven children. He later marries.

3. The king is moral, and he believes that keeping promises is important. He lives in a nice home and loves his children. The father in *The Toad-Bridegroom* is a poor father who is greedy, mean, and superstitious.

Page 196

I.
1. B
2. C
3. D
4. A
5. A or B
6. B
7. C or A
8. D

II.
1. In the end the princess does not marry the prince but still seems to be happy.
2. Accept reasonable answers.
3. "Do not judge a book by its cover" is the moral. It means that what is on the inside of a person is more important than what is on the outside. It also means that insides and outsides do not always match.
4. Accept reasonable answers.